GW00373909

THE INSIDER'S GUIDE TO

FLORIDA

U.S. IMMIGRATION
160-LOS C-4125

MAY 23 1989

ADMITTED_____
UNTIL   (CLASS)

INSIDER'S GUIDES

AUSTRALIA • BALI • CALIFORNIA • CHINA • EASTERN CANADA • FLORIDA • HAWAII •
HONG KONG • INDIA • INDONESIA • JAPAN • KENYA • KOREA • NEPAL • NEW ENGLAND • NEW
ZEALAND • MALAYSIA AND SINGAPORE • MEDITERRANEAN FRANCE • MEXICO • PORTUGAL •
RUSSIA • SPAIN • THAILAND • TURKEY • VIETNAM, LAOS AND CAMBODIA • WESTERN CANADA

Insider's Guide Florida
(Second Edition)

© 1995 Kümmerly + Frey A.G.

Moorland Publishing Co Ltd
Moor Farm Rd., Airfield Estate, Ashbourne, DE61HD, England
First Published 1991
Second Edition published 1995
by arrangement with Kümmerly + Frey A.G.

ISBN: 0 86190 581 4

Created, edited and produced by Allan Amsel Publishing
53 rue Beaudouin, 27700 Les Andelys, France
Editor in Chief: Allan Amsel
Original design concept: Hon Bing-wah
Picture editor and designer: Jean R. Johnston
Text and artwork composed and information updated
using Xerox Ventura software

Printed by Samhwa Printing Co Ltd, Seoul, Korea

THE INSIDER'S GUIDE TO
FLORIDA

by Donald Carroll
Photographed by Nik Wheeler

MPC

Contents

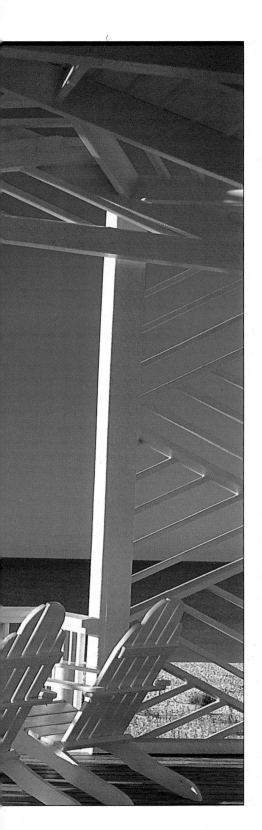

Welcome
to
Florida

IT IS FASHIONABLE — almost obligatory — to begin a travel guide by describing the area of one's travels as a "land of contrasts". As a rhetorical device it's very handy; it allows the writer to gather up in a few sentences disparate phenomena that might otherwise require many paragraphs, if not pages, of laborious explanation. With "contrasts" one is able to envelop and summarize a place in one giant parenthesis, and then move briskly along.

Unfortunately — for the writer, that is — Florida is by no stretch of the imagination a

"land of contrasts". It is a land of spectacular sameness. True, the oldest city in the United States, St. Augustine, is just up the coast from the headquarters of the Space Age, Cape Canaveral; while in the middle of ancient Indian territory is the 28,000-acre (over 11,600 ha) reservation known as Walt Disney World. And no one has ever mistaken the antebellum Southern charms of Tallahassee for the Latin rhythms of Miami, any more than have the literati of Key West been confused with the glitterati of Palm Beach. And where other states have a generation gap, Florida has a generation chasm — between the young who flock there to live it up, and the elderly who migrate there to die.

Nonetheless, the overall impression is, if not of sameness, of minor variations on a few major themes. The principal theme, of course, is sunshine: Florida is very aptly nicknamed the Sunshine State. Another theme is flatness: Florida's highest point is only 345 ft (105 m) above sea level. Another is wetness: quite apart from the vast swampland of the Everglades, Florida has 30,000 lakes and 10,000 miles of rivers, and of course its 1,350 miles of coast is lapped by the sea. Now, when you add to this the fact that most of the restaurants in the state (30,000 of them!) are distinguishable from one another only by their prices, or that most of the hotel rooms are distinguishable only by their addresses, or that most of the beaches are distinguishable only by their names, or that most of the roads are distinguishable only by their numbers, you can see why it would be difficult to speak convincingly of Florida as a land of great variety.

Why, then, with all this standardization and uniformity, do 40 million people visit Florida annually? Simple: because standardization is highly desirable if the standards are high, because uniformity is a good thing if things are uniformly good. That's Florida's secret. People know exactly what to expect. When you know that the weather will be sunny, and the beaches will be lovely, and the people will be friendly, and the service efficient, and the accommodation comfortable, and the prices reasonable, then you know why Florida is the most popular tourist destination in the world. No other place in the world can deliver all of this and Mickey Mouse, too.

However, while such consistency and dependability make Florida a very easy place to visit, they make it a difficult place to write about. When the level of quality is so evenly maintained, picking and choosing becomes even harder, and more subjective, than usual. And then there's the problem of quantity. Take hotels, for example. In Miami Beach, a narrow strip of land only seven miles (11.3 km) long, over 300 new hotels were built in one year alone! Or golf courses. In the vicinity of Fort Lauderdale, a city of modest size, there are 60 golf courses! With such a superabundance of tourist amenities, where does one begin the winnowing process?

Well, for better or worse, one begins with one's own set of preferences — all right, prejudices — as well as a sense of the sort of information I personally would have found valuable before going there.

A word about this information. While I have endeavored to make it as precise as I possibly could, there is one area of deliberate imprecision: hotel and restaurant prices. This is because each establishment's prices fluctuate enormously according to a number of factors. For instance, the price of the

guidebook as the memoirs of a demented accountant.

I have therefore divided hotels and restaurants into three categories according to the *range* of prices you can expect. With hotels, **Luxury** means you can expect to pay over — sometimes way over — $120 for a double room; **Mid-range** hotels will tend to charge between $60 and $120; **Inexpensive** hotels will cost under — sometimes way under — $60 for a double room. Restaurants listed as **Expensive** will cost you over $50 per person, excluding wine; **Moderate**

same hotel room could vary by as much as 100 percent depending on the time of year (summer is regarded as the off-season, except in the north), the number of occupants, the length of occupancy, whether special discounts are available, and whether sales tax (currently 6 percent) or tourist tax (currently 2 percent) is included. Restaurant prices are similarly variable; many restaurants, for example, offer substantial discounts to those willing to eat early in the evening. And none of this takes into account the fact that hoteliers and restaurateurs throughout the world have been known to put up their prices without consulting me first. Thus, to try to be precise about these prices would make this seem not so much a

restaurants will generally charge between $20 and $50; **Inexpensive** restaurants will be below $20, often well below. The categories are fuzzy, I know, but at least they are not misleading. When it comes to taking responsibility for the spending of your money, I would rather be vaguely right then precisely wrong.

One thing, however, I can predict with absolute certainty: you will find much to enjoy in Florida. In fact, if you can't enjoy yourself in Florida, don't bother to try anywhere else.

OPPOSITE: Greek girl at Tappon Springs.
ABOVE: The pier at Naples reaches out into the Gulf of Mexico.

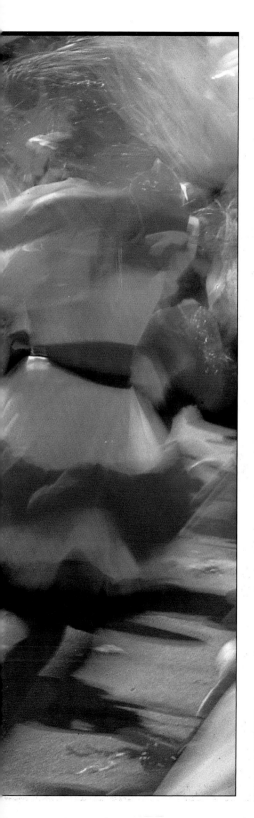

The State and Its People

THE HISTORICAL BACKGROUND

It is perhaps appropriate that the world's most visited vacation spot should itself be populated mostly by new arrivals. Only about a third of Florida's nine million inhabitants were actually born there. And none of its inhabitants are descended from the native peoples who had been living there for over 10,000 years before the Europeans arrived in the sixteenth century and began the systematic extermination of the original Indian population.

Although Columbus claimed the territory for Spain, sight unseen, in 1492, the first European actually to lay eyes on Florida was almost certainly the English cartographer John Cabot, who sailed down the east coast of America on behalf of King Henry VII in 1498. The first European to set foot in Florida was the Spanish explorer Ponce de León, who landed near present-day St. Augustine on April 2, 1513, while looking for the legendary "Isle of Bimini", which according to folklore had a miraculous "fountain of youth". Having arrived at Easter, he named the new land after Spain's Easter celebration, **Pascua Florida**, or "Feast of Flowers".

Ponce then sailed down the coast, out around the Florida Keys (which he called **Los Martires**, because they appeared to him like kneeling martyrs in the water), and back up the west coast as far as Charlotte Harbor, near present-day Fort Myers. He returned to Florida in 1521 with 200 settlers and attempted to establish a settlement near Charlotte Harbor. However, the local Indians were in no mood to see the white man encroaching on their territory, and they launched a ferocious attack on the settlement, in the course of which Ponce himself was badly wounded. The entire party was forced to withdraw to Cuba, where Ponce died of his wounds.

Seven years later another Spaniard, Pánfilo de Narváez, landed at Tampa Bay with 300 would-be colonists. He led them on a march up to the Panhandle, where they were to rendezvous with his ships after conducting a search for the gold he was certain he would find en route. He found no gold, nor did he find his ships waiting for him. With his party now much reduced by the hostile attentions of the Indians they had encountered on their march, they decided to build their own boats and set sail for Mexico. They never arrived.

Undeterred by the fate of his two predecessors, Hernando de Soto sailed from Cuba in 1539 with 600 troops, landing at Tampa Bay and marching northwards more or less in the footsteps of Pánfilo de Narváez, searching for the same gold treasure that the Spanish were convinced was there somewhere. When he didn't find it, he just kept going and kept looking. He died on the banks of the Mississippi three years later.

In 1559 the conquistador Don Tristán de Luna arrived with 1,500 men at Pensacola Bay, where he attempted to establish a colony. After two years of struggle, he gave up and went home.

Ironically, it was the French who were indirectly responsible for the first Spanish success at colonization in Florida. In 1562, Jean Ribault explored the mouth of the St. Johns River and claimed the area for France. Within two years there was a colony of 300 Huguenots living there in the newly-built Fort Caroline. Not amused by the presence of these French squatters — and Protestant ones at that — on "their" territory, the Spanish dispatched a former smuggler, Pedro Menéndez de Avilés, to found a settlement nearby and to deal with the French. He accomplished both tasks.

Landing south of Fort Caroline on August 28, 1565, the feast day of San Augustin, Menéndez named his new settlement in honor of the saint and then led his men northward to sort out the French. Unfortunately for the little Huguenot community, Jean Ribault had had the same idea with regard to the Spanish, and had set sail with his men to destroy the fledgling settlement of St. Augustine. Thus Menéndez found Fort Caroline virtually undefended and captured it easily, killing all but women and children. Meanwhile, Ribault's force had run into a storm at sea and were shipwrecked before they could reach St. Augustine. The spot where Menéndez later found the survivors is known to this day as

Replica of *HMS Bounty* moored at Miami.

Matanzas — Spanish for "killings" — for he took no prisoners.

For the rest of the century the Spanish labored feverishly to consolidate and expand their hold on the peninsula. A chain of forts was established, along with a network of Fransciscan missions to convert the Indians. Although Sir Francis Drake succeeded in burning down St. Augustine in 1586, two years before he defeated the Spanish Armada, the English as well as the French were loath to challenge Spain's colonial supremacy in Florida throughout

the seventeenth century. At the same time, Indian resistance to Spanish domination was crumbling rapidly. Those who weren't killed by Spanish firepower succumbed to the European diseases the Spanish brought with them—smallpox, diphtheria, and syphilis — while others were taken into slavery for the plantations in the West Indies. Thus for over a century the Spanish were the acknowledged overlords of Florida.

By 1700, however, there were signs that Spain's grip on Florida wasn't all that secure after all. To the north, English colonies were proliferating—and flourishing. To the west, LaSalle had claimed the entire Mississippi River valley for France. Then the War of the Spanish Succession in 1702 brought English

troops into Florida, where, with the help of the Creek Indians, they overran most of Spain's military outposts in the north and destroyed almost all of her missions. Then the French captured Pensacola in 1719. Although they handed it back soon afterwards, purely to keep it out of English hands, the writing was on the wall for Spain.

Finally, in 1763, after France's defeat in the French and Indian Wars left England as the undisputed master of the American continent, Spain ceded Florida to England in exchange for Havana, which the English had captured. By this time all of the native Indians had vanished, to be replaced by renegade Creeks from neighboring territories to the north and west. They were called Seminoles, from the Spanish words for renegades or runaways, *cimarrones*. The English got on well with the Seminoles, cultivating them as trading partners rather than exterminating them as savages, but England's ambitious plans for developing Florida had to be put on hold as the rebellion in the 13 colonies to the north approached revolution.

If the British colonial presence in Florida was brief — two decades, from 1763 to 1783 — it was also benign, as indicated by the fact that Florida did not join in the American Revolution, and indeed provided a haven for prominent English Tories fleeing the war. But when the war was lost, Britain traded Florida back to Spain in 1783 in exchange for the Bahamas.

In the years following the War of Independence citizens of the newly-sovereign United States of America began to develop a keen and acquisitive interest in this Spanish-owned territory dangling below the infant nation. The Seminoles, still loyal to their erstwhile British landlords, and (rightly)mistrustful of the intentions of the Americans who were buying up land in big chunks all around them, made violent nuisances of themselves to the new settlers — so much so that in 1817 Andrew Jackson led a small army into northern Florida to punish the Indians. This became known as the First Seminole War. Apart from teaching the Indians an unhappy lesson, it taught the Spaniards that they were manifestly incapable of protecting their territory. They sold Florida to the United States in 1821.

Andrew Jackson — an obvious choice — was created military governor of the newly annexed territory. Less obviously, Tallahassee was created its capital. It happened thus: because the British had divided the territory for administrative purposes into East Florida and West Florida, with capitals in St. Augustine and Pensacola respectively, the two settlements had rival claims to be the capital of a united Florida. To settle the issue, the territorial legislature came up with a novel solution. One man was dispatched from St. Augustine to Pensacola, and another man was dispatched from Pensacola to St. Augustine. Wherever they met up would be the new capital. They met in the forest at Tallahassee.

As the influx of new settlers from the north increased, the resistance of the Seminoles stiffened, prompting Congress in 1830 to pass the Removal Law, which required that all Indians be removed to the Arkansas Territory west of the Mississippi. Again the Seminoles resisted, and when Seminole warriors ambushed and wiped out a detachment of 139 U.S. troops under Major Francis Dade near Tampa in 1835, now-president Andrew Jackson had just the excuse he needed to go in and get rid of the Seminoles once and for all. But yet again the white man had underestimated the fighting spirit and determination of the red men. The Second Seminole War lasted for seven bloody years, even though the Seminoles' brilliant chief Osceola had been captured in 1837 while negotiating with the U.S. commander under a flag of truce.

In 1842, most of the surviving Seminoles were removed along the "Trail of Tears" to what is now Oklahoma. Even then, several hundred refused to capitulate, escaping into the Everglades where they and their descendants remained defiantly independent until the U.S. finally signed a treaty with them in 1934.

In 1845 Florida joined the Union as the twenty-seventh state, with a population of about 80,000, of which almost half were black slaves and almost none were Indians.

Unsurprisingly, given the state's geography and plantation economy, Florida sided with the Confederacy during the Civil War. Equally unsurprisingly, given the state's historical vulnerability to outside occupation, no major battles were fought there as the Union forces marched in and captured all the strategic spots without too much difficulty. The period of Reconstruction was also less traumatic than in other southern states — and briefer, thanks to a wealthy Philadelphia industrialist named Hamilton Disston, who in 1881 was persuaded to buy four million acres of south-central Florida swampland for $1 million,

thus erasing the state's debt burden in one stroke.

The next few years saw several developments which were to put Florida firmly on the road to becoming, a century later, the world's premier holiday playground. First, the American Medical Association declared St. Petersburg to be the healthiest spot in the United States. Then the youngish but infirm inventor Thomas Edison forsook New Jersey for Fort Myers, where he built an estate with America's first modern swimming pool. Then along came Henry Bradley Plant,

OPPOSITE: A typical sight in Pensacola's historic Seville Quarter. ABOVE: The Old Capitol in Tallahassee, now a museum.

a Connecticut Yankee who built the Atlantic Coastline Railroad from Richmond, Virginia to Tampa — the single greatest attraction of which was Plant's Tampa Bay Hotel, a phantasmagorical hostelry stretching for a quarter of a mile under minarets, cupolas, and domes. Simultaneously, Henry Morrison Flagler, a retired Standard Oil executive, was building his Florida East Coast Railroad down the other side of the peninsula. He laid his tracks to St. Augustine, and then to Ormond Beach, and then to Palm Beach, and then to the little hamlet of Miami, and then,

eventually, by way of a series of arched bridges, over the ocean and the Florida Keys to Key West. At every important stop along the way Flagler left behind at least one stunning hotel to accommodate the people his railway was transporting down from the north: the Ponce de León and the Alcazar in St. Augustine, the Ormond in Ormond Beach, the Royal Poinciana in Palm Beach, and the Royal Palm in Miami. In the course of his triumphal march to the southernmost tip of the United States, Flagler also created two future cities: Palm Beach and Miami.

In 1912, the year before Flagler died, a millionaire from Indianapolis, Carl Fisher, discovered a barrier sandbar in Biscayne Bay, where he bought a large tract of land and then added to it with the help of a dredge. A few hotels and golf courses and tennis courts later, Miami Beach was in business. To the south of Miami George Merrick created Coral Gables, the nation's first fully planned city, while up the coast the eccentric architect Addison Mizner was putting up mansions in Palm Beach and buying up scrubland which was to become Boca Raton. At the same time, swampland in the Everglades was being drained to create rich farmland.

All of this activity led to a spectacular land boom in the early 1920s. People poured into the state from all over the country to get a piece of the action. As prices spiraled wildly upward, con-men sold the same parcels of land over and over. Others bought and resold land on the same day. Many bought land sight unseen, only to discover later that the land was underwater. As a result of this feeding frenzy, by 1925 two and a half million people had invested in Florida land. But the following year the bottom fell out of what had come to be known as the "surreal estate" market.

The boom was bound to go bust in any case, but its collapse was hastened by the fact that the railways simply couldn't handle the enormous demand for building materials, and many builders went bankrupt as a consequence. Then one of the boats bringing materials to Miami capsized, blocking Miami's harbor and bankrupting more builders. The final blow, literally, came on September 17, 1926, when a savage hurricane blew into Miami, damaging over half the buildings and leveling nearby developments. The party was now over, and three years later when the stock market crash brought on the Great Depression, the lights were turned out.

They flickered back on again during World War II, when the U.S. military decided to take advantage of Florida's climate and use it as a year-round training ground. Not only did this give thousands of young soldiers their first tantalizing glimpse of this sunlit, sub-tropical land, but it also produced corollary benefits such as a much-improved system of roads and airports which made it possible for growers to ship their produce all over the country. Equally importantly for the state's economy, military research led to the development of coolants that were to give Florida efficient air conditioning for its sweltering summers as well as a means of creating frozen concentrates out of its vast citrus crops. The war was definitely good for Florida.

So too, belatedly, was the land bust of 1926, because when people and prosperity began to return to Florida in the post-war years, the lessons of 1926 were remembered. Property transactions were regulated, developments controlled, subdivisions properly planned. Consequently, Florida is still enjoying the remarkable growth that was

launched at roughly the same time as the first rocket was launched from Cape Canaveral in 1950.

There are, it is true, those who think that this growth has been achieved in part at the expense of the environment, that too little attention has been paid to the natural beauty that made the state so attractive in the first place. Others point to the paradox by which the state's glorious climate is starting to become a financial burden: by luring so many retirees away from less hospitable climes, it ensures that the costs of health care and programs for the elderly will have to grow as well.

As of now, however, these are mere sunspots on the sun that shines on Florida.

The State and Its People

GEOGRAPHY AND CLIMATE

At first glance, it would seem rather pointless to write about Florida's geography and climate. After all, there must be very few travelers anywhere in the world who couldn't find Florida on a map or who wouldn't know what sort of weather they could expect to find when they got there. Nonetheless, there are aspects of Florida's geographical and climatic conditions that may still come as a surprise to the visitor.

By American standards the state is not very large — less than 60,000 sq miles (97,000 sq km), about the size of England and Wales combined. Nor, as I have said, is it topographically very diverse. Most of Florida is either swampland or former swampland surrounded by coastal plains. Offshore these plains continue to surface intermittently as islands, sand bars, or coral reefs. At its edges, where Florida rejoins the sea whence it emerged some 20 million

OPPOSITE: Sunset in Panhandle.
ABOVE LEFT: The Panhandle town of Seaside.
ABOVE: Rockets on parade at the Kennedy Space Center.

years ago, the beaches don't vary significantly in either texture or appeal. Along the northern Atlantic coast they tend to be broad and the sand is rather tightly packed; along the southern Atlantic coast they are still broad but softer; along the Gulf Coast they are narrower and softer still, and strewn with shells in the south; in the Panhandle, from Pensacola to Panama City, the beaches are sugary, almost powdery, both in color and consistency.

Within these sandy margins, there are over 300 species of trees, over 400 species and subspecies of birds, and at least 80 different land mammals. Florida's official state tree is the wonderful sabal palm, which can be found almost everywhere in the state, but in different regions its preeminence is challenged variously by pines, cypresses, magnolias, and live oaks. And of course there are the vast citrus groves in the central and south-central parts of the state.

Of the permanent bird population, the most spectacular inland (and usually swampland) residents are the ibises, egrets, herons, ospreys, cormorants, cardinals, roseate spoonbills, and flamingos. Along the shoreline you will find a somewhat less exotic array of sandpipers, terns, and pelicans. Then there are those birds, such as ducks and geese, who just like wintering in Florida.

The most interesting mammals are, sadly but predictably, also the rarest: gray foxes, black bears, pumas, and wildcats. There is, however, one mammal that is both very interesting and very common: the friendly dolphin, which can often be seen disporting itself near the beach or beside the boat. Other familiar figures in the landscape, markedly less friendly, include those huge, waddling handbags called alligators (or, by Floridians, just 'gators).

Although Florida was named for the Easter "Feast of Flowers" in Spain, it could just as appropriately have been named for the feast of flowers which it offers its beholders. This is especially true in the spring, when the bougainvillea, poincianas, orchid trees, geraniums, azaleas, trumpet vines, and tiger lilies conspire to incite a riot of color.

The climate — well, you already know about the climate or you wouldn't want to know about everything else. It is sunny all year round, with temperatures in most places ranging from fairly warm to very warm. In mid-winter in the northern parts of the state it sometimes, but rarely, plunges to 50 °F (10 °C); otherwise the thermometer tends to hover around 60 °F (15 °C). You add degrees as you move south: it can easily be 75 °F (24 °C) in Key West in January.

In the summer it is correspondingly warmer in different parts of the state, but — here's the good news — *not all that much warmer*. It seldom reaches 90 °F (32 °C) anywhere, and all the coastal areas are naturally air conditioned by the ocean breezes. (Every interior space untouched

by the ocean breezes has been air conditioned by man.) And more good news: the waters around Florida, thanks partly to the Gulf Stream, are agreeably warm all year round.

And the bad news? You have to dial H to get any bad news: Humidity and Hurricanes. Neither, however, constitutes a serious inconvenience. The humidity can be avoided by staying indoors or in the water around midday in mid-summer; the hurricanes can be avoided by staying indoors. Fortunately, hurricanes are relatively infrequent, even in the hurricane season (late summer-early autumn), and their arrival is announced well in advance by the news media. Moreover, the buildings are built to withstand high winds (as in California

they are built to withstand earthquakes). As a result, Floridians have become so blasé about hurricanes that whenever one is imminent thousands of "hurricane parties" are organized, as it were, against the wind.

Basically, though, there is nothing in Florida that can come between you and the sea and the sun.

Sunset, soft sand and serenity on the beach at Seaside, Florida.

Miami
and
Environs

ON JULY 28, 1890 the small fishing and farming community of Miami, with a population of 343 people, was incorporated as a city. By 1920 the population had grown to 30,000, and Miami's development as a major resort was well under way. Nowadays, nearly two million people live in the 26 municipalities which make up the Greater Miami area. These municipalities include Miami Beach, with its Art Deco hotels and miles of sand; the South Pacific-like Virginia Key and Key Biscayne islands below Miami Beach; Coral Gables, colloquially known as the "Miami Riviera" because of its Mediterranean-style buildings and High Society contingent; Coconut Grove, which is noted for the quality of its shops and its nightlife; and Little Havana, west of the downtown area, the city's Cuban district. Greater Miami now contains 2,040 sq miles (3,284 sq km) of land — of which 1,423 acres (58 ha) are public beaches along a 15-mile (24-km) stretch of coast between Key Biscayne and Bal Harbour — and 354 sq miles (570 sq km) of water.

The area's ethnic mix is 36 percent white, 18 percent black, and 46 percent Hispanic. The majority of the Hispanics are of Cuban origin, but there are also considerable numbers from Panama, Colombia, El Salvador, and Nicaragua, as well as some 150,000 French-speaking Haitians. The influx of foreigners into Miami has given rise to the sobriquet "America's Casablanca", as some of the immigrants are political or economic refugees, particularly those from Latin American countries and the Caribbean.

Despite the tensions involved in such a racial mixture, and despite its (largely undeserved) reputation for crime and vice, the Miami area has just been judged the twentieth most desirable place to live in the U.S. among the 333 cities surveyed in Rand McNally's *Places Rated Almanac*. The almanac ranks cities according to the level of crime and the quality of such things as health care, the environment, public transportation, education, recreation, the arts, and the climate. By these criteria, Miami ranks among the best cities in the country.

The Miami International Airport is the second busiest in the nation, handling up to 850 flights a day, and the Port of Miami is indisputably the cruise ship capital of the world, welcoming over two and a half million cruise passengers every year. But the crucial number — the number that attracts all these numbers of people — is 76 °F (24 °C). That's the average annual temperature in the Greater Miami area.

MIAMI

BACKGROUND

The first American settler in the area was a Carolina planter named Richard Fitzpatrick, who in 1826 brought a group of slaves to work the land on the banks of the Miami River. Fitzpatrick's Miami holdings were inherited by his nephew, William English, in 1842, the same year in which the Second Seminole War came to an end. English saw clearly the place's potential and began drawing up plans for a village by the mouth of the Miami River. He decided to call the new settlement "Miami", a corruption of the Tequesta Indian word mayaime, meaning "very large", which is what the Indians once called Lake Okeechobee to the northwest.

Through newspapers in the state's northern cities, English advertised lots of sale at $1 each. Reassured that the Seminoles were no longer a threat, small but growing numbers of people were lured south by the bargain offer. Homesteads were established and the community grew steadily until 1855, when the Third Seminole War broke out.

During the Civil War the Miami area became a refuge for spies, deserters, and blockade runners, but the actual battles were confined to the northern part of the state. New settlers arrived after the war, and the area's growth resumed: agricultural communities were established at Lemon City, Coconut Grove, Buena Vista, and Little River, while a merchant named William Brickell set up a trading post near the mouth of the Miami River, which did a lively trade with the local Indians.

The "Mother of Miami", (so called because she is said to have "conceived" the city), a wealthy widow named Julia Tuttle, arrived in 1875. She set herself up in William English's old house and over the next 15 years became the area's most important landowner. She was persistent in her efforts to persuade Henry Flagler to extend his Florida East Coast Railroad to Miami, and even tried to tempt him with an offer of 300 acres of land free, but to no avail. In 1895, however, freak weather conditions came to Mrs. Tuttle's aid. That was the year of the Great Freeze, which wiped out 90 percent of the state's citrus crop but left the Miami area relatively untouched.

The effects of the Great Freeze cut Flagler's railway profits and severely damaged the image of his resorts on the coasts to the north. Seeing her chance, Mrs. Tuttle sent a bouquet of Miami orange blossoms to Flagler as a little reminder that the Miami area had a climate dependable enough to produce citrus crops all year round. Flagler got the point, and his railway reached Miami the following year, 1896. Developers soon followed, building hotels and condominiums, and Flagler himself further invested in the new city by putting up the Royal Palm Hotel.

The real estate boom quickly accelerated and by 1910 the population had grown to 5,000, including some very rich people who had built some very fancy houses along Brickell Avenue overlooking Biscayne Bay. James Deering's elaborate Villa Vizcaya, still ogled by tourists today, was probably the most impressive of these private palaces. By 1920 the planter John S. Collins and his partner, the businessman and speedway mogul Carl Fisher, had bought up most of the 1,600 acres of mangrove island just off the coast, drained it, and developed it into Miami Beach. The decade of the Twenties was a major boom period for Miami: in the winter season of 1924–25, 300,000 tourists visited the city, and the population swelled to 100,000. In 1926, however, the boom came to an abrupt end and the financiers and developers who had fueled the boom rapidly began disinvesting.

Still, the development continued at a modest pace through the Depression years. George Merrick established Coral Gables as one of the most exclusive suburbs in the

area, and Glenn H. Curtiss made Hialeah and Miami Springs into popular resort centers for winter vacationers. In Miami Beach, marvelous Art Deco hotels rose from the sands. In the 1937–38 winter season, more than 800,000 tourists came to Miami. The city expanded relentlessly to accommodate the ever-increasing numbers of visitors and new residents, until — like Los Angeles on the other coast — it became difficult to decide where the city stopped and the rest of the country began.

After the Cuban revolution in 1959 Miami began receiving waves of refugees: more than half a million over the next few years. The Cubans added a whole new dimension to the appearance and the socio-cultural character of the city. Miami's architecture,

food, music, politics, media, and, of course, language were all profoundly affected by the new arrivals. They also brought considerable entrepreneurial skills with them, reinforcing the city's economic base and helping to establish it as one of America's most important financial centers. In addition to the hundreds of banks and insurance companies in Miami, many multinational corporations have their Latin American headquarters in the city because of its unrivaled airline connections to the Caribbean and South America.

Like all big cities, Miami has its problems. But I think it's fair to say that there are few cities in the world that wouldn't willingly swap their problems for Miami's — especially if the climate was part of the deal.

GENERAL INFORMATION

Comprehensive information on hotels, transportation, sporting events, and special attractions in the Miami area can be obtained from the Greater Miami Convention and Visitors Bureau, Barnett Tower, Suite 2700, 701 Brickell Avenue, Miami FL 33131. ((305) 539-3000. For more detailed information on where to stay, contact the Greater Miami Hotel and Motel Association, DuPont Plaza Center, Suite 719, 300 Biscayne Boulevard Way, Miami FL 33131. ((305) 371-2030.

Downtown Miami's bold skyline reflects its status as one of America's most important financial centers.

For specific information on the most popular tourist areas, contact one or more of the following chambers of commerce: The Key Biscayne Chamber of Commerce, 95 West McIntire, Key Biscayne, ((305) 361-5207; the Coconut Grove Chamber of Commerce, 2820 McFarland Road, Coconut Grove, (444-7270; the Coral Gables Chamber of Commerce, 50 Aragon Avenue, Coral Gables, ((305) 446-1657; the South Miami Chamber of Commerce, 6410 Southwest 80th Street, South Miami, ((305) 661-1621; and the Bal Harbour Chamber of

Commerce, 655 96th Street, Bal Harbour, ((305) 866-4633.

If you need still more information, you can find out what's happening and where to find it in Miami by checking the "What You Can Watch" and "What You Can Do" sections of the *Miami Herald*.

Useful telephone numbers (all in area code 305):

Miami International Airport	876-7077
Metro Taxicabs	944-4422
Yellow Cabs	885-5555
Central Taxicab Service	534-0694
Physician Referral Service	326-1177
Dental Referral Service	285-5470
Weather/Surf Information	661-5065

WHAT TO SEE AND DO

Sights

There are so many things to see in Miami that the best approach is to take one area at

a time. A good place to start is downtown, the commercial and business center of the city. Here you will find the **Center for Fine Arts** at 101 West Flagler Street, ((305) 375-1700, where 15 different national and international exhibitions of painting, sculpture, photography, and the decorative arts are mounted each year. Admission is $4 for adults and $2 for children.

The history of the region is brought into focus at the **Historical Museum of Southern Florida**, which is in the same complex as the Center for Fine Arts at 101 West Flagler Street, ((305) 375-1492. The museum has displays which illuminate the lifestyles and culture of both the Indians and the nineteenth-century settlers; a photography and film exhibition shows how Miami emerged as a major city. Admission is $4 for adults and $2 for children aged three to 12.

Those who are more enthralled by modern technology than by art or history should head for the **Miami Museum of Science and Space Transit Planetarium**, which has over 100 hands-on exhibits examining the natural sciences, biology, and human anatomy; there are also live scientific experiments, displays of advanced computer technology, and an Animal Exploratorium with a collection of rare natural history specimens. The Planetarium has a dome 65 ft (20 m) high which houses astronomy and laser shows, and the Weintraub Observatory for evening star gazing. The museum is at 3280 South Miami Avenue, ((305) 854-4247, and is open from 10 am to 6 pm daily, with separate late openings at weekends for the observatory. Admission is $6 for adults and $3 for children aged three to 12.

Two other downtown attractions worth visiting are the **H.M.S. Bounty** at 401 Biscayne Boulevard in Bayside Marketplace, ((305) 375-0486, which is the fully rigged-out replica of the eighteenth-century tall ship used in the filming of MGM's *Mutiny on the Bounty*, and the **Vizcaya Museum and Gardens** at 3251 South Miami Avenue, ((305) 579-2708, where antiques, paintings, and Oriental decorations adorn the interior of James Deering's 34-room Italian Renaissance villa. The European-style formal gardens and fountains surrounding the villa are among the most beautiful in the country.

ABOVE: The *Heritage of Miami* under full sail passes a cruise liner in Biscayne Bay. OPPOSITE: Getting around, Miami style.

Opening hours are daily from 9:30 am to 5 pm, and admission is $8 for adults and $4 for children aged six to 18.

To reach Virginia Key and Key Biscayne take Rickenbacker Causeway from the mainland at Brickell Avenue and Southwest 26th Street, across Biscayne Bay. There are parks and beaches on both keys, with swimming and sporting facilities, and you can also see pockets of old mangrove swamp of the kind which once covered Miami Beach to the north. The first thing to see on Virginia Key is **Planet Ocean** at 3979

is open from 9:30 am to 6:30 pm daily. Admission is $17.95 for adults and $12 for children under 13.

On Key Biscayne you can take a look at the outside of **President Nixon's Home** at 485 West Matheson Drive, which was Nixon's holiday retreat for a number of years. The house is not open to the public. On the southern tip of the Key at 1200 South Crandon Boulevard is the **Bill Baggs Cape Florida State Recreation Area**, which has nature trails and beaches in addition to the oldest structure in south Florida, the 95-ft

Rickenbacker Causeway, ((305) 361-5786, which is the world's largest marine science museum. There are icebergs on display, simulated hurricanes, and the sailing vessel *April Fool*, which at six feet (1.83 m) long is the smallest ever to cross the Atlantic. The museum is open daily from 10 am to 6 pm; admission is $8.50 for adults and $5 for children aged six to 12. At 400 Rickenbacker Causeway on Virginia Key is the **Miami Seaquarium**, ((305) 361-5705, home to a performing killer whale called Lolita as well as Flipper the porpoise, veteran of films and a television series. There are regular dolphin shows, a shark pool, sea lions, and thousands of other sea creatures in dozens of aquariums at the Seaquarium, which

(30-m) high **Cape Florida Lighthouse**. You can climb to the top of the lighthouse and enjoy the view over Biscayne Bay and the Atlantic beyond.

Back on the mainland, to the southwest of the downtown area on Bayshore Boulevard is the bayside community of Coconut Grove, a haven for hippies during the Sixties but now home to an altogether more sophisticated set who enjoy the exclusive shops, French-style cafés, and trendy nightlife. The main sights in "The Grove" include **Silver Bluff**, which is a fascinating rock formation dating back thousands of years: it is on Bay Boulevard between Crystal View and Emathia Streets. The **Barnacle State Historic Site** at 3485 Main Highway,

((305) 448-9445, is a tranquil five-acre estate which has in its grounds one of the region's oldest houses, built in 1870, where you can see authentic period furniture and historical photographs.

A few miles further down the coast is Coral Gables, known as the "Miami Riviera" because of its Mediterranean-style architecture and well-heeled inhabitants. For a good example of the architecture, visit the **Coral Gables House** at 907 Coral Way, a coral rock structure built at the turn of the century as a home for George Merrick, the founder of

Stanford Drive, ((305) 284-3536, there are several El Greco paintings among a fine collection of Renaissance and Baroque art.

Continuing on down the coast from Coral Gables, you come to the area of Greater Miami known as South Dade County, which has some of the most popular tourist attractions in the whole region. The largest cageless zoo in the nation, **Metrozoo**, at 12400 Southwest 152nd Street, ((305) 251-0401, features very rare — and very beautiful — white Bengal tigers, koala bears, and over 300 exotic birds in a free-flight aviary.

the community. At 2701 DeSoto Boulevard, ((305) 442-6483, is the **Venetian Pool**, a lagoon carved out of rock, with caves, stone bridges, and a sandy beach. It is a delightful place to laze away an afternoon, and admission is only $3.50 for adults and $1.50 for children under 13.

The **Fairchild Tropical Garden** is the nation's largest tropical botanical garden, and has hourly train rides through its 83 acres of exotic flora. The plant house contains rare specimens and a miniature "rain forest". You can find all this vegetation at 10901 Old Cutler Road, ((305) 667-1651; admission is $7 for adults and free for children under 12. It is open daily from 9:30 am to 4:30 pm. At the **Lowe Art Museum**, 1301

The animals live in natural habitats separated from the public by moats. Admission is $6 for adults and $3 for children; opening hours are from 10 am to 5:30 pm daily. Still more exotic birds — over 1,000 of them — can be seen at **Parrot Jungle**, 11000 Southwest 57th Avenue, ((305) 666-7834, where the birds fly around a sub-tropical jungle. It is open daily from 9:30 am to 5 pm; admission is $10.50 for adults and $6 for children under 14. Caged walkways cross **Monkey Jungle**, a unique colony of apes and monkeys living semi-wild in a natural tropical

OPPOSITE: Villa Vizcaya, John Deering's Italian Renaissance villa, ABOVE its sculptured stone barge.

habitat. There are also daily shows featuring performing chimps. This primate enclave is at 14805 Southwest 216th Street, ((305) 235-1611, and can be visited daily from 9:30 am to 5 pm, for $10.50 adults and $6 children aged five to 12.

The **Weeks Air Museum** at 14701 Southwest 128th Street, ((305) 233-5197, is a new and increasingly popular attraction, housing 35 immaculate civilian and military aircraft dating from the earliest days of aviation. There are also exhibits and photographs depicting aviation history. The

museum is open from Wednesday to Sunday, 10 am to 5 pm, and admission is $6 for adults and $3 for children under 13. Another interesting collection can be seen at the **Gold Coast Railroad Museum**, 12450 Southwest 152nd Street, ((305) 253-7834, which has historic trains on display and features a ride around the museum's grounds in a steam locomotive.

A good way to see a lot of Miami in a little time is to take one of the **Old Town Trolley Tours of Miami**. These tours leave on a two-hour narrated trip every half-hour from 14 different places in the city. Call (305) 374-8687 for information. There are numerous cruise lines offering a wide variety of cruises out of the Port of Miami, the most popular

being the half-day cruises, evening dinner cruises, and full-day cruises to Bimini and the Bahamas. The prices are very reasonable, ranging from $50+ for half-day cruises to $100+ for full-day cruises. *Sea Escape* cruises sail from Pier 6, 1080 Port Boulevard, Port of Miami, ((305) 379-0000; *Tropicana/Sea Venture* cruises leave from Pier 12, Port of Miami, ((305) 477-5858.

Sports

Football fans can watch the Miami Dolphins of the NFL play between September and January in Joe Robie Stadium at 2269 Northwest 199th Street, Greater Miami North. There are tours of the 75,000-seat stadium — call (305) 623-6183 for details — and for ticket information dial (305) 620-2578. The Miami Heat **basketball** team of the NBA plays from November to April at the Miami Arena, 721 Northwest First Avenue, Miami, ((305)577-4328. Miami's new professional minor-league **baseball** team is the Miami Miracle, who play at the FIU University Park Campus, Sunblazer Arena, 11200 Southwest Eighth Street, on the Tamiami Trail east of Miami, ((305) 220-7040. The baseball season runs from April to early October.

Horse racing takes place in the lovely surroundings of Hialeah Park, which has a French Mediterranean-style clubhouse and grand-stand. There is a Metrorail station in the grounds of the park, which is at 105 East 21st Street, Hialeah, ((305) 885-8000. For horsepower of a mechanical nature, go to the Hialeah Speedway, which holds weekly **stock car races** in the winter season at 3300 Okeechobee Road, off U.S. 27, in Hialeah, ((305) 821-6644. The Miami Sharks of the American **Soccer** League play from August to November at 11201 Coral Way, off Southwest 24th Street, Miami, ((305) 477-2050. **Jai alai** enthusiasts can see the sport played at the Miami Jai Alai Fronton, 3500 Northwest 37th Avenue, Miami, ((305) 633-6400. There are 13 games each evening, and it is legal to bet on the games. You can see many of the world's top **tennis** players in action at the Lipton International Players Championship, which is the fifth richest two-week tennis tournament in the world, offering prize money totaling $3.1 million. The tournament is held in March at the tennis center on Key Biscayne, 7300 Crandon Boulevard, ((305)361-5252.

For those who want to play rather than watch sport, there are 34 public **golf** courses in the Greater Miami area, including the Fontainebleau Golf Course at 9603 Fontainebleau Boulevard in Miami, ((305) 221-5181, the Country Club of Miami at 6801 Northwest 186th Street in Miami, ((305) 821-0111, the Key Biscayne Golf Course at 6400 Crandon Boulevard on Key Biscayne, ((305) 361-9129, the Biltmore Golf Course

also give you information on both tennis courts and golf courses: call (305) 579-6916.

There is, as you might expect, terrific **fishing** in the waters off Miami. To arrange a fishing trip, contact Ocean Type Fishing Charters, 4035 Southwest 11th Street, Coral Gables, ((305) 446-8445, or Sandskipper, 4000 Crandon Boulevard, Key Biscayne, ((305) 361-9740. **Sailing** boats can be rented from Easy Sailing, Dinner Key Marina, Coconut Grove, ((305) 858-4001, where you can also rent powerboats and scuba diving equipment. **Diving** charters

at 1210 Anastasia Avenue in Coral Gables, ((305) 442-6485, and the Palmetto Golf Course at 9300 Southwest 152nd Avenue in South Dade County. **Tennis** players are also well catered for in the Miami area. There are 11 public tennis centers to choose from, including the Biltmore Tennis Center at 1210 Anastasia Avenue in Coral Gables, ((305) 442-6565, which has 10 hard courts, and the International Tennis Center on Key Biscayne at 7300 Crandon Boulevard, ((305) 361-8633, which has 17 hard courts.

More information on tennis facilities in and around Miami can be obtained from the Florida Tennis Association at 9620 Northeast Second Avenue, Miami Shores, ((305) 757-8568. Miami's recreation department will

(and lessons) which go to various offshore reefs can be arranged through Diver's Paradise, 4000 Crandon Boulevard, Key Biscayne, ((305) 361-3483, which also rents equipment. **Windsurfing** equipment and jet skis are available from Windsurfing Place on Key Biscayne at 3501 Rickenbacker Causeway, ((305) 361-1225.

Shopping

For the widest range of choices in North Miami go to the **Adventura Mall** at 19501 Biscayne Boulevard, which contains several

ABOVE: Some inhabitants of Parrot Jungle greet a visitor. OPPOSITE: A Latina inhabitant of Miami.

department stores and 150 shops selling just about everything. Another impressive shopping plaza is the **Bayside Marketplace** downtown at 401 Biscayne Boulevard. It is an open-air complex with brick walkways lined with tropical trees and plants; its 100 shops specialize in women's fashions, jewelry, gifts, African and Oriental arts and crafts, and personalized souvenirs. In Little Havana you can findCuban arts and crafts shops along the colorful **Southwest Eighth Street** between Route 95 West and 35th Street. For more upmarket

shopping go the the **Mayfair Shops** plaza at 2911 Grand Avenue in Coconut Grove, or to the **Miracle Mile** between Douglas Road and Lejeune Road in Coral Gables. While you're there, go to the **Miracle Center**, a futuristic shopping mall at 301 Coral Way.

Nightlife

There are many cultural events to illuminate the Miami night. For a comprehensive listing you should consult the Arts Section of the *Sunday Miami Herald* and the monthly *Miami's Guide to the Arts*. Most of

the major events are staged at the **Gusman Center for the Performing Arts**, which is home to the **Miami City Ballet**, ((305) 532-7713, and the **Philharmonic Orchestra of Florida**, the state's foremost symphony orchestra, ((305) 945-5180. The center also hosts the **Miami Film Festival** every February. For information on all events, contact the center at 174 East Flagler Street, Miami, ((305) 372-0925. Opera lovers should know that the **Greater Miami Opera** is the seventh largest in the country, and regularly attracts the likes of Pavarotti and Domingo. Performances are at the Dade County Auditorium, 2901 West Flagler Street, Miami, ((305) 854-7890. The Florida Shakespeare Festival and the Hispanic Theatre Festival both take place at the **Minorca Playhouse** 232 Minorca Avenue, Coral Gables, ((305) 446-1116.

The liveliest popular nightlife in the region occurs in downtown Miami, Little Havana, and Coconut Grove. **Tobacco Road** is one of the oldest watering holes in Miami, which features live blues bands. It is downtown at 626 South Miami Avenue, ((305) 374-1198. For the samba sounds and tropical drinks of Brazil, you should head for the **Jardin Brasilien** in the Bayside Marketplace at 401 Biscayne Boulevard, ((305) 374-4748.

All the action in Little Havana is along Southwest Eighth Street. At № 971 is **La Tranquera**, ((305) 856-9467, where you can hear Latin jazz and marengue music. At № 2235, flamenco dancing accompanies mariachi music in **Cacharrito's Place**, ((305) 643-9626. At № 3604, Latin musicians perform throughout the night at the **Copacabana Supper Club**, ((305) 443-3801.

In Coconut Grove, a particularly lively venue is **Biscayne Baby** at 3336 Virginia Street, ((305) 445-3751, which features a dining area straight out of the 1950s as well as a disco. The **Hungry Sailor** at 3064-1/2 Grand Avenue, ((305) 444-9359, is an English-style pub serving English food, ales, and beers along with its jazz, reggae, and folk music. **Regine's** in the Grand Bay Hotel, 2669 South Bayshore Drive, ((305) 858-9600, attracts the same trendies to its disco/lounge as its counterparts in other cities.

ABOVE: The Bayfront Park in downtown Miami. OPPOSITE: Bahamian dancer at Miami Pasco.

WHERE TO STAY

Luxury

It's a short taxi ride from the airport to the **Doral Resort and Country Club** at 4400 Northwest 87th Avenue, Miami, ((305) 592-2000, toll-free (800) 327-6334, which is one of the largest golf resorts in the world with five championship courses in its 2,500-acre grounds. There are also 15 tennis courts, and you can receive instruction from the resort's resident tennis pro, former Wimbledon

champion Arthur Ashe. Other exceptional facilities include the four-story Doral Spa, complete with steam rooms, saunas, Turkish baths, and gyms, and the 24-stable Doral Equestrian Center, which offers riding lessons. If you are still stuck for something to do, the hotel provides a regular shuttle service to the beach. Near the Bayside Marketplace downtown is the **Hotel Inter-Continental Miami** at 100 Chopin Plaza, ((305) 577-1000, toll-free (800) 327-0200, a 34-story triangular building with 645 attractive rooms and suites, a theater, and a rooftop recreation area with tennis and racquetball courts, a swimming pool, gardens and a jogging trail. In the hotel's lobby it is hard to miss the 70-ton sculpture by Henry Moore.

Downtown luxury can also be found at the **Omni International Hotel**, 1601 Biscayne Boulevard, ((305) 374-0000, which has over 500 ultra-modern rooms — many of them with stunning views of the Miami skyline and Biscayne Bay — and its own leisure complex with expensive boutiques, bars,

and night clubs. Over on Key Biscayne at 350 Ocean Drive, ((305) 361-2021, toll-free (800) 3430-7170, is the **Sonesta Beach Hotel**, a popular hotel with families because it has a comprehensive program of activities for children. All the rooms and suites have balconies overlooking the island or the Atlantic, and the 28 villas in the grounds are full efficiencies with private swimming pools.

Two of the best hotels in the area can be found in Coconut Grove. The **Mayfair House** has its own shopping mall with designer boutiques, nine restaurants, and a central atrium with fountains and plants. The hotel's 181 suites each has a Japanese hot tub or a jacuzzi, and the rooftop facilities include a swimming pool and a solarium. Newspapers come with breakfast, and complimentary caviar is served in the Tiffany Bar. This glamorous and extremely non-budget hotel is at 3000 Florida Avenue, ((305) 441-0000, toll-free (800) 433-4555. The elegant **Grand Bay Hotel** at 2669 South Bayshore Drive, ((305) 858-9600, toll-free (800) 327-2788, has English and French suites with baby grand pianos, and in every room new arrivals are greeted by flowers and complimentary champagne. The service is splendid, and you can arrange golf, tennis, or sailing through a very helpful concierge. The hotel's Grand Café is one of the best restaurants in Miami.

In Coral Gables is the Moorish castle-like **Biltmore Hotel** at 1200 Anastasia Drive, ((305) 445-1926, toll-free (800) 445-2586. The hotel's grand rooms with antique furnishings and vaulted ceilings adorned with frescoes are matched outside by the beautiful grounds featuring a golf course, tennis courts, and an enormous swimming pool.

Mid-range

Moderately priced and near the airport, the **Hotel Sofitel Miami** offers a sauna, tennis courts, Continental breakfasts, and soundproof rooms at 5800 Blue Lagoon Drive, ((305) 264-4888. In North Miami, the **Inn on the Bay** at 1819 79th Street Causeway, ((305) 865-7100, is a family-oriented hotel with small but immaculate rooms, only a few minutes away from the beach. The **Everglades Hotel** downtown at 244 Biscayne Boulevard, ((305) 379-5461, has just been given a comprehensive face-lift, and has very comfortable, very modern rooms, while the rooftop has a swimming pool and a bar. Also downtown near the Bayside shops is the **Biscayne Bay Marriott Hotel and Marina** at 1633 North Bayshore Drive, ((305) 374-3900, where the marina has boating, fishing, and windsurfing facilities; the other amenities include five restaurants, a games room, and free in-room movies.

The **Coconut Grove Hotel** is one of the few in Coconut Grove which caters to the not-quite-wealthy. And it does it very well,

west Eighth Street, ((305) 266-1727. But the best choice can be found along Biscayne Boulevard, which at N° 340 has the **Best Western Marina Park Hotel**, ((305) 372-2862, and at N° 3400 the **Mardi Gras Motel Apartments** ((305) 573-7700, and at N° 3530 the **Bay Point Motel,** ((305) 573-4444, and at N° 6330 the **Economy Inn,** ((305) 633-6916.

WHERE TO EAT

Expensive
Il Tulipanò at 11052 Biscayne Boulevard in

with two excellent restaurants, tennis courts, a sauna, water sports facilities, and its own shops. It is at 2649 South Bayshore Drive, ((305) 858-2500, toll-free (800) 327-8771. In Coral Gables the best not-quite-expensive hotel is the **Hotel Place St. Michel** at 162 Alcazar Avenue, ((305) 444-1666. Every room is tastefully appointed, including European antiques, and apart from the complimentary Continental breakfasts the hotel's French restaurant is of a very high standard, as is the service throughout the hotel.

Inexpensive
Most of the budget-priced hotels in Miami are in and around the downtown area, including the **Sunnyside Motel** at 6024 South-

North Miami, ((305) 893-4811, is the creation of Filippo Il Grande, whose veal dishes and shellfish (especially the clams) are a delight. The **Pavillion Grill** at the Hotel Inter-Continental, 100 Chopin Plaza, ((305) 372-4494, should offer a map with its menu: the specialties include Key West tuna, Carolina pheasant, Texan cactus, Wyoming rabbit, and Hawaiian sweet onions. Another excellent hotel restaurant downtown is **Veronique's** at the Biscayne Bay Marriott, 1633 North Bayshore Drive, ((305) 374-3900, where you should definitely order the Cajun-style seafood.

The huge swimming pool ABOVE in the Moorish castle setting of the Biltmore Hotel in Coral Gables and OPPOSITE its interior.

Southwest Eighth Street in Little Havana has two (among many) distinguished restaurants. At N° 740 the **Malaga**, ((305) 858-4224, features such Cuban specialties as *arroz con pollo* (chicken with rice), spicy fried veal and pork, white bean and sausage soup, and other delicious concoctions. At N° 2499 **El Bodegon de Castilla** ((305) 649-0863, specializes in Spanish cooking — mostly Castillian, obviously, but some Catalan.

In Coconut Grove I would strongly recommend the **Mayfair Grill** in the Mayfair House Hotel, 3000 Florida Avenue, ((305) 441-0000. The star attraction on the menu — I'm not joking — is the grilled buffalo. In Coral Gables, go to **Chez Maurice**, where Maurice Cambin runs a very good French Provincial restaurant at 382 Miracle Mile, ((305) 448-8984.

Moderate

There is a selection of fine Italian restaurants along Biscayne Boulevard in North Miami, and among the best of them is **La Lupa** at 11220 Biscayne Boulevard, ((305) 893-9531, which features both northern *and* southern Italian cuisine. For authentic Nicaraguan food, you should go to **La Parilla** at 9611 West Flagler Street in Little Managua, about 10 miles west of downtown Miami. The restaurant, ((305) 553-4419, has a fascinating fried pork with yucca and red snapper in Creole sauce. For Spanish food try **Las Tapas** at 401 Biscayne Boulevard downtown at the Bayside waterfront, ((305) 372-2737. The house specialty is of course *tapas*, which can easily and infinitely be expanded into a wonderful main course.

For Cuban food I would single out **Centro Vasco** at 2235 Southwest Eighth Street, ((305) 643-9606, if only for their delicious stuffed squid in black bean sauce.

On Key Biscayne I like **La Choza**, an Argentinian steak house at 973 Crandon Boulevard, ((305) 361-0113. In Coconut Grove I'm partial to **Señor Frog's** at 3008 Grand Avenue, ((305) 448-0999, which serves some of the best Mexican food in the Miami area. Also, if you order prudently,

you can eat more or less economically at the splendid **Grand Café** in the Grand Bay Hotel, 2669 South Bayshore Drive in Coconut Grove, ((305) 858-9600. In Coral Gables, devotees of Thai food (and I'm certainly one) are grateful for the presence of **Bangkok, Bangkok** at 157 Giralda Avenue, ((305) 444-2397, just as fans of Indian food (I'm one of those, too) sing the praises of the **House of India** at 22 Merrick Way in Coral Gables, ((305) 444-2348.

Inexpensive

In North Miami, **Nick and Maria's** is casual, welcoming, and serves some marvelous Greek dishes at 11701 Northeast Second Avenue, ((305) 891-9232. If you are particularly health-conscious, the place to go to in downtown Miami is **Granny Feelgood's** at 190 Southeast First Avenue, ((305) 358-6233, where you can expect some wonderful salads, *inter alia*. At the other end of the spectrum — *fry! fry!* — is **The Big Fish** at 55 Southwest Miami Avenue Road, ((305) 372-3725. But for genuinely inexpensive, genuinely tasty meals, your best bet is simply to walk up and down Southwest Eighth Street in Little Havana: you will be amazed (and tantalized) by the number and range of budget-priced eateries.

On Key Biscayne, **The English Pub** at 320 Crandon Boulevard, ((305) 361-5481, is deservedly popular, mixing basic English and American cooking. In Coconut Grove, **Monty Trainer's Bayshore** is a big local favorite, with its outdoor raw bar overlooking a marina, and its reggae and calypso bands at the weekend. It is at 2560 South Bayshore Drive, ((305) 858-1431. In Coral Gables, you will find a very reasonably priced meal to your liking if you simply walk along Coral Way: it is crowded with many cheap and cheerful places to eat.

HOW TO GET THERE

More than 80 national and international airlines fly into Miami International Airport, which is only six miles west of downtown. Numerous taxi and limousine companies serve the airport. A taxi takes about 20 minutes to reach the middle of Miami, and charges about $16. There is also a Metrobus

---

OPPOSITE: Automotive and architectural reminders of the past in Miami Beach's Art Deco district.

station at the airport, which operates a shuttle downtown much more cheaply.

If you are traveling from the north by car you have several options: I–95 and Route 1 come directly down the coast, and I–75 ("Florida's Turnpike") comes through central Florida and Orlando on its way to the southeast. Route A1A, Ocean-skirting and island-hopping, is the slow and scenic way to approach Miami from the north. From the west you will take Route 84, Everglades Parkway, also known as "Alligator Alley".

MIAMI BEACH

Miami Beach is a narrow strip of land a little over seven miles (11 km) long and only a mile (about 1.6 km) wide at its widest point. It is separated from mainland Miami by Biscayne Bay, and connected to it by three causeways. It probably has more hotels than any other comparable patch of land in the world, and in a few blocks at the southern end of the island it has the largest concentration of Art Deco buildings in America. And then there is the beach itself, running along the entire eastern side of the island. Not only that, but it is getting bigger all the time: at this writing there is a dredging operation pumping offshore sand on to the island to create a strip of beach over 300 ft (91 m) wide at some points.

BACKGROUND

In 1912 Miami Beach was an offshore mangrove and palmetto swamp inhabited mostly by crocodiles. The only inhabitant of note was a horticulturist named John S. Collins who had bought some land there and established an avocado and citrus plantation. He founded the Miami Beach Improvement Company in 1912, initiated some land sales on the island and began the construction of a bridge to the mainland.

Collins ran out of money the following year, 1913, and the unfinished bridge became known as "Collins' Folly". Undaunted, Collins set up in partnership with Carl Fisher, who, in exchange for large areas of land on the island, injected much-needed capital into the development company, enabling the bridge to be completed and further development to be launched. Fisher set about clearing the swamps from his land and creating new acreage by draining the shallow bays. What slowly emerged was a tropical island with a wide swath of beach, which Fisher and Collins immediately recognized as a potential resort. They spurred the development of the island into the Twenties, building shopping plazas, hotels, golf courses, and tennis courts.

Elderly people came here to retire, while vacationers began to arrive in their thou-

Seven miles (11 km) of beach, the winter sun and a lot of enterprise transformed a former mango and palmetto swamp into Miami Beach, one of America's leading resorts.

sands. Then, in the Thirties, after the worst of the Depression was over, a new building boom began at the southern end of the island. Pastel, geometric, streamlined buildings started to appear: Art Deco had arrived with a vengeance. Today over 100 Art Deco houses and hotels are to be seen in what is one of the most architecturally striking pockets in the country. Since the 1930s Miami Beach's story has been one of steady growth and development into one of the leading resorts in America, as hordes of tourists swarm in to enjoy the beaches and the winter sun. At the same time, more and more northerners are choosing to retire there, while from the south Latin Americans continue to arrive and to do their part to invigorate the island's growth.

GENERAL INFORMATION

The Miami Beach Chamber of Commerce is at 1920 Meridian Avenue, Miami Beach, ((305) 672-1270. For 24-hour information on hotels, car rentals, cruises, and the island's principal attractions, contact the Miami Beach Resort Hotel Association at 407 Lincoln Road, Suite 10G, Miami Beach, ((305) 531-3553.

WHAT TO SEE AND DO

Sights
Undoubtedly the main sight in Miami Beach is the **Art Deco district**, which is a block north of Sixth Street between Lummus

Miami and Environs

Park and the beach at the southern tip of the island. Each of the curved, multi-colored buildings has its own unique character, and if you would like to learn more about them you should get in touch with the Miami Design Preservation League, ((305) 672-2014, which organizes tours of the district. Three of the largest and most impressive Art Deco hotels in Miami Beach are on **Collins Avenue**, which is more or less the spine of the island: they are the Delano, the National, and the Ritz Plaza, which resemble, respectively, a spaceship, a balloon, and a submarine.

The most impressive hotel, however, is the majestic **Fontainebleau Hilton**, which is set among tropical vegetation, lagoons, and waterfalls, and has a huge, wonderful mural on one of its exterior walls.

The only art museum of note on the island is the **Bass Museum of Art** at 2121 Park Avenue, ((305) 673-7533, which has Renaissance, Baroque, Rococo, and modern works in its collection, including especially interesting works by Rubens and Toulouse-Lautrec. The museum is open from 10 am to 5 pm Tuesday to Saturday and from 1 pm to 5 pm on Sunday; admission is $3 for

ABOVE AND OPPOSITE: Art Deco buildings in Miami Beach.

adults and $2 for children. The **Miami Beach Garden Center and Conservatory** at 2000 Garden Center Drive is a place of great natural charm and beauty in which you can relax for no charge, seven days a week from 10 am to 3:30 pm, or you can stroll along the **Boardwalk** which runs beside the beach from 21st Street to 46th Street.

Different parts of the beach seem to have developed distinct personalities. The beach around **21st Street**, for example, has been colonized by young people and couples with small children; the beach at **35th Street** attracts a quieter, older group, and many of its beachfront hotel bars are open to the public; around **46th Street** you get the Very Important Tourists from the Fontainebleau and other top hotels; while up at **53rd Street** and **64th Street** you will find probably the quietest beaches on the island.

Sports

There are several public golf courses in Miami Beach: Normandy Shores at 2401 Biarritz Drive, ((305) 673-7775, the Bayshore Golf Course at 2301 Alton Road, ((305) 673-7706, and the Haulover Beach Golf Course in the northern part of the island at 10800 Collins Avenue, ((305) 940-6719. **Tennis** players should go to Flamingo Park at Michigan Avenue and 12th Street, ((305) 673-7761, where there are 17 public courts open from 9 am to 9 pm; there are also public courts at North Shore Park, 350 73rd Street, ((305) 673-7754. The Miami Beach Recreation Department can give you further information on golf and tennis facilities; call (305) 673-7700.

If you are keen on **deep-sea fishing**, all sorts of cruises, from a few hours to a few days, can be chartered from the Kelly Fishing Fleet at 10800 Collins Avenue, ((305) 945-0944. For **scuba diving** enthusiasts, equipment rental, instruction, and chartered excursions are all available from Aquanauts at 677 Southwest First Street, ((305) 534-7710. If **boating** appeals to you, you can hire a boat from Beach Boat Rentals at 2380 Collins Avenue, ((305) 534-4307, from where you can cruise Biscayne Bay and the adjoining canals; yachts can be hired from Florida Yacht Charters and Sales at 1290 Fifth Street, ((305) 532-8600. The best place for **surfing** is

Miami and Environs.

at Haulover Beach at the north end of the island, but you shouldn't expect a major surfing experience as the area is not famed for its surf.

Shopping

There is no shortage of shops selling beach paraphernalia in Miami Beach. Chocolate, 119 Fifth Street, and Tommy at the Beach, 450 Ocean Drive, are as well-stocked as any of them. The best selections of "serious" shops are in the **Bal Harbour Shops** at 9700 Collins Avenue. For antiques, arts and crafts, galleries and that sort of thing you should go to either **Española Way** or to the **Lincoln Road Mall** on Lincoln Road between Collins Avenue and Michigan Avenue.

Nightlife

Most of the after-dark action in Miami Beach takes place in the Art Deco district. New Wave music pounds through the night at **Joseph's on the Beach**, 323 23rd Street, ((305) 673-9626, while at **Penrod's**, 1 Ocean Drive, ((305) 538-1111, you can choose from various dance floors offering reggae, jazz, and rock music. For mellower sounds try the sidewalk café **The Tropics International**, 960 Ocean Drive, ((305) 531-5335, which features live jazz on some nights. At the **Irish House Bar**, 1430 Alton Road, ((305) 672-9626, a place full of "character" as well as characters, the odd song is played on the elderly juke box but the patrons mainly shoot pool and drink beer.

The bistro decor and the solo guitarist combine to give the **Café des Arts** a whiff of Parisian nightlife at 918 Ocean Drive, ((305) 534-6267. Another attractive, quasi-bohemian night spot is the **Wet Paint Café** at 915 Lincoln Road Mall, ((305) 672-3287, where the nicely decorated cellar echoes to the sounds of live jazz and Caribbean music. Reggae features heavily at the **Club Bamboo** in the Eden Roc Hotel at 4525 Collins Avenue, ((305) 538-5803, while music of the Fifties tops the bill at **Chevy's on the Beach**, 8701 Collins Avenue, ((305) 868-1950.

WHERE TO STAY

Luxury

There are 18 acres of beautifully landscaped grounds surrounding the famous **Fontainebleau Hilton** at 4441 Collins Avenue, ((305) 538-2000, which also has 300 ft (91 m) of its own beach, seven tennis courts, several swimming pools and waterfalls, a giant spa with mineral baths, saunas, and jacuzzis, not to mention 1,200 splendidly appointed rooms. There is also a specially supervised program for children. At the **Doral-on-the-Ocean** resort guests are welcomed with complimentary chocolates and a fruit basket in their rooms. The Doral's many amenities include an Aqua Sports Center offering water- and jet-skiing, snorkeling and scuba diving instruction, windsurfing, and sailing. It is at 4883 Collins Avenue, ((305) 532-3600.

The luxury suites at the **Alexander Hotel**, 5225 Collins Avenue, ((305) 865-6500, are elegantly (and antiquely) furnished, and each one has a private balcony overlooking the ocean and the hotel's 600 ft (183 m) of beach. Then there is the quirky and delightful old **Eden Roc** at 4525 Collins Avenue, ((305) 531-0000, with its 1950s furnishings, its New York deli with Israeli music, and its marvelous ocean-view restaurant. My favorite, though, is the **Hotel Cavalier** in the Art Deco district at 1320 Ocean Drive, ((305) 531-6424, toll-free (800) 338-9076. From the moment its limousine picks you up at the airport, it provides a joyful experience.

Mid-range

Although most of the hotels in the Art Deco district are as highly priced as they are highly desirable, there are some notable exceptions. One is the **Park Central Hotel** at 640 Ocean Drive, ((305) 538-1611, which has a ceiling fan in each room, and an excellent, uncomplicated restaurant, Lucky's. There is also the **Edison Hotel** at 960 Ocean Drive, ((305) 531-0461, where the rooms are modern and immaculate.

Away from the Art Deco district, there is the **Hawaiian Isle** at 17601 Collins Avenue, ((305) 932-2121, toll-free (800) 327-5275, which has lots of bamboo and tropical plants, as well as volleyball, tennis, and basketball courts, water sports facilities, and 400 ft (122 m) of beach. **Chateau by the Sea** has, incongruously, a country flavor to it. It also has a large swimming pool and its own shops; it is located at 19115 Collins Avenue, ((305) 931-8800. Even more incongruously, you will find a covered wagon and horses at 17201 Collins Avenue, which means you have arrived at the **Desert Inn**, a Wild West theme resort with a swimming pool and outside dining areas, and answers to ((305) 947-0621, toll-free (800) 327-6362.

Inexpensive

The friendly, family-run **Beachcomber Hotel** offers clean and comfortable rooms in the Art Deco district at 1340 Collins Avenue, ((305) 531-3755. I would also recommend the **Beach Motel** at 8601 Harding Avenue, ((305) 861-2001, which has both rooms and efficiencies, plus the obligatory swimming pool, and the **Ocean Roc** at 19505 Collins Avenue, ((305) 931-7600, which has lovely, airy rooms with balconies, and a nice bar with its restaurant.

WHERE TO EAT

Expensive

If you are going to pay a lot of money for your dinner, you might as well have it at **Café Chauveron**, 9561 East Bay Harbor Drive, ((305) 866-8779, where Roger Chauveron and his staff provide French food and service of the highest standard. Another outstanding French restaurant is **Dominique's** in the Alexander Hotel at 5225 Collins Avenue, ((305) 861-5252, where chef Dominique D'Ermo specializes in nouvelle cuisine enlivened by the odd American eccentricity such as wild boar sausage or sautéed alligator tail. **The Forge** having recently undergone a $2 million face-lift, now has a decor—chandeliers and stained glass and antiques — to match its rich menu and even richer wine list. The Forge is at 432 Arthur Godfrey Road, ((305) 538-8533.

Two Art Deco restaurants well worth a visit are the **Carlyle Grill** at 1250 Ocean Drive, ((305) 534-2135, which features Americanized nouvelle cuisine, and **Joe's Stone Crab** at 227 Biscayne Street, ((305) 673-0365, where the specialty is obvious (although for me the *real* specialty is their key lime pie).

Moderate

There are two Italian restaurants in the Art Deco district well worth a visit: **Tiramesu** at 500 Ocean Drive, ((305) 532-4538, and **Gino's Italian Restaurant** at 1906 Ocean Drive, ((305) 532-6426.

For excellent Chinese food go to **Christine Lee's Gaslight** at the Thunderbird Hotel, 18401 Collins Avenue, ((305) 931-7700. For cooking that can best be described as Continental-Californian, with an ambience and clientele to match, check out **The Strand** at 671 Washington Avenue, ((305) 532-2340. For eclecticism run riot, but deliciously so, try **Pineapples** at 530 Arthur Godfrey Road, ((305) 532-9731, where your grilled ginger dolphin could be preceded by a Chinese egg roll and accompanied by an Italian salad with Greek cheese.

Inexpensive

If you have finished a hard day's tanning on the beach near the Art Deco district, you can eat well and cheaply at **The Palace**, 1200 Ocean Drive, ((305) 531-9077. It is anything but palatial, being a 1950s-style diner, but it *is* a treat. The **News Café** at 800 Ocean Drive is a bit more sophisticated, or at least tries to be, but is equally good value. If you are feeling piggish, but want quality with your quantity of food, probably the best place in town is **Wolfie Cohen's Rascal House** at 17190 Collins Avenue, ((305) 947-4581. Another good place for budget grub is **Pumperniks** at 12599 Biscayne Boulevard, ((305) 891-1225.

HOW TO GET THERE

First you have to get to Miami: see earlier section. Then from the mainland take the Broad Causeway to the Bay Harbour Islands and over to Bal Harbour, the John F. Kennedy Causeway to northern Miami Beach, the Julia Tuttle Causeway to central Miami Beach, and the MacArthur Causeway to southern Miami Beach.

The
Gold
Coast

DRIVING along the 60-mile (97-km) stretch of coastline known as the Gold Coast, where glittering resorts confront the ocean across golden sandy beaches, it is hard to believe that less than a century ago this was mosquito-infested swampland.

Indeed, the only mark left on the Gold Coast by earlier centuries is the name itself. It derives from the most lucrative business enterprise to occupy the inhabitants of this area in the nineteenth century: salvaging gold from the frequent shipwrecks offered up by Mother Nature on the rocks offshore. These salvage operations, known as "wrecking", proved to be so profitable that the "wreckers" are said to have taken not just to praying for shipwrecks but to praying for particular *kinds* of shipwrecks — according to the demands of the market at any given time. And when Mother Nature failed to oblige, they were even known to indulge in a little do-it-yourself shipwreck-making, by luring passing ships on to the rocks.

Wrecking largely died out towards the end of the century, with the advent of more sophisticated maritime navigational equipment and the arrival of Henry Flagler's Florida East Coast Railroad. Now it became the turn of the land to supply the riches. Flagler himself started the new gold rush in 1894 by erecting the enormous Royal Poinciana Hotel in Palm Beach, to which he enticed some of the richest families in America. The hotel, since demolished, had 1,150 rooms and a staff of 1,400. Two years later he built The Breakers in Palm Beach, which twice burned down but which now, in its third incarnation, stands as one of the most famous hotels in the world. That same year, 1896, Flagler extended his railway to Fort Lauderdale, and in 1902 built himself his own 55-room marble mansion in Palm Beach. Thus, by the turn of the century, the ground had been prepared for this once-inhospitable bit of coast to become one of the most popular and celebrated resort areas in the world.

Among the first to see the possibilities here was the flamboyant architect Addison Mizner, who arrived a few years later and decided that what the place needed was a lot of pastel stucco buildings designed by him. Whether it needed them or not, it got them — as well as many more by other architects trying to imitate his style. That style has been variously described as "Italianate", "Pseudo-Spanish", "Mediterranean Revival", "Spanish-Moorish" and, my favorite, "Bastard Spanish-Moorish-Romanesque-Gothic-Renaissance-Bull Market-Damn the Expense" style. Mizner's *chef-d'œuvre* was the Cloister Inn in Boca Raton, now the Boca Raton Hotel and Club, a wonderful pink confection that remains one of the most expensive hotels ever built. To this palace Mizner lured as many of the rich and famous as he could attract, and they in turn attracted the multitudes. As Mizner had predicted, "Get the big snobs, and the little ones will follow."

Meanwhile, to the south, in Fort Lauderdale another visionary was doing his part to add luster to the Gold Coast. Charles Rodes, a property developer from West Virginia, suddenly came up with the "Venetian Solution" to the problem of what to do with all that swampland: he began dredging a series of "finger canals" that converted sodden, useless land into prime waterfront real estate. As a result, today the *soi-disant* "Venice of America" has almost 200 miles (322 km) of inland waterways to go along with its seven miles (11 km) of beautiful beach.

By the 1920s the allure of the Gold Coast had set off a feeding frenzy among property speculators, developers, investors, builders, prospective retirees, and would-be winter migrants from the north. There followed a land boom of incredible proportions, at the height of which over 2,000 people a day were arriving to stake their claim to a little bit of paradise. For most of them, however, that paradise was lost in 1926 when the boom abruptly collapsed.

For the next two decades, through the years of the Depression and the Second World War, some of the shine went off the Gold Coast (though none of the sunshine: there are 3,000 hours of it every year, with an average annual temperature of 75 °F, or 24 °C). Then paradise was regained after the war, and for the second half of this century it has been an irresistible magnet for countless millions of pleasure-seekers.

The Atlantic horizon, in a latticework frame.

FORT LAUDERDALE

Although sunny by disposition as well as by climate, Fort Lauderdale has long had an image problem. For decades it had to put up with being called Fort Liquordale, a sobriquet it earned during Prohibition when its bars and night clubs were awash in illicit alcohol smuggled in from the Bahamas. Then, in 1960, the old image was given a new twist in the film *Where the Boys Are*, which depicted the place as America's party headquarters for college students on their spring break. Although the new image had only a fractional basis in reality, the film succeeded in creating the phenomenon it was ostensibly portraying, so that for many years afterwards Fort Lauderdale was visited annually by migratory swarms of fun-seeking collegians. Now, to the manifest relief of the natives, most of the Eastertime action seems to have shifted north to Daytona Beach.

BACKGROUND

Fort Lauderdale's early history has vanished as completely as the fort which Major William Lauderdale built near the mouth of the New River in 1838 to protect settlers from attack by the Seminoles. What *is* known is that the first settler, Charles Lewis, arrived in 1793 and established a plantation by the New River. Exactly 100 years later another settler, Frank Stranahan, arrived and established a trading post for doing business with the Indians, as well as a general store and a ferry system. When he married a few years later, Stranahan converted the general store into a residence, which has since been restored and is open to visitors.

Although the arrival of Flagler's railway in 1896 opened up the area to accelerated settlement, there were still fewer than 200 residents when Fort Lauderdale was incorporated in 1911. It was not until the land boom of the Twenties that the city's spectacular growth began in earnest. Today, with upwards of 30,000 pleasure craft roaming its rivers and canals, and

A Fort Lauderdale welcome for yachts on the Round-the-World race.

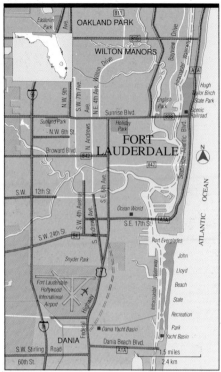

For recorded information you can dial (305) 765-8068. The Broward Parks and Recreation Division also has a special-events number: ((305) 563-PARK.

Other useful telephone numbers (all in area code 305):

Fort Lauderdale/Hollywood	
International Airport	357-6100
Yellow Cabs	527-8600
Checker Cabs	485-3000
Broward County Medical	
Association	525-1595
Broward County Dental	
Association	772-5461
Physician Information Service	966-DOCS
24-Hour Doctors' House Calls	748-5900

untold thousands of bodies from all over the world glistening on its beaches, the ghosts of Henry Flagler and Charles Rodes must be blinking in wonder.

GENERAL INFORMATION

The Greater Fort Lauderdale Convention and Visitors Bureau is at 200 East Las Olas Boulevard, Suite 1500, Fort Lauderdale FL 33301. ((305) 765-4466. The Greater Fort Lauderdale Chamber of Commerce is at 52 Northeast Third Avenue, Fort Lauderdale FL 33301. ((305) 462-6000. The Broward County Hotel/Motel Association is at 701 Central East Broward Boulevard, Fort Lauderdale FL 33301. ((305) 462-0409. The association is represented in Europe by Sastel International Ltd., 18 Buckingham Palace Road, London SW1 0PQ. ((0171) 630-5995.

For up-to-the-minute information on local events and attractions, check the listings in the *Fort Lauderdale News/Sun Sentinel* or in the free magazines, *See*, *Key*, and *Where*.

OPPOSITE: Wearing big smiles: a bikini contest in Fort Lauderdale.

WHAT TO SEE AND DO

Sights

It is not often that the most entertaining means of seeing the sights are themselves major tourist attractions, but this happens to be the case in Fort Lauderdale, where two large paddlewheel riverboats, the *Jungle Queen* and the *Paddlewheel Queen*, cruise the waters in and around the city.

The 550-passenger *Jungle Queen* has two three-hour cruises daily, at 10 am and 2 pm, leaving from the Bahia Mar Yachting Center, 801 Seabreeze Boulevard, ((305) 462-5596. The cruise includes a stop at Indian Village where the sights include rare birds, monkeys, and alligator wrestling. In the evening there is a four-hour dinner cruise, which leaves Bahia Mar at 7 pm and features a vaudeville revue and other entertainment. The dinner, served on an exotic island in the New River, is an all-you-can-eat affair of barbecued ribs, chicken, and shrimp. Prices for the daytime cruises are $12.95 for adults and $6.50 for children; for the evening cruise $22.95 for everybody.

The 400-passenger *Paddlewheel Queen* has an afternoon cruise leaving at 2 pm from 2950 Northeast 32nd Avenue, one block south of Oakland Park Beach Bridge and two blocks west of A1A, the coast road, ((305) 565-6260. It costs $9.95 for adults and $6 for children. There is also a dinner cruise, featuring a charcoal broiled steak dinner and dancing under the stars to a live band, which costs $26.50 for adults and $21.50 for children.

For sightseeing on your own by water there is available for rent just about every type of boat imaginable, though I'm partial to the **motorized gondolas** myself. They can seat up to six people, can be hired for any length of time you want, and are available from Gondolas of America, Inc., Bahia Mar Yachting Center, South Docks, 1007 Seabreeze Boulevard, ((305) 522-3333.

The best way to see Fort Lauderdale by land is on the **Voyager Sightseeing Train**, a string of canopied, rubber-wheeled cars pulled by a little white Jeep. There are 90-minute tours daily at 10 am, noon, 2 pm, and 4 pm, leaving from 600 Seabreeze Boulevard, ((305) 463-0401.

Among the sights particularly worth seeing I would put the **Museum of Discovery & Science** at the top of the list. It is a science and nature museum with hands-on exhibits that allow you to watch bees at work in a glass-fronted hive, go cave crawling, bend rays of light, and touch a star, among other things. Children love it. There is also an IMAX cinema with a 55 ft by 75 ft (17 m by 23 m) screen. It is at 401 Southwest Second Avenue, ((305) 467-6637. Admission is $6.

Also well worth a visit is the city's new multimillion-dollar **Museum of Art** at 1 East Las Olas Boulevard, ((305) 525-5500. It has an extraordinary collection of ethnographic art, including pre-Columbian, West African, Oceanic, and American Indian art; its Dutch and Flemish collections are quite strong as well. The museum stays open late on Tuesdays, and is closed on Sunday mornings and Mondays. Admission: adults $4, students $1.

The **Stranahan House**, ((305) 524-4736, Fort Lauderdale's oldest remaining structure, is where Frank Stranahan traded with the Indians and sold to the settlers at the turn of the century before he converted it into a home. It has been lovingly and immaculately restored to its pre-World War I condition, and is open to the public on Wednesdays, Fridays, and Saturdays from 10 am to 3:30 pm, and on Sundays from 1 to 3:30 pm. The house is just off Las Olas Boulevard at the New River tunnel. Admission is $3.

To get an idea (but only an idea) of how some of the Indians lived with whom Stranahan traded, go to the **Seminole Okalee Indian Village** at the corner of Stirling Road and Route 7. The Indians support themselves by selling arts and crafts and — believe it or not — running bingo games.

For a close-up look at some of the native fauna, **Ocean World** at 1701 Southeast 17th Street, ((305) 525-6611, has continuous shows featuring trained dolphins and sea lions, plus a three-story-high aquarium for viewing all kinds of marine life. Tickets are $10.95 for adults and $8.95 for children. **Butterfly World** in Tradewinds Park, 3600 West Sample Road, ((305) 977-4434, is home to over 150 species of butterflies and features a screened-in tropical rain forest where thousands of exotic "flying flowers" flutter by. Admission is $8.95 for adults and $6 for children. **Flamingo Gardens**, at 3750 Flamingo Road, ((305) 493-2955, features a jungle tram ride, crocodiles, alligators, monkeys, tropical birds, a petting zoo and, of course, pink flamingos. Admission is $7 for adults, $4.50 for young people under 18. Improbable as it may seem, Fort Lauderdale is one of the best places to see and savor the Wild West as it really (more or less) was. The suburban community of Davie has turned itself into an authentic cowtown, complete with cowboys and cowgirls and, every Friday night, a rodeo in the **Davie Rodeo Complex** at Orange Drive and Davie Road, ((305) 434-7062.

Sports

If you are a **baseball** fan, you should know that the New York Yankees hold their spring training here in February/March, during which they play exhibition games at Lockhart Stadium, 5301 Northwest 12th Avenue, ((305) 776-1921. If you like more fast-paced action, combined with legal betting, you can see **jai alai** at Dania Jai Alai, 301 East Dania Boulevard, ((305) 949-2424, from late June until mid-April.

Golf enthusiasts will be pleased to learn that there are no less than five dozen (yes, *dozen*) golf courses in the Fort Lauderdale area. There are 11 public courses within the city limits of Fort Lauderdale alone, not to mention the many private courses that welcome non-members. Among the most attractive and challenging courses are the

American Golfers Club near the beach at 3850 North Route 1, ((305) 564-8760, the Bonaventure course at 200 Bonaventure Boulevard, ((305) 384-5020, and the Deer Creek Golf and Tennis Club at 2801 Deer Creek Country Club Boulevard, Deerfield Beach, ((305) 421-5550.

Tennis players are equally well catered for, with over 170 public tennis courts, including the lighted ones at George English Park, 1101 Bayview Drive, ((305) 566-0664, and Holiday Park at 1400 East Sunrise Boulevard, ((305) 761-5391. For comprehensive

467-2822, and Pro Dive at the Bahia Mar Yachting Center, ((305) 761-3413.

Shopping

For maximum choice you should head for the **Galleria**, a huge shopping mall over one million sq ft (or almost 305,000 sq m) at 2500 East Sunrise Boulevard, a few blocks from the ocean. It has over 150 shops and restaurants, in addition to such department stores as Neiman-Marcus, Lord & Taylor, Jordan Marsh, Saks Fifth Avenue, and Brooks Brothers.

information about the availability of both golf courses and tennis courts, contact the Fort Lauderdale Parks and Recreation Department, ((305) 761-2621.

Scuba diving and snorkeling can be enjoyed at more than 80 different dive sites along the bit of coast stretching about 12 miles (19 km) in each direction north and south of Fort Lauderdale. These include coral reefs, sunken wrecks, and ships that were deliberately scuttled to create artificial reefs. Of the many stores offering classes in diving and daily diving trips, as well as scuba and snorkeling equipment, are Force E at 2104 West Oakland Park Boulevard, ((305) 735-6227, Lauderdale Diver at 1334 Southeast 17th Street, ((305)

For maximum chic, palm-lined **Las Olas Boulevard** boasts an infinite variety of handsome (and occasionally offbeat) boutiques. For maximum craftsy shopping you should try the **Seminole Okalee Indian Village** at 5791 South Route 7. Here you will find the Anhinga Indian Museum and Art Gallery, ((305) 581-8411, the Thunderbird Trading Post, ((305) 585-2281, and the Flying Bird Gift Shop, ((305) 792-3445.

Nightlife

The "in" place these days — or those days, when I was there — is **Shooter's** at 3031 Northeast 32nd Avenue, ((305) 566-2855.

Seaside promenade at sunset.

What makes it "in" is not only that it is very attractive both inside and outside (where it sits beside the Intracoastal Waterway) but that, if you can't get in, it is also in between two other popular night spots, the **Bootlegger** (℃ (305) 563-4337), which has its own swimming pool, and **Durty Nelly's** (℃ (305) 564-0720).

Jazz fans won't want to miss the **Musician Exchange Café** at 200 South Andrews Avenue, ℃ (305) 764-1912, which usually features regional performers during the week and more famous musicians at the weekend. If you like country-and-western, **Do-Da's** at 700 South Route 7, ℃ (305) 791-1477, has four different theme rooms with dance floors, a Mexican restaurant, and a corral bar. The well-known bands play at the weekend.

If you want a good laugh, **The Comic Strip** at 1432 North Route 1, ℃ (305) 565-8887, is a great place to catch acts that haven't yet made it as well as those that have. Note: Sunday and Monday nights are amateur nights. Further up the road is **Casey's Comedy Club**, 6000 North Route 1, ℃ (305) 491-4423, which often features well-known American comedians.

Those who would prefer to be entertained by the sights rather than the sounds of the night should go up to the **Pier Top Lounge**, which rotates above the 17-story Pier 66 Resort and Marina at 2301 Southeast 17th Street, ℃ (305) 525-6666. Although there is a band and a small dance floor, the main attractions here are the ocean and the sunsets. For sea-level imagery drop in at **Shirttail Charlie's** and watch the boats go by on the New River. It's at 400 Southwest Third Avenue, ℃ (305) 463-3474. And the food is delicious.

WHERE TO STAY

Luxury

What do you say about a hotel that has 1,100 ft (335 m) of beach frontage, 8,000 sq ft (2,438 sq m) of free-form swimming pool (with waterfall), five restaurants and five tennis courts, three boutiques and three lounges, and you name-it? You say it is **Marriott's Harbor Beach Resort** and it is at 3030 Holiday Drive and its telephone

number is ℃ (305) 525-4000, toll-free (800) 228-9290. The **Bahia Mar Resort and Yachting Center** can also boast some impressive numbers: a 40-acre yacht basin, a 350-slip marina, a small fleet of charter fishing boats, but only (sigh) four tennis courts. It is located at 801 Seabreeze Boulevard, ℃ (305) 764-2233, toll-free (800) 327-8154. The **Pier 66 Hotel and Marina** at 2301 Southeast 17th Street, ℃ (305) 525-6666, toll-free (800) 327-3796, was Fort Lauderdale's first luxury high-rise hotel, and is still one of its finest, with a 142-slip marina and facilities for water sports rivaled only by Bahia Mar. Away from the beach — indeed, away from it all — is the **Bonaventure Resort and Spa** 17 miles (27 km) west of Fort Lauderdale at 250 Racquet Club Road, ℃ (305) 389-3300, toll-free (800) 327-8090. Set in 1,250 acres (506 ha), it has four restaurants, five swimming pools, 24 tennis courts, two 18-hole golf courses, a 160-seat amphitheater, a bowling alley, a roller-skating rink, riding stables, and a massive spa. Perhaps the most charming hotel in Fort Lauderdale — certainly the one with the most charming and solicitous staff — is the **Riverside Hotel** at 620 East Las Olas Boulevard, ℃ (305) 467-0671, toll-free (800) 325-3280. More Southern Comfortable than nouveau ritzy, it is in the heart of the city's most fashionable shopping area, with a swimming pool and gardens in the back beside the picturesque New River.

Mid-range

Some might argue that the **Lago Mar Hotel** belongs in the above category, but for what you get it is definitely not expensive. And what you get, most of all, is the peace and quiet that comes from being on the exclusive south end of the beach, far from the madding crowds. The hotel, at 1700 Southeast Ocean Boulevard, ℃ (305) 523-6511, has a lagoon on one side and the Atlantic on the other, with two swimming pools, four tennis courts, and a putting green in between. The **Casa Alhambra**, by contrast, has only five rooms in a restored Mediterranean-style house of the Thirties. The owner/manager, Victoria Feaman, serves a Continental breakfast in the morning and complimentary cocktails and hors d'œuvres in the evening, and in general makes guests feel like they are what she considers them to be: her guests. This happy place is at 3029 Alhambra Street, only a few yards from the beach, ((305) 467-2262.

Just south of Fort Lauderdale there is another delightfully out-of-the-ordinary hotel, **DiVito By the Sea**, at 3500 North Boardwalk, Hollywood, ((305) 929-7227. Known affectionately as "the Palace of Kitsch", it resembles a riverboat painted by someone who was both color-blind and in a hurry, and which is towing (or pushing) a replica of the Leaning Tower of Pisa. Among its other eccentricities is that it only likes letting rooms on a weekly basis, it only likes children from April to December, and it doesn't like any credit cards. Yet it's still a very likeable place. More predictable (which is not, by the way, a criticism) are the **Holiday Inns**. In price they range downward from the one on the ocean at Nº 999 North Atlantic Boulevard, ((305) 563-5961, to the one at 4900 Powerline Road, ((305) 776-4480. Bracketing these two, with both lower and higher rates than either, is the Holiday Inn Hotel and Conference Center at 5100 North Route 8, ((305) 739-4000.

Inexpensive

Two of the best bargains in Fort Lauderdale are within a few blocks of each other. The **Sherwood Motel**, 2201 North Route 1, ((305) 564-9636, and the larger **Berkeley Inn**, 1055 North Route 1, ((305) 565-4821, toll-free (800) 348-3769. Both have swimming pools and large, comfortable rooms. Similarly, there is a stretch of North Birch Road, just two blocks away from the beach, that has dozen of inexpensive motels, with pools, side by side. Two of the nicest of these are the **Sea View Resort Motel** at 550 North Birch Road, ((305) 564-3151, and the **Sea Chateau** at 555 North Birch Road, ((305) 566-8331.

WHERE TO EAT

Expensive

Occupying the 12th-floor penthouse of the Four Seasons condominium at 333 Sunset Drive, just off Las Olas Boulevard, ((305)

463-3303, **Le Dome** is one of the finest restaurants in Florida, with sensational views to match its dishes. The **Left Bank**, despite its name, is more American than Parisian, and more romantic than bohemian, but no matter. Owner/chef Jean-Pierre Brehier has created a superb restaurant at 214 Southeast Sixth Avenue, ((305) 462-5376. The cuisine inclines towards the nouvelle, and is memorably delicious. Visitors hungry for more traditional French cooking are advised to take their appetites to the corner of Route 1 and East Sunrise Boulevard, where they will find not one but two marvelous restaurants. **La Ferme**, at 1601 East Sunrise Boulevard, ((305) 764-0987, is the creation of Henri and Marie-Paule Terrier, a delightful Lyonnais couple who will make you feel at home — that is, if you could get food like theirs at home. A few steps away from La Ferme is **La Coquille** at 1619 East Sunrise Boulevard, ((305) 467-3030, an enchanting little bistro run by Jean and Hélène Bert. **Casa Vecchia** is just what the name says it is: an old house. And much more: in this beautifully re-decorated old house beside the Intracoastal Waterway, at 209 North Birch Road, ((305) 463-7575, restaurateurs Leonce Picot and Al Kocab have established a splendid Italian restaurant specializing in the more subtle cuisine of northern Italy.

Moderate

To avoid praising the same people twice in one paragraph, I have decided to cheat and list as "moderate" the fairly expensive **Down Under**, also the creation of Messrs Picot and Kocab. The restaurant is "down under" the Oakland Park Boulevard Bridge, at 3000 East Oakland Park Boulevard, ((305) 563-4123, and offers a menu that is really an anthology of other restaurants' greatest hits. It works. Louis Flemati's **Café de Paris**, at 715 East Las Olas Boulevard, ((305) 467-2900, is deservedly popular with the locals, as much for its cheery atmosphere (which includes strolling musicians) as for its tasty food. Just down the street, but half a world away, is the wonderful **Lagniappe Cajun House** at 230 East La Olas Boulevard; the food is authentic Cajun/Creole, the decor is New Orleans Revival, and Saturday

and Sunday brunches are accompanied by Dixieland bands. Equally if differently fun is the aptly-named **Sea Watch** restaurant on the ocean at 6002 North Ocean Boulevard, ((305) 781-2200. Here, among lots of brass, wicker, and greenery, and within earshot of the waves, you can dine handsomely and reasonably on all kinds of fresh seafood.

Inexpensive

If you don't mind — or even if you do mind — eating off paper plates and using paper napkins, paper cups, and plastic forks, you should make for the **Southport Raw Bar** at 1536 Cordova Road, just off the 17th Street Causeway, ((305) 525-2526. Noisy and ugly, its only attractions are the most glorious oysters, shrimp, and clams you have ever tasted at prices you won't believe. If it's something meatier and spicier you're after, try **Ernie's Bar-B-Que** at 1843 South Route 1, ((305) 523-8636. Whatever you order here, you *must* try Ernie's conch chowder. Somewhat swankier and more specialized, **Bobby Rubino's Place for Ribs** is, well, the place for ribs. It's at 4100 North Route 1, ((305) 561-5305. If you are a devotee of Tex-Mex food, as I am, you can't do better than **Carlos and Pepe's 17th Street Cantina** at 1302 Southeast 17th Street, ((305) 467-7192. Celestial food at bargain-basement prices. A word of warning, however: I am not the first person to have discovered the cantina, so unless you go early you could have a bit of wait at the bar (not such a bad fate, actually).

HOW TO GET THERE

Fort Lauderdale/Hollywood International Airport is served by a large number of national and international airlines, although many people prefer to fly in to Miami's airport, about an hour's drive to the south. Taxi fares from the Fort Lauderdale airport to most of the beach hotels should be under $12. There are a dozen rental car companies with offices in or near the airport.

Approaching Fort Lauderdale by car from the north or south, drivers can take Florida's Turnpike (a tollway), or I–95, or Route 1 (also known as Federal Highway), or Route A1A, which snakes slowly and scenically along the coast. The main road

from the west is Route 84, a tollway also known as Everglades Parkway or, more colloquially, Alligator Alley.

PALM BEACH AND BOCA RATON

In a sense, Palm Beach is a mirage, because its special appeal is very much in the eye of the beholder. To some, it is an oasis of taste and style, a chic enclave for the upper classes, an island paradise for the mega-wealthy. To others, it is a 12-mile (19-km) long shrine

to vulgarity and excess, an offshore game reserve where cash-laden social climbers and penniless aristocrats can prey on each other in peace. That globetrotting chronicler of high society, Taki, has called it, rather harshly, "a Gulag for the rich, the last refuge of the lifted, a Mecca for the monosyllabic."

To be honest, there is some merit to both views. But whichever view you take, there is no denying that the place *is* special, if not unique. Where else would you find flocks of (specially imported) parrots where you would normally find pigeons, or find an

ABOVE: Consuming is conspicuous along Worth Avenue in Palm Beach. OPPOSITE: The palms of Palm Beach.

artificial reef offshore anchored by a Rolls Royce and a yacht, or find a city ordinance banning outdoor clotheslines because they are unsightly? Exactly.

BACKGROUND

The first settlers arrived in Palm Beach during (and probably because of) the American Civil War, but the palms didn't arrive until 1878, when a Spanish ship carrying a cargo of coconuts, the *Providencia*, ran aground on the island. The coconuts were planted, and

During the Twenties Palm Beach became the place where anybody who was Anybody went for the winter season. Mansions sprouted among the palms. West Palm Beach was created, on the mainland, across from the island, by Flagler "for my help" — the army of servants required to staff the hotels and private homes. Since automobiles were prohibited as disturbers of peace, the gliterrati were ferried to and from by blacks in wicker rickshaws known as "Afro-mobiles". Palm Beach became the ultimate Fantasy Island for The Haves. Today its

before long the place had a name as well as some distinctive flora. Then in 1894 Henry Morrison Flagler arrived with his railway, built the Royal Poinciana and The Breakers hotels, and set about attracting the well-born and well-heeled. He succeeded. Not only did Vanderbilts, Wanamakers, Rock-efellers, Guggenheims, Goulds, Astors, Posts, Huttons, Chryslers, DuPonts and other names out of the *Social Register* go there, but so did talented eccentric Addison Mizner, whose architectural creations were to give Palm Beach and Boca Raton their characteristic, pastel-tinted look.

ABOVE: "Italianate" style buildings in downtown Palm Beach. OPPOSITE: Exterior and interior views of the Henry M. Flagler Museum.

social cachet may have been diluted somewhat by the infiltration of certain high-decibel, high-visibility *parvenus*, but it nonetheless remains a wonderful example of the happiness that money can buy.

GENERAL INFORMATION

The Palm Beach County Convention and Visitors Bureau is at 1555 Lakes Boulevard, Suite 204, West Palm Beach FL 33401. ((407) 471-3995. The bureau has a European office at AM Hauptbahnhof 10, 6000 Frankfurt/Main 1, Germany, ((069) 234098, and is represented in Britain by Travel Markets International, Wrencote House, 119-121 Croydon High Street, Croydon,

Surrey CR0 0XJ, ℭ (081) 688-1451. The Chamber of Commerce of the Palm Beaches is at 501 North Flagler Drive, P.O. Box 2931, West Palm Beach FL 33401. ℭ (407) 833-3711. The Boca Raton Chamber of Commerce is at 1800 North Route 1, Boca Raton, ℭ (407) 395-4433.

Other useful telephone numbers (all in area code 407):

Palm Beach International Airport	471-7400
Yellow Cabs	689-4222
Doctor referral service	433-3940

1100 South Ocean Boulevard, the 118-room Moorish extravaganza built for cereal heiress Marjorie Merriweather Post in the Twenties and now owned by Donald Trump, and the 55-room marble palace built by Henry Flagler in 1902, which was originally called Whitehall but is now the **Henry M. Flagler Museum**. As the Trump mansion is not open to the public, and only its 75-ft (23-m) tower is clearly visible from the road, the visitor's time is better spent inspecting Mr. Flagler's palatial edifice on Coconut Row. There are seven

WHAT TO SEE AND DO

Sights

Mansion-gazing is by far the most popular form of sightseeing in Palm Beach, and the best way to gaze at the mansions is from the water. Narrated sightseeing cruises go every day from Steamboat Landing — as do luncheon, cocktail, and dinner cruises with live entertainment. Ticket prices vary from $3 up to $45, so it's best to check in advance with Empress Dining Cruises, Inc., Steamboat Landing, 900 East Blue Heron Boulevard, Riviera Beach FL 33404. ℭ (407) 842-0882.

Among the mansions themselves, the two most noteworthy are **Mar-A-Lago** at

kinds of rare marble in the foyer alone, and each guest bedroom is decorated in the style of a different period in world history. Parked outside the mansion is Flagler's private railway car. The museum, ℭ (407) 655-2833, is closed on Mondays; admission is $5 for adults and $2.50 for children.

Considering that most of the expensive art in Palm Beach is in private homes, the **Norton Gallery of Art** at 1451 South Olive Avenue in West Palm Beach, ℭ (407) 832-5196, has a surprisingly impressive collection, particularly of the French Impressionists and of twentieth-century American art. It also has a delightful outdoor sculpture garden. It is closed on Mondays.

Animal lovers and people with bored children will want to visit the **Dreher Park Zoo** at 1301 Summit Boulevard in West Palm Beach, ((407) 533-0887. Among its more unusual animals are an endangered Florida panther and a 100-pound capybara, the world's largest rodent. About 15 miles further west on Southern Boulevard is the 500-acre (over 200 ha) **Lion Country Safari**, where you can drive along eight miles (13 km) of paved roads past African lions, elephants, zebras, giraffes, white rhinos, antelopes, and chimpanzees, to name only a few of the animals that roam free here. There is also a petting zoo as well as a number of free rides, games, and boat cruises. If you don't have a car, or are a little uneasy about driving your nice car past hundreds of wild animals, you can rent a car here for $5 an hour. Worth noting, too, is that there is an excellent campground right next to the park. The postal address of both the park and the campground is P.O. Box 16066, West Palm Beach FL 33416. ((407) 793-1084. Admission is $11.95 for adults and $9.95 for children under 16 (under three, free).

Sports

Two major-league **baseball** teams hold their spring training in West Palm Beach, the Montreal Expos and the Atlanta Braves. They play at the Municipal Stadium, Lakes Boulevard and Congress Avenue, ((407) 684-6801. You can watch **jai alai** from the first of the year until about the middle of May at the Palm Beach Jai Alai Fronton, 1415 West 45th Street, West Palm Beach, ((407) 844-2444.

The spectator sport most closely associated with Palm Beach is, of course, **polo**. It is played from November until late April at the Palm Beach Polo and Country Club, 13198 Forest Hill Boulevard, West Palm Beach, ((407) 793-1113, Gulfstream Polo Grounds, Lake Worth Road, ((407) 965-9924, and Royal Palm Polo Club, 6300 Clint Moore Road, Boca Raton, ((407) 994-1876.

With upwards of 80 **golf** courses in the area, golfers have plenty of choice. The first choice of most is the famous course at the PGA Sheraton Resort, 400 Avenue

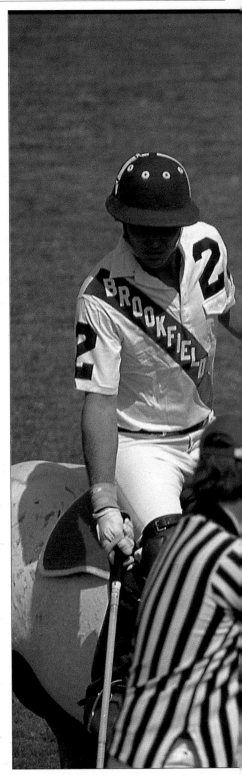

RIGHT: Polo players in Boca Raton.

of the Champions, Palm Beach Gardens, ℂ (407) 627-2000.

Tennis players will find no shortage of courts, many of them free. The Lake Worth Racquet and Swim Club at 4090 Coconut Road, Lake Worth, ℂ (407) 967-3900, will let you use one of their lighted courts for $10 an hour per player. For information on public courts near you in either Palm Beach or Boca Raton call the Palm Beach County Parks and Recreation Department, ℂ (407) 964-4420. There are countless opportunities for **scuba diving** and **snorkeling** along this coast. My

advice would be to call or visit one of the half-dozen Force E stores in the Palm Beach-Boca Raton area. Not only do they rent the equipment you will need, but they also provide instruction if you need it as well as dive boats for charter. In West Palm Beach there is a Force E at 1399 North Military Trail, ℂ (407) 471-2676, and in Boca Raton there is one at 7166 Beracasa Way, ℂ (407) 395-4407, and at 877 East Palmetto Park Road, ℂ (407) 368-0555.

Shopping

If you know anything about Palm Beach, then you already know about **Worth Avenue**. It is to Palm Beach what Bond Street is to London, Rodeo Drive is to Beverly Hills, the Rue du Faubourg St. Honoré is to Paris, and the Via Condotti is to Rome. It is where beautiful objects go to find the Beautiful People who will want to own them.

Although it is only three blocks long, with the Atlantic at one end and Lake Worth at the other, the street is home to over 250 stores and boutiques, ranging in size from

Saks Fifth Avenue (30,000 sq ft or 9,144 sq m) to Tally Ho Antiques (25 sq ft or 7½ sq m). For sheer, concentrated opulence, there is no street anywhere that can match it. Even the fire hydrant is chrome-plated. Worth Avenue is definitely worth a visit, if only for window-shopping.

Nightlife

Most Palm Beach nightlife revolves around private entertaining, not surprisingly, and therefore interesting night spots are in short supply. Apart from **Ta-Boo**, a fashionable supper club at 221 Worth Avenue, ℂ (407) 655-5562, the best places to go are the lounges at the big hotels, especially the one at The Colony. Boca Raton has rather more to offer after dark. The **Royal Palm Dinner Theater** at 303 Golfview Drive, ℂ (407) 392-3755, presents Broadway musicals, with occasional guest stars, all year round. The **Top of the Bridge Lounge** at 999 Camino Real, ℂ (407) 368-9500, gives you a lovely view of the Intracoastal Waterway along with the live music. Right on the Intracoastal Waterway is **Wildflower** at 551 East Palmetto Park Road, ℂ (407) 426-0066. A restaurant as well as a lounge, it features spectacularly unconventional decor as well as a disk jockey playing dance music. **Tugboat Annie's** at 6909 Southwest 18th Street, ℂ (407) 394-9900, is your place if you like good rock and reggae in a relaxed atmosphere.

WHERE TO STAY

Luxury

Hotels don't get much more luxurious than these. To begin with, there is **The Breakers**. This twin-towered, Italianate palace, modeled on the Villa Medici in Florence, was rebuilt (after two fires) in 1926. Ever since it has served as the unofficial community center for Palm Beach's glitterati, all the while retaining its reputation for graceful formality. The hotel is at 1 South County Road, ℂ (305) 655-6611, toll-free (800) 833-3141, and in addition to almost half a mile of beachfront there are 19 tennis courts, two 18-hole golf courses, and a swimming pool. Matching — some would say surpassing — The Breakers in upper-crustiness is **The Colony**, where the Duke and Duchess of Windsor usually stayed and John Lennon didn't (having been turned away on grounds of scruffiness). Although the hotel's *look* is distinctly, but tastefully, Floridian, it *feels* European: the service is excellent, understated, just right. Locals describe it admiringly as "a hundred rooms and a reputation". It is at 155 Hammon Avenue, ((305) 655-5430.

One might think that the above hotels would be impossible acts to follow, but the **Brazilian Court Hotel** is right up there with them. Built in the same year as The Breakers, and extensively renovated a few years ago, it is the sort of place where you wouldn't be surprised to see Cary Grant or Gary Cooper — both of whom, in fact, did stay here. Like The Colony, it combines the best of New and Old World hospitality. It's at 301 Australian Avenue in west Palm Beach, ((305) 655-7740. The fourth member of this dazzling quartet is the **Boca Raton Hotel and Club** at 501 East Camino Real in Boca Raton, ((305) 395-3000, toll-free (800) 327-0101, also built in 1926. Originally named the Cloister Inn, this was undoubtedly Addison Mizner's masterpiece. It has since expanded outwards and upwards (only 100 of the hotel's 1,000 rooms are in the original building), and now includes four swimming pools, 22 tennis courts, a golf course, a 23-slip marina, seven restaurants, and over a mile of beach. Yet its standards of excellence remain as high as ever, which explains why it is still one of the world's great hotels.

Mid-range

In the upper part of the middle range is the **Howard Johnson Motor Lodge** at 2870 South County Road in Palm Beach, ((305) 582-2581, toll-free (800) 654-2000. Nearby (in price as well) is the **Beachcomber Apartment Motel** at 3024 South Ocean Boulevard, ((305) 585-4648. A little further north in Riviera Beach there is the **Rutledge Resort Motel** at 3730 Ocean Drive, Riviera Beach, ((305) 848-6621, and the **Best Western Seaspray Inn** at 123 Ocean Avenue, ((305) 844-0233, toll-free (800) 528-1234. The **Best Western University Inn** in Boca Raton is another good bet. It is at 2700 North Route 1, ((305) 395-5255.

Inexpensive

The **Boca Raton Motel** at 1801 North Route 1, ((305) 395-7500, toll-free (800) 453-4511, is excellent value. In the same area I would also recommend the **Shore Edge Motel** at 425 North Ocean Boulevard, ((305) 395-4491. From here to Palm Beach there are countless dozens of economy motels to choose from. The best bargain I came across was the **Harbor Lights Apartments** on the water at 200 Inlet Way in Palm Beach Shores, ((305) 844-5377. It has only seven rooms, all very reasonably priced.

WHERE TO EAT

Expensive

Like the Casa Vecchia in Fort Lauderdale, **La Vieille Maison** is another "old house" restored and refurbished by the redoubtable Leonce Picot and Al Kocab. An elegant, two-story, artifact-filled honeycomb of alcoves and intimate spaces, the restaurant specializes in wonderfully imaginative French Provincial cuisine. It is at 770 East Palmetto Park Road in Boca Raton, ((305) 391-6701. Also in Boca Raton is **Chez Marcel** in Royal Palm

ABOVE: The Breakers, a Palm Beach landmark since the turn of the century. OPPOSITE: Worth Avenue.

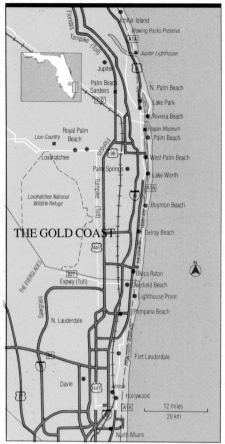

1440, because most of the natives you meet will do it for me. For celebrity-spotting at all hours of the day or night, as well as for an amazing array of dishes in a splendid setting, plus live (and lively) music at night, you won't do any better than this. A few miles to the north on the Jupiter inlet is another local treasure, **Harpoon Louie's**, 1065 Route A1A, ((305) 744-1300. Here you can enjoy a terrific view of the inlet and the famous Jupiter Lighthouse while gorging yourself on Louie's massive portions of seafood. For a completely different sort of atmosphere, and food, try the pub-like **Doherty's** at 288 South County Road in Palm Beach, ((305) 655-6200. It's very good, and very jolly. Finally, if you are as passionate about Thai food as I am, you are in for a treat at the **Siam Garden** in Oaks Plaza, 680 Glades Road, Boca Raton, ((305) 368-9013. Not only is it truly garden-like, but its food is authentic — which means delicious.

Inexpensive

For your basic down-home cookin with all the fixins, go to **Tom's Place** at 7251 North Route 1 in Boca Raton, ((305) 997-0920. Ribs, fried chicken, stew, catfish, hush puppies, that sort of thing. Like Tom's, **Original Grandma Sarah's** at 1301 North Route 1 in West Palm Beach, ((305) 833-6369, provides hearty meals in a friendly atmosphere at friendly prices. **Hamburger Heaven** at 314 South County Road in Palm Beach, ((305) 655-5277, serves, yes, heavenly hamburgers. And **Toojay's** at 313 Poinciana Plaza in Palm Beach, ((305) 659-7232, serves scrumptious crab cakes and meat loaf.

How to Get There

Although Palm Beach International Airport is only minutes away from Palm Beach itself, the Fort Lauderdale airport is served by many more airlines with many more flights into the area.

The principal north-south roads into Palm Beach and Boca Raton are the same as for Fort Lauderdale. The main road from the west is Route 98, which becomes Southern Boulevard as it approaches Palm Beach.

Plaza, Route 1 and Southeast Fourth Street, ((305) 368-6553. The creation of Marcel Wortman, from Strasbourg by way of Costa Rica, it is as unpretentious as its menu is rich. For classic French cooking with an intriguing twist to it, go to **Le Monegasque**, at the President condominium, 2505 South Ocean Boulevard in Palm Beach, ((305) 585-0071. This utterly delightful restaurant is, both gastronomically and decoratively, an *hommage* to owner Aldo Rinero's native Monaco. By contrast, **The Dining Room**, which graces the Brazilian Court Hotel, celebrates many different cuisines, often in arresting new combination. For excellent taste wedded to excellence you can taste. The Dining Room, ((305) 655-7740, is the place to go .

Moderate

It is probably a waste of space to recommend **Chuck & Harold's Café** at 207 Royal Poinciana Way in Palm Beach, ((305) 659-

Facing the Atlantic: beach huts stand sentinel.

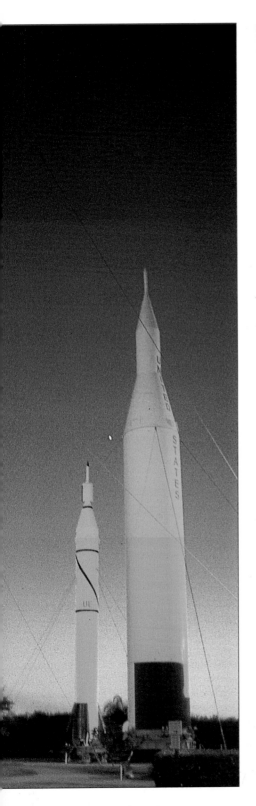

The Atlantic Coast

STRETCHING for over 300 miles from Palm Beach to the Georgia state line, Florida's Atlantic coast has attractions ranging from the oldest city in the country — St. Augustine — to the extremely High Tech marvels at the Kennedy Space Center on Merritt Island near Cape Canaveral.

Following in the wake of Columbus, the Spanish explorer Ponce de León led an expedition across the Atlantic in 1513 to try to discover the fabled waters of a "fountain of youth", rumored to exist somewhere near present-day St. Augustine. He was successful only to the extent that nowadays you can find a Fountain of Youth Discovery Park in the city's tourist guides.

By 1562 a small expeditionary force of French Huguenots had settled at what was to become Fort Caroline near the mouth of the St. Johns River, around which Jacksonville now stands. Responding to this challenge, King Philip II of Spain sent Pedro Menéndez de Avilés to Florida with orders to drive the French out of the northeast and establish a garrison town on the coast. At the end of August 1565 Menéndez spotted a strategic point overlooking a bay and some days later landed there. Thus began the long history of St. Augustine. Wasting no time, Menéndez marched against Fort Caroline and routed the garrison, and then destroyed what remained of the French forces on his way back to St. Augustine.

Although this confirmed Spain as the dominant power in the region, it by no means assured the Spanish of control in perpetuity. Indeed, Fort Caroline was retaken only two years later, and Amelia Island, just above Jacksonville, has seen no fewer than eight flags raised above it since 1562. The whole area was tossed around between the Spanish, French, and English for a few centuries, and Mexico even laid claim to it for a brief period before the Union wrenched it away from the Confederacy.

In the years following the end of the Civil War the coast began to prosper from the north downwards. Jacksonville rose to prominence as a port, and the arrival of Henry Flagler's Florida East Coast Railroad in the 1880s secured the city's position as the state's shipping and industrial center. As his railway crept further south Flagler

dotted the coastline with luxury hotels to cater to the expensive tastes of the wealthy northerners who began wintering in Florida. Resort towns soon developed to accommodate the increasing flow of tourists to the region. Nor were all the new arrivals tourists: it was the now-famous climate that attracted NASA to Florida's Atlantic coast in the 1960s.

THE SPACE COAST

The Kennedy Space Center has become one of the most popular sightseeing destinations in Florida. Every year over 1.5 million people visit Spaceport USA (the name given to the public visitation program at the space complex), and many of them plan their visit to coincide with the launch of a spacecraft. Although the Space Center is clearly the main attraction, the coast also has resort towns with excellent beaches, and there is an abundance of wildlife — including such rare species as the southern bald eagle and the West Indian manatee — on Merritt Island itself.

BACKGROUND

Ais and Timucan Indian tribes were the original inhabitants of the Cape area. The name "Canaveral" is derived from an Indian word meaning "canebearer", as the Indians' arrows were made from reed or cane. To this day, large areas of the region remain a wilderness of mosquito-infested swamp, savannah, and rugged coastline. In fact, most of Merritt Island is a national wildlife refuge; of the 140,000 acres of the island owned by NASA only seven percent has been developed for the space program. The rest is an extension of the wildlife refuge — a fact that NASA is keen to emphasize. Old Indian burial mounds have also been left untouched and lie next to the bunkers and buildings of the Space Center.

Hard on the heels of the Soviet Union's *Sputnik*, America's first satellite, *Explorer I*, was launched from Cape Canaveral on January 31, 1958. The National Aeronautics

A Saturn 5 rocket at the Kennedy Space Center.

and Space Administration (NASA) was created the following year, originally operating from the Cape itself but moving over to Merritt Island in 1964. By 1968 the Apollo program was well under way and came to fruition on July 20, 1969 with Neil Armstrong's first step on the moon. Such local towns as Cocoa Beach (which is opposite Cape Canaveral, unlike the town of Cocoa which is on the mainland across Indian River) were transformed by the influx of scientists, technicians, and workers from the Space Center.

GENERAL INFORMATION

The offices of the Cocoa Beach Tourism and Convention Council are on Merritt Island at 400 Fortenberry Road, ✆ (407) 459-2200, where you can get any needed information as well as free maps and brochures.

If you would like to be at the Cape for the launch of a spacecraft, call NASA toll-free (800) 432-2153 for information on launch dates and best vantage points. A limited number of passes, which enable you to drive into the grounds of the Space Center and park within five miles of a launch pad, are available for the shuttle launches. To make a reservation for a launch date, phone (305)

452-2121 between 8 am and 4 pm or write to: NASA Visitors Services Branch, PA-V1C, John F. Kennedy Space Center, Florida 32899. (Do remember that there are plenty of vantage points outside the Space Center where you can park to watch a launch, especially along Route 1 in Titusville.)

WHAT TO SEE AND DO

Sights

The Kennedy Space Center's *Spaceport USA* promotional leaflet puts it like this: "Here you can experience it all. The excitement. The glory. The awe-inspiring achievements. What's more, you can relive it free. Free parking. Free admission. Free kennel facilities. Even free use of a camera." This breathless recitation of the FREEdoms at Spaceport USA is a little bit misleading, because not every service is free by any means.

Take Route 405 from Titusville to enter the Space Center at Gate 3, or take Route 3 from Cocoa Beach to enter at Gate 2; guards at each gate provide a pass for Spaceport USA. The **Visitors Center** is on the south side of the NASA Parkway on Merritt Island. Among the many exhibits you will be able to see in the Visitors Center are a piece of the moon, an Apollo capsule, a lunar module, and the flight deck of a space shuttle. The Hall of History contains a detailed account of the whole space program and the IMAX Theater shows a half-hour film of the launch and landing of the space shuttle *Columbia* — at an admission price of $4 for adults and $2.50 for children aged three to 12. It's advisable to make an advance booking for the show as well as for the bus tour of the outlying grounds in order to avoid lengthy queues.

The **bus tour** takes two hours and costs $7 for adults and $2.50 for children under 12. A guide will answer any questions, ranging from the fuel consumption of the shuttle rocket at take-off (considerable) to the toilet conditions for an astronaut (problematic). You will get to visit the **Vehicle Assembly Building**, which is one of the largest buildings in the world, and the massive transporters which carry the completed rocket to the launch pad. The tour moves on to the launch pads at Complex 39 and then to the **Astronaut Training Building**, where conditions of actual space flight are simulated. The cumulative effect of all this is, one has to agree, awe-inspiring.

After the Space Center you can come back down to earth with a driving tour through the island's wildlife refuge. Reservations for an official tour bus can be made by calling (407) 867-0667, or you can guide yourself along the **Black Point Wildlife Drive** by entering the refuge via County Road 402, off Route 1 in Titusville. Bird-

Shopping

The best shopping in the area is at Cocoa Village in downtown Cocoa (not Cocoa Beach). Over 50 shops offer a variety of goods in an Old World market atmosphere that retains the charm and sense of ease that so many modern malls have lost. The Wine Experience at 316 Brevard Avenue has a good selection of Australian and Californian wines. At Handwerk House, 206 Brevard Avenue, you will find a collection of beautifully-crafted stuffed animals and rag dolls. At the Indian River Pottery,

watchers will be particularly excited by the variety of species to be seen along the route, including a bird called the anhinga which swims underwater with its head above the surface.

If you really want to get away from it all, you can take the half-hour airboat ride up the St. Johns River and get a close-up look at the alligators hanging out on the riverbank. Despite their air of complete indifference, they have a way of giving the impression that they're really contemplating the next painful and inconsiderate thing they can do to something smaller and less toothy than they are. The boat leaves from the **Lone Cabbage Fish Camp** at Route 520, six miles west of I–95, Cocoa, ((407) 632-4199.

116-B Harrison Street, artisans produce a range of household utensils which go straight from the potter's wheel, via the kiln, into the shop window next to the caged singing birds. Not far away, at 4151 North Route A1A, is what is reputed to be the largest surf shop in the world, the Ron Jon Surf Shop, which sells and rents everything you might need in or on the water. It never closes.

Nightlife

The Cocoa Banana at 900 North Route A1A, Cocoa Beach, ((407) 799-3700, is one

---

OPPOSITE AND ABOVE: Two iews of the Rocket Garden at the Kennedy Space Center.

The Atlantic Coast

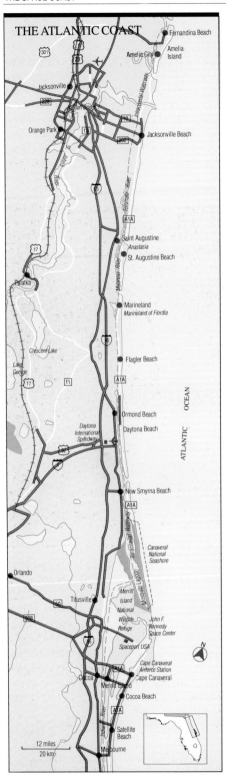

THE ATLANTIC COAST

of the area's most popular night spots, featuring a disco, bar, electronic games room, and pool tables. Appealing to a slightly more mature crowd, **Coco's** at 1550 North Route A1A in the Hilton Hotel, Cocoa Beach, ((407) 799-0003, is a small disco lounge/bar playing the light soul sounds of the Sixties. At **Dino's Jazz Piano Bar**, 315 West Route 520, Cocoa Beach, ((407) 784-5470, one can happily waste some after-dark hours in a relaxed atmosphere listening to good jazz.

WHERE TO STAY

Luxury

There are no surprises about the **Cocoa Beach Hilton**, 1550 North Route A1A, Cocoa Beach, ((407) 799-0003, toll-free (800) 445-8667. Its facilities are typically Hiltonesque, and many of its 300+ rooms overlook the sea. If you are lucky (or clever) enough to be there at the right time, you can witness space launches from the second-floor rooms at the **Inn at Cocoa Beach**, 4300 Ocean Beach Boulevard, Cocoa Beach, ((407) 799-3460, a beautifully preserved residence which manages to combine luxury with a cozy atmosphere.

Mid-range

A good choice for families is the **Crossway Inn and Tennis Resort** at 3901 North Route A1A in Cocoa Beach, ((305) 783-2221, where children under 12 can stay free. The hotel has a games room, a swimming pool, and tennis and basketball courts. The **Polaris Beach Resort Inn**, 5600 North Routh A1A, Cocoa Beach, ((305) 783-7621, toll-free (800) 962-0028, has both a croquet lawn and a beach. Efficiency apartments are very well-equipped at the Polaris, as they are at **Surf Studio Beach Apartments**, 1801 South Route A1A, Cocoa Beach, ((305) 783-7100, which has 11 moderately priced units and personal, friendly service.

Inexpensive

As an alternative to staying in Cocoa Beach, and still only five kilometers (three miles) from the Kennedy Space Center, the **Rodeway Inn** at 3655 Cheney Highway, Titusville, ((305) 269-7110, toll-free (800) 228-2000, is remarkably good value, with a pool and a complimentary Continental breakfast. Still on the mainland, the **Brevard Hotel** at 112 Riverside Drive, Cocoa, ℭ (407) 636-1411, is a quiet place overlooking the Indian River but within walking distance of the bustle of Cocoa Village. Another good budget choice is the **Ocean Suite Hotel** at 5500 Ocean Beach Boulevard, Cocoa Beach, ℭ (407) 784-4343, next to the Canaveral Pier.

WHERE TO EAT

Expensive

The elegant **Black Tulip** at 207 Brevard Avenue, ℭ (407) 639-8343, is probably the most fashionable restaurant in Cocoa Village. The starters are particularly delicious, and include crab cakes served on Kaiser rolls and artichoke hearts in mustard sauce. The beef, poultry, and seafood entrees are less interesting, but still very edible. **Bernard's Surf** at 2 South Route A1A in Cocoa Beach, ℭ (305) 783-2401, has a big reputation and even bigger menu, on which you will find such culinary curiosities as bear meat and chocolate-covered ants. Their crab and lobster are deservedly celebrated locally, but my favorite dish was the freshwater salmon, batter-dipped and fried and served with toasted almonds.

Moderate

The **Dixie Crossroads** at 1475 Garden Street, Titusville, ℭ (407) 268-5000, is a large, family-oriented restaurant specializing in — what else? — seafood. Hint: try the smoked mullet. For a meal before or after your visit to the Space Center you could drop in at the **Kountry Kitchen**, 1115 North Courtenay Parkway, Merritt Island, ℭ (407) 459-3457, which serves up hearty bacon-and-egg breakfasts and mountainous dinners, or at **Victor's Family Restaurant**, 320 North Courtenay Parkway, ℭ (407) 459-1656, which — surprisingly — has a selection of tasty Greek dishes.

Inexpensive

At **Desperadoes**, 30 North Route A1A, Cocoa Beach, ℭ (407) 784-3363, chef Manuel Mercado rustles up some of the tastiest *chimichangas, tamales* and *tostadas* on the Atlantic coast, which you can wash down with Mexican beer or — heresy! — with wine. You can sit in the sun at the **Pasta Garden**, 220 Brevard Avenue, Cocoa Village, Cocoa, ℭ (407) 639-8343, and enjoy fairly straightforward Italian food and seafood. The **Peking Garden** at 155 East Route 520, Merritt Island, ℭ (407) 459-2999, serves quite decent Chinese food. But if your priority is to quieten the kids, let me recommend the **Village Ice Cream and Sandwich Shop** at 120-B Harrison Street in Cocoa Village, ℭ (407) 632-2311.

HOW TO GET THERE

The Melbourne International Airport (about 30 miles, or 48 km, south of Cape Canaveral), ℭ (407) 723-6627, is regularly served by a large number of national airlines. Hertz, ℭ (407) 723-3414, and Avis, ℭ (407) 723-7755, both have offices at the airport.

The three north-south routes to the Space Coast are the same three as for the entire eastern Florida coast: I–95, Route 1, and Route A1A.

Relaxing in the shadow of the Rocket Garden.

DAYTONA

Daytona and Ormond Beach, a few miles to the north, emerged from the great Florida Sun Rush at the end of the nineteenth century as two of the resorts most favored by prosperous northerners. The expanse of hard-packed, white beach between the two resorts must surely be the only beach in the world which owes its fame to being driven upon. It all began at the turn of the century when two motoring enthusiasts called R.E. Olds and Alexander Winton — watched by their friend Henry Ford from his rocker on the veranda of the Ormond Hotel — raced their cars down the beach in what has become known as America's first drag race.

BACKGROUND

By extending his Florida East Coast Railroad to the area in the late 1880s, Henry Flagler laid the tracks which property developers and winter-weary northerners were soon to follow. Flagler enlarged his own hotel empire by buying and renovating a venerable hostelry in Ormond Beach, the Ormond Hotel. Also in Ormond Beach, John D. Rockefeller established a winter residence, The Casements, where he spent much of his later life.

The resorts continued to develop and to attract the rich in increasing numbers. Organized racing began in 1904 with an event called the Winter Speed Carnival, which drew speed merchants and their society financiers from all over the world to the Daytona and Ormond beaches. In 1928 Malcolm Campbell, a slightly dotty and speed-obsessed English millionaire, arrived at Daytona with a car powered by an aircraft engine. He waited for the surf to create a sufficiently flat beach, then accelerated across it at an record speed of 206.96 mph (333 kph). He subsequently raised this record to 444 kph (276 mph) on the beach at Daytona.

They no longer race on the beach, but Daytona's love affair with machines and speed continues with stock-car racing and speedway. The speed limit on the beach these days is 16 kph (10 mph) and the fastest thing you'll see is a surfer riding the waves.

GENERAL INFORMATION

The Daytona Beach Chamber of Commerce is at 126 East Orange Avenue, P.O. Box 2775, Daytona Beach FL 32015. ((904) 255-0415. Its staff will give you information on accommodation or attractions. For a free copy of the *Daytona Beach Resort Area Visitors Guide*, call toll-free (800) 535-2828. The Ormond Beach Chamber of Commerce is at 165 West Granada Street, P.O. Box 874, Ormond Beach FL 32074. ((904) 677-3454.

Other useful telephone numbers (all in area code 904):

Daytona International Airport   255-8441
Volusia County Medical Association 258-1611
Dental service   734-1355

WHAT TO SEE AND DO

Sights

First, **the beach**. It's big (23 miles or 37 km long, 500 ft or 152 m wide) and it's a highway (but remember, no faster than 10 mph or 16 kph).

You can drive on to the sand at Ormond Beach, and you can go as far south as Ponce de León Inlet. Stick to the main track, avoid the water, and heed the warning signs about soft, unsafe areas of the beach. You can park anywhere you like on the beach.

For those who drive in the fast lane Daytona is something of a Mecca. From January onwards there are the qualifying rounds for the **Daytona Grand National Stock Car Race** held in mid-February. The track gives way to a **Motorcycle Classic** in the first week of March, and the speedway (car racing) culminates at the end of June with the **Paul Revere 255** and the **Firecracker 400**. All the action is at the **Daytona International Speedway**, Volusia Avenue, near the airport off Route 92, five kilometers (three miles) west of Daytona, which took over from the beach in 1959 as the venue for the races. Tickets for the races start at $15 and rise to $65. For further information contact the Daytona International Speedway, P.O. Drawer S, Daytona Fl 32015. The **Birthplace of Speed Museum** in Ormond Beach houses

Daytona Beach, where the speed limit is now a stately 10 mph.

famous cars which have raced on the beach over the years and also traces the history of the beach races. It's open from noon to 4 pm, Monday to Saturday. Admission is $2.

The **Museum of Arts and Sciences** at 1040 Museum Way, Daytona Beach, ((904) 255-0285, houses one of the world's finest collections of Cuban art and sculpture. The main attraction of the science collection is a Pleistocene mammal which weighed in at five tons and was a good few meters taller than most of the unfortunate creatures it encountered. In neighboring Ormond

Timucan village of Nocoroco. The *Dixie Queen II* riverboat will take you in comfort along the Halifax River (which is the name given to the section of the Intracoastal Waterway which flows between mainland Daytona and the barrier islands). Sunset and moonlight cruises, with dinner, are especially popular. The *Dixie Queen II* leaves from 841 Ballough Road, Daytona Beach, ((904) 255-1997.

Sports

Daytona has a dozen **golf** courses within a

Beach you can visit John D. Rockefeller's old winter house, **The Casements**, at 25 Riverside Drive, ((904) 676-3216. The house, which was built opposite a hotel which hadn't treated the great man with the proper respect, is now a cultural center exhibiting Hungarian and Italian artifacts and American art; admission is free and the center is open Monday to Thursday 9 am to 9 pm, Friday 9 am to 5 pm and Saturday 9 am to 12 pm.

If you want to get some idea of how the Timucan Indians used to live, visit the **Tomoka State Park** just north of Ormond Beach on North Beach Street, off Route 40, ((904) 676-4050. A museum there has exhibits showing the history of the ancient

couple of miles of the beach. Some Daytona hotels have discount green fees for their guests and will happily arrange tee-off times for you as well. Three courses are particularly recommended: Tomoka Oaks Country Club, Route 1 and Nova Road, Ormond Beach, ((904) 677-7117; Indigo Lakes, Route 92 at I–95, Daytona Beach, ((904) 254-3607; and Daytona Golf and Country Club, 600 Wilder Boulevard, Daytona Beach, ((904) 250-3119.

There are eight public **tennis** courts; the city's recreation department, ((904) 253-9222, will direct you to the one nearest you.

For those keen on **water sports**, pontoon boats and jet skis can be rented at the

Dixie Queen Marina, 841 Ballough Road, ((904) 255-1997, and surfboards at Daytona Beach Surf Shops, 520 Seabreeze Boulevard, ((904) 253-3366.

Shopping

Seabreeze Boulevard is where you will find the best choice of shops in Daytona Beach. There is, for example, an enormous range of sports and swimwear at the Bikini Company at N° 504, ((904) 253-1120, and much for the chiclets at Touché just down the street at N° 310, ((904) 252-2365.

the **Club Mocambo** at 637 North Route A1A, Daytona Beach, ((904) 258-9413. The collegiate crowd tends to congregate at **P.J.'s**, 400 Broadway, Daytona Beach, ((904) 258-5222, where there is always cheap beer to go with the rock music during happy hour (6 to 7 pm).

WHERE TO STAY

Luxury

The **Daytona Beach Hilton** at 2637 South Route A1A, Daytona Beach, ((904) 767-

Nightlife

The **Clarendon Plaza Hotel** at 600 North Route A1A, Daytona Beach, ((904) 255-4471, has three night clubs. There is the rock-video music of Penrod's; there are live bands and early-hours disco at the Plantation Club and the 701 offers recorded rock music throughout the night. Earlier in the evening you can do your warm-up exercises at the **Oyster Pub**, 555 Seabreeze Avenue, Daytona Beach, ((904) 255-6348. **Finky's** at 640 North Grandview Avenue, Daytona Beach, ((904) 255-5059, reverberates to the live sounds of southern rock and country bands, while for those who prefer their music in the middle of the road as well as the middle of the dance floor there is

7350, toll-free (800) 445-8667, has 215 spacious rooms, the larger among them having their own private balconies overlooking the sea. There's a games room for children, and a swimming pool, and two restaurants, one of which is on the roof of the hotel offering panoramic views of the city and the sea. Eight kilometers (five miles) out of Daytona is the **Indigo Lakes Resort** at 2620 West International Speedway Boulevard, Daytona Beach, ((904) 258-6333, toll-free (800) 223-4161. The idyllic grounds contain a championship golf course, 10 tennis courts, and a health institute and spa.

OPPOSITE: The pier at Daytona Beach.
ABOVE: A snake-like bridge lights the way to Daytona Beach.

The trouble is that the resort's restaurant is so good, with so many sinfully tempting dishes, you will need these sport and health facilities.

Mid-range

Perry's Ocean Edge has oceanfront rooms and enclosed garden rooms in addition to ones overlooking the solarium swimming pool, whirlpool, and solar-heated spa. It can be found at 2209 South Route A1A, Daytona Beach, ((904) 255-0591. Along this main road you will find quite a selec-

tion of medium-sized hotels with well-appointed rooms and swimming pools, all very conveniently located for the beach. Among the nicest: the **Treasure Island**, ((904) 255-8371, toll-free (800) 874-7420, the **Daytona Sands**, ((904) 767-2551, and the **Sun Viking Lodge**, ((904) 252-6252, toll-free (800) 874-4469.

The **St. Regis Hotel** at 509 Seabreeze Boulevard, Daytona Beach, ((904) 242-8743, overlooks a green lawn instead of a sandy beach, and is wonderfully quiet. The **Nautilus Inn** at 1515 South Route A1A, Daytona Beach, ((904) 254-8600, has very handsome rooms, each with its own balcony, and a beachfront location — and is still moderately priced.

Inexpensive

A new and increasingly popular hotel is the **Captain's Quarter Inn** at 3711 South Route A1A, Daytona Beach, ((904) 767-3119, which has earned its reputation for being especially welcoming. Another friendly welcome awaits guests at the **Del Aire Motel**, 744 North Route A1A, Daytona Beach, ((904) 252-2563, right next to the beach. The **Econo Lodge** at 2250 Volusia Avenue, Daytona Beach, ((904) 255-3661, is cheaper than these two and nearer the speedway.

WHERE TO EAT

Expensive

The **St. Regis Hotel Restaurant** at 509 Seabreeze Boulevard, Daytona Beach, ((904) 252-8743, has one of the most elegant dining rooms in Daytona to go with its classic French cuisine. **La Crêpe en Haut**, on the upper floor of a courtyard mall next door to the Birthplace of Speed Museum at 142 East Granada Boulevard in Ormond Beach, ((904) 673-1999, is renowned for its crepes and sweetbreads but also has some superb steaks. Fresh fish is what draws people to **The Chart House**, 645 South Beach Street, Daytona Beach, ((904) 255-9022. The same, but Italian-accented, goes for the **King's Cellar** at 1258 North Route A1A, Daytona Beach, ((904) 255-3014.

Moderate

It can be unsettling to walk into a restaurant and see *Isten Hozott* ("God welcomes you") written above the entrance, but God has clearly smiled on Marie and Hugo Tischler, who have splendidly recreated the menu and ambience of Marie's old Budapest restaurant at the **Hungarian Village**, 424 South Ridgewood, Route 1,

agreeable restaurant overlooking the harbor.

Inexpensive

Also to be found in Ponce de León Inlet, at Timmon's Fishing Camp, ((904) 761-4831, is **Down the Hatch**, which has its own fleet of boats bringing in seafood from the ocean. In the Outlet Mall in South Daytona Beach is **Duff's Smörgasbord**, ((904) 788-0828, which is a simple, unfussy eat-as-much-as-you-like (for under $6) place. Cheaper still is the **Piccadilly Cafeteria** in the Volusia

Daytona Beach, ((904) 253-5712. Four miles (six and a half kilometers) west of Route A1A on Route 92, **Gene's Steak House**, ((904) 255-2059, offers seven different kinds of prime steak cooked over hickory coals. At **Aunt Catfish's**, 4009 Halifax Drive, Daytona Beach, ((904) 767-4768, you can have your catfish cooked in any of a number of ways: garlicky, Cajun-style, fried, or blackened. "Aunt" Jim Galbreath also has a specialty called "Florida Cracker" — a concoction of chicken, crab fritters, catfish fingerlings, shrimp, and coleslaw. Seven miles (11 km) south of Daytona on Route A1A is the small village of Ponce de León Inlet, where you will find the **Inlet Harbor**, ((904) 767-4502, an extremely

Mall at 1700 Volusia Avenue, Daytona Beach, ((904) 258-5373.

HOW TO GET THERE

Daytona International Airport is served by a number of national airlines. An alternative is to fly into Orlando Airport, which is better served than Daytona, and then take the Daytona-Orlando Transit Service (DOTS) to the coast.

OPPOSITE: Close-up of a bronze cannon at the Castillo de San Marcos in St. Augustine. ABOVE: The castle, begun in 1672, was completed in 1756.

ST. AUGUSTINE

The juxtaposition of the old and the new is one of the most striking features of St. Augustine. Some of the nation's oldest buildings and churches stand next to modern shopping malls, bars, and restaurants. The city also presents a pleasing blend of grand houses with walled courtyards, balconies overhanging winding lanes, and wide tree-lined avenues. Much of the old city is built of *coquina* — a material con-

Menéndez de Avilés. He named the colony after San Augustin, having first sighted the coast on August 28, the saint's feast day. The town was intended to be Spain's principal military base along Florida's northeast coast. Nine wooden fortresses were built, all of which succumbed to hostile forces (one of them being a British squadron led by Sir Francis Drake) or to the elements, before construction of the Castillo de San Marcos commenced in 1672. The final touches were put to the castle in 1756.

sisting of seashells embedded in a lime mortar — which adds to its distinctive appearance. Near the old city gate is the massive fortress, Castillo de San Marcos, built over a period of 70 years by the Spanish, which often served as a refuge for the townspeople during a siege. Nowadays the only invaders who lay siege to the city are the hordes of tourists who have come to appreciate the charms of this lovely city.

BACKGROUND

St. Augustine was founded on September 8, 1565 — 42 years before the British established Jamestown in Virginia — by the Spanish admiral and ex-smuggler Pedro

During the eighteenth century the city was controlled in turn by the English, French, and Spanish (all of whom left their architectural marks on the place). It endured many sieges before being ceded — along with the rest of Florida — to the United States by Spain in 1821. After the Civil War the city began to flourish as a commercial seaport for the nearby plantations, and the arrival of Henry Flagler's railway in the early 1880s brought trainloads of rich tourists from the north into town. Flagler built the luxurious Ponce de León and Alcazar hotels to accommodate them, and used the city as the base from which to push his railway-and-hotel empire south along the length of Florida's east coast.

GENERAL INFORMATION

The St. Augustine Chamber of Commerce at 1 Riberia Street, St. Augustine FL 32084, ((904) 829-6477, will furnish you with maps and brochures listing all the city's attractions. Even more detailed information is available from the St. Augustine Visitor Information Center at 10 Castillo Drive, St. Augustine FL 32085, ((904) 824-3334. Guided tours of the city are available from Spanish Heritage Tours; call (904) 829-3726 for further details.

WHAT TO SEE AND DO

Sights

St. Augustine is dense with sightseeing attractions, especially in the labyrinthine streets of the old town. A tour in a horse-drawn carriage is a pleasant way of seeing the city: **Colee's Carriages** leave from 1 Castillo Drive, charging $6 for adults and $3 for children aged five to 11. Alternatively, you can take one of the **Sightseeing Trains** from 170 San Marco Avenue, ((904) 829-6545, for a narrated tour which allows you to disembark at any point along the route and rejoin a later train. The trains run every 15 minutes and tickets are $5 for adults and $2 for children aged six to 12.

You could conduct your own tour on foot by passing through the **Old City Gate**, near the Information Center on Castillo Drive, to the **Castillo de San Marcos**, a Spanish castle which remained unconquered throughout its military history. Admission is $2, for which you receive a guided tour through exhibits that re-create the castle's history; the view from the ramparts is in itself worth the price of admission. Opening times are 8:45 am to 4:45 pm daily.

Facing the castle, centered around St. George's Street, is the **San Augustin Antiguo**, a quarter of the city where the houses and environment of an eighteenth-century Spanish colonial town have been re-created. The crafts and activities of the time are demonstrated by costumed artisans. The quarter contains some of the oldest buildings in America, including the Oldest

Wooden **Schoolhouse** at 14 St. George Street, which dates from 1778 and is the oldest wooden building in the city. The conditions of an eighteenth-century classroom have been re-created inside the schoolhouse.

Dating from 1723, the **Oldest House** at 14 Francis Street is, well, the oldest house in the city. The Spanish, French, and British refurbishments that have taken place over the centuries can be seen room by room in both the decor and the furnishings. Next door to the house is the **Webb Museum**,

which contains exhibits from all periods in the city's colonial history. Admission to both house and museum is $5 for adults and free for children under 12; they are both open from 9 am to 5 pm daily.

The tiny **St. Photios Chapel** on St. George Street has a stunning altar surrounded by frescoes and Greek icons; there is also a display outlining the history of Greeks in America. The **Basilica Cathedral of St. Augustine** on Treasury Street can be toured daily, and has the oldest parish records in the country. Ponce de León once

OPPOSITE: Seeing the sights of St. Augustine in a horse-drawn carriage. ABOVE: The Bridge of Lions, St. Augustine leads visitors to some of the oldest buildings in the nation.

searched for the legendary waters in this area, but you should have less trouble finding the **Fountain of Youth Discovery Park** at 155 Magnolia Avenue, which has a planetarium, space globe, a re-created Indian village, and a fountain—all for $4.50 adults and $2.50 children, and it's open from 9 am to 5 pm daily. Or you can marvel at the thousands of fascinating and thought-provoking exhibits at **Ripley's Believe It or Not** at 19 San Marco Avenue, ((904) 824-1606.

One of Florida's best collections of antiques, decorative arts and crafts, and musical instruments can be seen at the **Lightner Museum** in the City Hall complex at King Street and Cordova Street, ((904) 824-2874; and if you can handle another dose of antiquity, the **Oldest Store Museum** at 4 Artillery Lane, ((904) 829-9729, is home to thousands of gloriously useless items of the kind which people have always bought from stores and then thrown in the attic, where they are found years later by great-grandchildren and donated to museums.

At the **St. Augustine Alligator and Crocodile Farm**, South Route A1A, ((904) 824-3337, you can see one of the state's most serious gangs of unhurried, unworried reptiles. A little further south down Route A1A you will find **Marineland of Florida** at 9507 Ocean Shore Boulevard, ((904) 471-1111, where you can watch dolphins show off, and see men of questionable sanity swimming around with hungry sharks and hand-feeding them. Admission is $8 for adults, $4 for children aged two to 11; it's open 9 am to 5 pm daily.

Shopping

The **Fiesta Mall**, at 1 King Street, has insinuated itself very successfully into its old Spanish surroundings despite being home to the trendiest boutiques in town. The traditionally produced crafts in **San Augustin Antiguo** are all for sale, and City Gate Crafts at 1 St. George Street has a range of tapestries, leather goods, and silver as finely crafted as anything in the old town. The best antiques around can be found at the Lightner Antique Mall, King and Granada streets, behind the Lightner

Museum. The mall is in the (now drained) swimming pool of Henry Flagler's old Alcazar Hotel and has stalls selling, for example, lovely linen and china at very reasonable prices.

Nightlife

Spanish food followed by Spanish music and dancing is to be found at **El Caballero** in the Fiesta Mall, ((904) 824-2096. The English influence can be seen at the **White Lion**, St. George and Cuna streets, ((904) 829-2388, where the ale flows copiously

during the "Lion's Roar Happy Hour". The **Conch House Marina Lounge** is a quieter place by the riverfront at 57 Comares Avenue, ((904) 829-8646, where the notes of a single guitar fill the air.

For those who would prefer to dance, the discs spin into the early hours at **Sister Sally's** in the Holiday Inn at 1060 South Route A1A, ((904) 471-2555, and until 1 am at **Mario & Chickies**, 180 Anastasia Boulevard, ((904) 824-2952.

OPPOSITE: The interior of St. Augustine's oldest house, dating from 1723. ABOVE: The Spanish facade of St. Augustine. OVERLEAF: St. Augustine's Bridge of Lions at night.

Sports

The best **golf** course in the area is the Ponce de León Shores on Route 1 North, ☎ (904) 829-5314, where a round costs $25 and hire of a golf cart $10. The city's recreation department, ☎ (904) 829-8807, can tell you all about the 20 public **tennis** courts in the city. **Surfers** can rent a board from Surf Station at 1020 Anastasia Boulevard, ☎ (904) 471-9011; Velasurf at 3639 South Route A1A, ☎ (904) 471-6228, rent sailboards.

WHERE TO STAY

Luxury

The **Casa de Salano** at 21 Aviles Street, ☎ (904) 824-3555, overlooks Matanzas Bay and has rooms furnished with local antiques; complimentary chocolates and a decanter of sherry are in every room also. The **Westcott House** is an elegant Victorian building dating from the 1880s, and its eight guest rooms have exquisite European and Oriental furnishings along with a complimentary bottle of wine for each new arrival. It is at 146 Avenida Menéndez, ☎ (904) 824-4301. The **Conch House Marina Resort** is a hotel with its own fishing pier and is at 57 Comares Avenue, ☎ (904) 829-8646, toll-free (800) 432-6256, where it also has suites with kitchen and dining facilities, two restaurants, outside beach bars, and a cocktail lounge built on pilings near the shore.

Mid-range

In the heart of the old town at 11 Cadiz Street, ☎ (904) 824-5214, the **Victorian Inn** has been transformed from a derelict boarding house into a quaint hotel, tastefully furnished and decorated. The **Casa de la Paz** at 22 Avenida Menéndez, ☎ (904) 829-2915, is a Mediterranean-style hotel with a stucco exterior and walled courtyard. It also has — a nice touch, this — a cozy and well-stocked library. One of the few hotels in St. Augustine with its own swimming pool is the **Kenwood Inn** at 38 Marine Street, ☎ (904) 824-2116, which also has a lovely patio shaded by a large pecan tree. Care and imagination have gone into the interior design, so that the rooms are decorated according to different "themes" —

English, maritime, honeymoon, and so forth. Also in the old town, with 10 comfortable, high-ceilinged rooms, plus a small pond in an attractive courtyard, is the **St. Francis Inn** at 279 St. George Street, ☎ (904) 824-6068.

Inexpensive

The bullfight paintings may be a bit off-putting, but otherwise the rooms at the **Monsoon Motor Lodge**, 32 Avenida Menéndez, ☎ (904) 829-2277, are very comfortable, and some come with a kitchen. There is less to

trouble one's aesthetic sensibility at the **Park Inn**, 116 San Marco Avenue, ☎ (904) 824-4352, apart from the view of the parking lot, but here again you get good value for money.

WHERE TO EAT

Expensive

The **Columbia** at 98 St. George Street, ☎ (904) 824-3341, offers delicious Spanish cuisine, including an especially tasty *paella Valenciana*, accompanied by Spanish guitar music. The German-Swiss Sinatsch family have a wildly eclectic but lovingly prepared array of dishes on their menu at **Le Pavillon**, 45 San Marco Avenue, ☎ (904) 824-6202. The **Raintree** at 102 San Marco Avenue, ☎ (904)

824-7211, is best known locally for its vast stock of beers and wines, but it also deserves mention for cooking the most basic food very well indeed.

Moderate
Scarlett O'Hara's at 70 Hypolita Street, ((904) 824-6535, has an imaginative variety of soups, salads, seafoods, and sandwiches to choose from. Conch chowder is the house specialty at **Captain Jim's Conch Hut** by the ocean at 57 Comares Avenue, ((904) 829-8646. For uncomplicated English-style

How to Get There
The nearest airport is Jacksonville International Airport. The principal road from the west is Route 207.

JACKSONVILLE

Embracing 840 sq miles on either side of the mouth of the St. Johns River, Jacksonville is the state's largest city (and one of the largest,

cooking, go to **Monk's Vineyard** at 56 St. George Street, ((904) 824-5888. For typically and satisfyingly American food, try the **Gypsy Cab Company** at 828 Route A1A, Anastasia Island, ((904) 824-8244.

Inexpensive
The **Café Alcazar** at 25 Granada Street, ((904) 824-2618, only serves lunch but it has an unusual and fun menu, including "crois-sandwiches". Fried shrimp lovers should head for **O'Steens** at 205 Anastasia Boulevard, ((904) 829-6974, while those looking for good hamburgers, fried chicken, or Mexican food will be happy to find themselves at **Panama Hattie's** on Route A1A South, near the beach, ((904) 471-2255.

in area, in America). It is also Florida's financial center. Amelia Island, with its 13 miles (21 km) of beach, and Fernandina Beach lie just to the north of Jacksonville, providing a quiet retreat from the city.

Background

A French garrison was established at Fort Caroline, by the mouth of the St. Johns River, in 1564, but in the following year it fell to a Spanish force from St. Augustine. Like St. Augustine, Jacksonville was controlled

ABOVE AND OPPOSITE: Eventide and endless tide.

by different European powers for the next two and a half centuries, until Andrew Jackson marched into the city in 1821 as the first American territorial governor of Florida — hence the name Jacksonville. The city assumed prominence during the Civil War as a strategic port, and later for the export of the citrus produce of the hinterland. The arrival of the Florida East Coast Railroad in 1883 ensured that the city became the principal industrial and shipping center of Florida.

GENERAL INFORMATION

The Jacksonville Chamber of Commerce is at 3 Independent Drive, Jacksonville FL 32202. ((904) 798-9148. The Amelia Island–Fernandina Beach Chamber of Commerce is at 102 Center Street, Fernandina Beach FL 32034. ((904) 277-0717.

Other useful telephone numbers (all in area code 904):

Jacksonville International Airport	741-2000
Yellow Cabs	354-5511
Duval Country Medical Society	335-6561
Dental Information and Referral Service	356-6642

WHAT TO SEE AND DO

Sights

Jacksonville has some of the finest art museums in Florida, including the **Jacksonville Art Museum** at 4160 Boulevard Center Drive, ((904) 398-8336, which houses an exceptional collection of Oriental porcelain and pre-Columbian artifacts. The world's largest collection of Meissen porcelain can be seen at the **Cummer Gallery of Art and Gardens**, 829 Riverside Avenue, ((904) 356-6857, which also houses a fine collection of European and Japanese art; in addition, the Italian-style gardens are a delight. The **Amelia Island Museum** at 233 South Third Street, Fernandina Beach, ((904) 261-7378, charts the complex military, political, and cultural history of the area, while the **Jacksonville Museum of Science and History** at 1025 Gulf Life Drive, ((904) 396-7062, will take you even further back in time.

A replica of the fort established by the French in 1564 can be seen at the **Fort Caroline National Memorial**, 12713 Fort Caroline Road, ((904) 641-7111, daily from 9 am to 5 pm, free of charge. To complete your historical overview visit the **Kingsley Plantation** on Fort George Island, County Road 105 off Route A1A, ((904) 251-3537, where Zephaniah Kingsley ran a worldwide slave trade and lived with his African princess wife. Open daily 9 am to 5 pm. Admission is free.

For the children, the **Jacksonville Zoo** at 8605 Zoo Road, half a mile east of Heckscher Drive, ((904) 757-4463, mostly dispenses with cages, employing moats to separate watcher and watched, and features elephant rides. Admission is $4 for adults and $2.50 for children. For a less elephantine pace overland, you can hire a horse, for $18 to $25 an hour, from **Sea Horse Stable** on Route A1A South, Amelia Island, and go galloping along the beach; call ((904) 261-4878 for a reservation. After the ride, you should go for a stroll among the new-Gothic and Victorian architecture of Fernandina Beach, Amelia Island's main village.

Back in Jacksonville you can relax along the **Riverwalk** on the south bank of the river, then cross the Main Street Bridge to reach **Jacksonville Landing** at 2 Independent Drive to soak up the street life of musicians, buskers, shops, bars, and cafés.

Sports

Golfers will be challenged by the links at the Dunes Golf Club, 11751 McCormick Road, Jacksonville, ((904) 641-8444, or the Jacksonville Beach Golf Club, Penman Road, Jacksonville Beach, ((904) 249-8600. On Amelia Island the City of Fernandina Golf Course at 2800 Bill Melton Road, Fernandina Beach, ((904) 261-7804, welcomes visiting players.

Tennis players should ring the city's recreation department, ((904) 633-2540, for information about the various municipal courts in Jacksonville.

You can hire a sailboat or receive **sailing** instruction at Amelia Island Charters, 116 Center Street, Fernandina Beach, ((904)

261-7086, while surfboards and sailboards can be hired from Aloha Wind 'n' Surf at 407 Route A1A, Atlantic Beach, ((904) 241-4886.

Shopping
There are over 100 medium-sized shops, catering to almost every taste, at the recently developed **Jacksonville Landing**, 2 Independent Drive, on the north bank of the St. Johns River, ((904) 353-1188, already mentioned. It is a festival marketplace on two levels, with a number of cafés and restaurants in which to retreat from the hurly-burly. On Amelia Island, Fernandina Beach's **Center Street** is the main artery of the shopping district.

Nightlife
Regular jazz combos perform in the snazzy surroundings of **Juliette's** in the Omini Hotel at 245 Water Street, ((904) 355-6644. At **57 Heaven**, 8136 Atlantic Boulevard, Atlantic Beach, ((904) 721-5757, you can boogie to dance music from the Fifties and Sixties. A younger crowd strut their stuff to mod-rock, heavy metal, and reggae at **Metropolis**, 43 West Monroe Street, ((904) 355-6410, while others prefer the live rock music at **Einstein-A-GoGo**, 327 North First Street, ((904) 249-4646.

On Amelia Island, serious drinking goes on until the early hours at what is reputed to be Florida's oldest bar, the **Palace Saloon**, 115 Center Street, ((904) 261-9068.

WHERE TO STAY

Luxury
The **Omini Hotel** at 245 Water Street, ((904) 355-6664, toll-free (800) 228-2121, is probably the fanciest in town, with superb service to match its sumptuous accommodation. Every room has a view of the beach at the **Sea Turtle Inn**, 1 Ocean Boulevard, Jacksonville Beach, ((904) 279-7402, toll-free (800) 831-6600. The hotel has a well-equipped games room and an excellent restaurant.

On Amelia Island is the residential resort complex, **Amelia Island Plantation**, Route A1A, ((904) 261-6161, toll-free (800) 342-6841. Accommodation ranges from rooms in the hotel itself to villas in the grounds

(some with private pools). There are shops and bars on the site and the leisure facilities include a golf course, 20 tennis courts, a beach, fishing lagoons, jacuzzis, and a gym. If you would like a room with a 360 degree view, you can have one at **The Lighthouse**, 748 Route A1A, Fernandina Beach, ((904) 261-5878. If you have the money you can rent all four floors and have the place to yourself — with service, of course.

Mid-range
Overlooking Riverwalk and the river is the **Jacksonville Hotel**, 565 South Main Street, ((904) 398-8800, which has rooms with private balconies and is well positioned for both the town and the beach. **Seaside Studios** at 222 14th Avenue North in Jacksonville Beach, ((904) 241-7000, has efficiency suites and a congenial central courtyard with a grill and loungers under small palm trees.

An inviting inn can be found at 28 South Seventh Street in Fernandina Beach, ((904) 261-5390, where the Victorian gables, porches, and towers of **Bailey House** greet the eye. The interior tastefully maintains an Old World feel, with antiques and lace curtains gracing spacious rooms. The **Seaside Inn** at 1998 South Fletcher Avenue, Fernandina Beach, ((904) 261-0954, has rather more character than its name suggests. Ceiling fans cool the air, baskets of fruit await new guests in their rooms, and complimentary afternoon tea is served on the veranda.

WHERE TO EAT

Expensive
Brett's at 501 South Eighth Street, Fernandina Beach, ((904) 261-2660, offers a Continental menu almost as lavish as the restaurant's surroundings. Chef Tim Felver of the **Florida Café**, 8101 Phillips Highway, Jacksonville, ((904) 737-2244, specializes in Californian cuisine; especially recommended are his mesquite-grilled meats, quail, and Alaskan salmon. The **Olive Tree** at 1249 Penman Road, Jacksonville, ((904) 249-1300, serves up some exceptional Spanish and Italian dishes, and the **Wine Cellar** at 1314 Prudential Drive, Jacksonville,

((904) 398-8989, is worth a visit for its game alone.

Moderate

If you like deep-fried chicken gizzards with sautéed peppers and onions you will be happy at the all-American **Homestead**, 1721 Beach Boulevard, Jacksonville Beach, ((904) 249-5240, where you can find other, less demanding dishes as well. Steak-lovers are advised to try the **1878 Steak House** at 12 North Second Street in Fernandina Beach, ((904) 261-4049. Those who prefer a more Iberian ambience should go to **Salud!** at 207 Atlantic Boulevard, Atlantic Beach, ((904) 241-7877, which has delicious gazpacho, conch fritters, and deep-fried crab wontons. **Crawdaddy's** at 1643 Prudential Drive, Jacksonville, ((904) 396-3546, includes alligator and traditional Cajun food on its menu.

Inexpensive

You will get very generous portions of Oriental pork, beef, and chicken at **Chiang's Mongolian Bar-B-Q**, 1504 North Route A1A, Jacksonville Beach, ((904) 241-3075. **The Slightly Off Center Bakery and Deli** at South Second Street on Amelia Island, ((904) 277-2100, is a convivial eatery offering sandwiches, hamburgers, and Cajun food. A good place for cheap Italian food is **Patti's** at 7300 Beach Boulevard, Jacksonville Beach, ((904) 753-1662, while sushi-lovers should make a bee line for **Ieyasu of Tokyo** at 23 West Duval, Jacksonville, ((904) 353-0163.

HOW TO GET THERE

Many national and international airlines fly in to Jacksonville International Airport. Airport limousines run from the airport and charges $10 to downtown Jacksonville. The principal north-south roads are still I–95 and Routes 1 and A1A, while the main highway from the west is I–10.

The mighty Castillo de San Marcos was never conquered.

Central Florida

EVIDENCE that Florida was once covered by the sea runs from north of Ocala south to Sebring, above Spring Lake, in the form of a limestone ridge which was once a prehistoric coral reef. This ridge is the backbone of the Florida peninsula and rises to about 330 ft (100 m) above sea level. Many of the hillsides along the ridge are lined with citrus groves, while the plains to either side form the state's vegetable garden. In the north, in the hills of Ocala, grass and corrals signify that this is horse country: while in the south, around the old cowboy town of Kissimmee, are the sandy scrublands of cattle country.

The agricultural plains are fed by the pellucid waters of thousands of springs, rivers, and lakes. The waters of Ocklawaha River, which runs through the Ocala National Forest, and the chain of lakes created by it are particularly pristine, thus making fishing and boating even more enjoyable than usual. The Ocala National Forest, the largest sandy pine forest in the world, is understandably very popular with riders, campers, and seasonal hunters.

Oh yes, there's also Walt Disney World.

BACKGROUND

Early settlers, known as "crackers" (derived from the crack of the cattle whips they used to drive cattle), were tough and industrious people who worked a living from the land, and herded the same breed of cattle which the Spanish had introduced to the region in the sixteenth century. The citrus and cattle industries established by the crackers became the foundation of the region's economy, ensuring that Orlando grew to become one of the state's most important commercial centers. The farmers and ranchers of the region lived alongside the warlike Seminole Indians. A band of them massacred 139 U.S. soldiers on December 28, 1835, igniting the bloody and bitter Second Seminole War. It is generally accepted that Orlando derives its name from one Orlando Reeves, a soldier who was killed fighting the Seminoles.

The coming of the steamboat encouraged tourism and greatly boosted the economy of central Florida, while the arrival of the railroads in the 1880s added further impetus to the area's development. So far, so good — and so quietly. Then, in 1971, something happened. Walt Disney World opened 20 miles (32 km) south of Orlando at Lake Buena Vista, and suddenly central Florida was the most popular holiday destination in the world.

WALT DISNEY WORLD

The Disney people chose the Orlando area as the site for their eastern U.S. theme park because of the availability of flat land at reasonable (read: cheap) prices, good transportation facilities, and a year-round sunny climate. Eventually, after much surreptitious wheeling and dealing, Disney's agents slowly, slowly acquired 28,000 acres — that's 42 sq miles, or 67 sq km, an area twice the size of Manhattan — because Disney wanted enough space to build a wholly self-contained and self-servicing complex which wouldn't attract the sort of ugly metropolitan collar that chokes Disneyland in California. Disney himself died in 1966, three years before work started on the site. The first visitor walked through the completed park's gates in the summer of 1971; by 1985 another 250 million had walked through, making it easily the greatest tourist attraction in the world.

A month-long celebration greeted the opening, in 1982, of Epcot Center, a futuristic showcase extension to the park. "Epcot" stands for Experimental Prototype Community of Tomorrow, and was Walt Disney's own brainchild: he envisioned a self-governing community existing alongside the theme parks. It has worked out pretty well as Mr. Disney planned it: the Walt Disney World Vacation Kingdom (to give it its full name) is known in the Florida statute books as the Reedy Creek Improvement District, which is the legal governing body of the whole Disney complex, with powers to enforce building codes, construct roads, and supervise the election of mayors to the district's two towns, Bay Lake and Lake Buena Vista.

OPPOSITE: The Magic Kingdom gives a surrealistic quality to the Disney World skyline.

The facilities and services of this Utopian kingdom are indeed highly advanced: the first fully electronic telephone system in the world, a land transport system based on an elevated, noiseless, and computerized monorail, supported by — Mr. Ripley would have loved this — a fleet of 400 ships, from steamboats to submarines, making it the fifth largest navy in the world.

GENERAL INFORMATION

For all enquiries about Disney World con-

Ticket Prices

The term "ticket" means that you get a single day's admission to either the Magic Kingdom or the Epcot Center (but not both); "passports" admit you to both attractions and grant you unlimited use of the internal transportation system. The prices: One-day ticket: $38.52 adults, $31.03 children; Four-day passport: $132.68 adults, $103.79 children; Five-day passport: $191.53 adults, $153.01 children.

Each day of entry your passport is stamped; the remaining days can be used at

tact Walt Disney World, Box 10000, Lake Buena Vista FL 32830, ((407) 828-3481. They will be happy to send you a copy of the *Walt Disney World Vacation Guide*.

Try to arrive at Disney World before 9 am as the place becomes packed very quickly. A $4 parking fee is paid at the entrance, after which you follow the signs either to the **Magic Kingdom** or **Epcot Center**, where you should be sure to remember the name of your lot and line number. Trams then take you to the **Ticket and Transportation Center** (TTC), where you buy tickets for entry to the parks.

The Disney World elevated monorail speeds past Space Mountain ABOVE to Epcot Center and Spaceship Earth OPPOSITE.

any time in the future. All tickets and passports can be bought from the Ticket and Transportation Center; registered guests can buy theirs from on-site hotels. A Disney World kiosk sells tickets and passports in the main terminal at Orlando International Airport or you can order them before you travel from Admissions, Walt Disney World, at the address above. Tickets take about five weeks to arrive. All prices are subject to variation but will be confirmed by Walt Disney World Information if you call (407) 824-4321.

Opening Hours

Disney World opens at 9 am all year round (although they often let you in early). To avoid the worst crowds, visit the Magic Kingdom in the afternoon — or, better still, in the evening — and Epcot in the morning, working your way back to the entrance gates from the more distant attractions. In the summer months the Magic Kingdom closes at midnight, Epcot Center at 11 pm (earlier in the winter). Monday, Tuesday, and Wednesday are the busiest days; Friday and Sunday the quietest. I don't know why. Late afternoon and evening are the best times of the day for getting on rides and getting served. Peak times are Christmas through New Year and all the major holidays. Late August is the summer's quietest period.

Transportation

The transport is both varied and efficient. The monorail operates daily from 7:30 am to 11 pm from the Transportation and Ticket Center (TTC), whence all other modes of transport depart to the various attractions. All buses are color-coded according to their destination. If you prefer to travel around by water, ferries and launches also leave from the TTC. For those staying in an on-site hotel, or for holders of a joint Magic Kingdom-Epcot Center passport, all transport is free.

Tips

It's almost impossible to see everything in the Magic Kingdom and Epcot Center in the same day. They are both huge and several miles apart. To relax, take three days over them, and five days if you want to take in the more outlying attractions of the complex, which include River Country, Discovery Island, the Shopping Village, and Hotel Plaza. Get a map from City Hall in the Magic Kingdom or from Earth Station in Epcot Center and plan some sort of route: it will help you to get more in. A good way to avoid the worst queues at the rides in the Magic Kingdom is to go during the daily parade of Disney characters which begins at 3 pm and lasts half an hour.

Useful telephone numbers (all in area code 407):

Guest relations	824-4500
Accommodation reservations	824-8000
Dining or Recreation Information	824-3737
Tours of Magic Kingdom and Epcot Center	827-8233
Magic Kingdom Lost and Found	824-4521
Epcot Center Lost and Found	827-8236
Shopping Village Information	823-3058
KinderCare Child Care	827-5444

For more comprehensive information, including many helpful hints, get a copy of Sehlinger and Finley's *The Unofficial Guide to Walt Disney World and Epcot*, published by Prentice-Hall.

WHAT TO SEE AND DO

Magic Kingdom

A monorail or ferry boat takes you from the TTC to the gates of the Magic Kingdom in a few minutes. You then walk through the gates into the **Town Square** which contains the City Hall, the information center, and the lost-and-found office, and a railway station from which you can take a 15-minute train journey around the 98 acres of the park's rides and attractions. The Town Square is a lively place with stalls, Dixieland bands, and Disney characters to welcome you.

Main Street, USA stretches away from the Town Square. It is a thoroughfare lined with arcades, ice cream parlors, cinemas, shops, cafés and restaurants with turn-of-the-century façades. The Disney characters parade down the street to the Town Square every day at 3 pm, and from 9 pm to 11 pm there's the *Electric Parade* of giant floats.

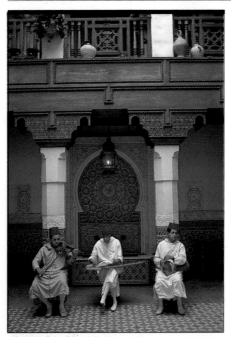

At the end of Main Street you cross a bridge over a moat and come to the 18-story *Cinderella's Castle*. The castle is at the heart of the Magic Kingdom; from here you can take any of the routes which lead to the various *Lands* — Main Street is the first such *Land*.

Adventureland

Adventureland is one of the most crowded in the kingdom. The top attractions are the *Pirates of the Caribbean*, which, among other buccaneering experiences, takes you through a cannon battle; the *Swiss Family Robinson Treehouse*, which is a labyrinthine concrete structure offering great views of the park; and the *Jungle Cruise*, which manages to go down the Nile and up the Amazon in one 10-minute journey.

Frontierland takes you back to the Old West of the Gold Rush days. The main attractions are the *Big Thunder Mountain Railroad*, a hair-raising runaway-train ride through a mine, and the *Country Bear Jamboree*, featuring singing, cavorting, audio-animatronic bears. For relative peace try

ABOVE TO OPPOSITE BOTTOM: The Moroccan, English, French and Chinese pavilions at Epcot Center.

Tom Sawyer Island, which can be reached by taking a raft.

The fourth *Land* is **Liberty Square**, which has as its themes Colonial and American history. Adults and older children will enjoy the *Hall of Presidents*, with animated figures of the nation's past leaders delivering famous speeches. There is also a 15-minute movie charting the history of the American Constitution. Slightly more attention-getting is

the popular *Haunted House* and the riverboat that takes you past scenes depicting the Old West.

Fantasyland is the farthest removed from the "real world" that the Magic Kingdom has to offer, and is easily the most popular with children. The attractions include a replica of Captain Nemo's submarine from *20,000 Leagues Under the Sea*, a trek through a forest to meet *Snow White and the Seven Dwarfs* and *Cinderella's Golden Carousel*. All of Disney's fairy-tale and cartoon characters will be encountered on the rides or streets of Fantasyland.

The last *Land* is **Tomorrowland**, where the roller-coaster ride — simulating space travel — at *Space Mountain* is heart-stopping (children under three cannot go on it and those under seven must be accompanied by an adult). The *Grand Prix Raceway* is popular with children who can get excited by a top speed of seven miles per hour.

From Tomorrowland you can take the route to Cinderella's Castle and Main Street back to the entrance gate. From there it's a three-mile (five-kilometer) monorail ride to Epcot Center.

Epcot Center

The *Experimental Prototype Community of Tomorrow* (Epcot) is an educationally-oriented complex, about twice the size of the Magic Kingdom, with two distinct areas — *Future World* and *World Showcase* — separated by a lagoon. It is best to explore World Showcase in the morning and Future World later in the day to get ahead of the crowds. You enter Epcot Center beneath *Spaceship Earth* (a 17-story spherical structure 180 ft or 55 m at its highest point) where you can

pick up a guide to both areas at *Earth Station*. Future World starts at Spaceship Earth, and World Showcase can be reached by taking the sidewalk which skirts the lagoon.

World Showcase is a collection of pavilions, each based around a replica of one of the host nation's landmarks or typical buildings (the Eiffel Tower, a Japanese pagoda, an English pub, that sort of thing). Displays, films, and exhibits portray the art, culture,

and general way of life of the country in question. There are daily displays in front of each pavilion of that country's crafts, as well as live folk music and dance, while inside there are stalls selling these crafts and other artifacts. Examples of the national cuisine are also served up, so be sure to visit the French and Mexican and Japanese pavilions.

The centerpiece of the World Showcase is the host pavilion, the **American Adventure**, which is based around a Colonial-style house and features a show in which audio-animatronic characters re-enact scenes from American history. The show's hosts are Mark Twain and Benjamin Franklin. The other pavilions fan out from American Adventure. The countries you can "visit" on your international tour are Mexico, China (with a brilliant reproduction of Beijing's Temple of Heaven), Germany, Italy (featuring a reproduction of St. Mark's Square in Venice), Japan, France, the United Kingdom (featuring the Rose and Crown pub with Guiness ale), Canada, Morocco, and Norway. Soon to come, at this writing, are pavilions from Spain, Israel, and Equatorial Africa.

Future World

Walk back around the lagoon to the Future World starting point in *Spaceship Earth*. Fu-

ture World features an educational and entertaining tour through the technological and scientific advances of man, exploring such subjects as transportation, communications, energy, and computers. In Spaceship Earth you are guided through displays and exhibits which show the history of man's attempt to communicate his ideas and make himself understood, from the time of the first cave paintings to the latest satellite technology.

Children will enjoy the educational computer games at **Innoventions**, where you can also gain an insight into the complex computer system which helps maintain the smooth functioning of the entire Disney World complex and amazing scientific develoments from around the world. The **Universe of Energy** dramatizes the formation of fossil fuels in prehistoric times with simulated earthquakes and volcanic eruptions; there are also audio-animatronic dinosaurs stalking around the display. **Horizons** is a journey through time in the opposite direction: solar-powered theater cars take you on a ride into the twenty-first century, where you will find farms run by robots, cities under the ocean, and zero-gravity baseball in space.

Journey into the Imagination features *Henry, I Shrunk the Audience*, in a fascinating thrilling ride. Characters called Dreamfinder and Figment then escort you through exhibits which try to show how art, literature, and films originate in one idea which expands and is modified to become the completed work. The least imaginatively named attraction at Future World is **The Land**, which will have greater appeal for adults than for children. The land covers six acres and offers walking tours through displays of the latest methods of food production, including one showing how food might one day be grown in outer space. Produce from The Land can be tasted at the Good Turn Restaurant. One of the most spectacular attractions in the whole of Disney World is **The Living Seas**, which features an underwater restaurant and "seacab" service in a six-million-gallon aquarium that is five fathoms deep and inhibited by hundreds of different kinds of sea life, including dolphins and barracudas.

OTHER THINGS TO SEE IN DISNEY WORLD

Blizzard Beach Water Park, a ski resort with slides down 90 ft (27 m) Mt. Gushmore into a tropical logoon.It is situated next to Disney's new All-Star Resorts.

River Country, at the Fort Wilderness Campground Resort by Bay Lake off Vista Boulevard, ((407) 824-3737, is an aquatic park with water slides, whitewater rapids, waterfalls, and swing ropes around a huge swimming pool. It's a very popular spot in the summer. Admission is $14.85 per day for adults and $11.66 per day for children aged three to nine.

Discovery Island is in Bay Lake and can be reached by boat from either the Magic

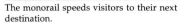

The monorail speeds visitors to their next destination.

Kingdom or River Country. It is a natural sanctuary for exotic flora, over 60 species of birds (such as the bald eagle and the stunning scarlet ibis), and small animals. Tickets can be bought from either the TTC, River Country, or on the island itself and are $10.07 for adults and $5.57 for children aged three to nine. The island's walkways and foot bridges offer a peaceful retreat from the rest of Disney World.

The Disney MGM Studios offer shows, rides, attractions and the fascinating studio tour which affords a chance to see Disney artists at work on animated features; film and television production techniques can also be studied, as can the fascinating special effects studio. A feature recently added to the studios is a George Lucas-created thrill ride through "space", in which you are strapped into seats that are on motion simulators similar to the ones used for training astronauts. A 3-D film by the creator of the Muppets, Jim Henson, starring Kermit the Frog, Miss Piggy, and all the gang, is also on view. Children particularly enjoy the newly-built playground based on the movie *Honey, I Shrunk the Kids*, which has grass 30 ft (nine meters) high, giant ants and spider webs. The latest attraction is the **Twilight Zone Tower of Terror**, a chilling 13 storey "drop" in a hotel lift. The studio is next to Epcot Center off Buena Vista Drive.

Shopping
If you have any money left, you might like to visit the **Walt Disney World Village** at

Lake Buena Vista (go west on Epcot Center Drive, then north on I–4). The village has a shopping complex with the latest fashions from around the world, electronic goods, and quality gifts. The prices, however, are high; you would be better off shopping in Orlando.

Nightlife

There is a good selection of nightlife in Disney World itself and in the nearby town of Kissimmee, five miles (eight kilometers) to the east on Route 192.

The **Polynesian Revue** and **Mickey's Tropical Revue** in the Polynesian Village Resort, Disney World, ((407) 824-8000, are shows with South Pacific themes featuring hula dancing which are held outdoors with barbecued dinner included. The **Giraffe Lounge** in the Hotel Royal Plaza, ((407) 828-2828, has live dance music every evening. In the Australian surroundings of the **Laughing Kookaburra Good Time Bar** in the Buena Vista Palace, ((407) 827-2727, you have a choice of over 100 beers; and for the best in German beers there is the **Biergarten** at the World Showcase in Epcot Center.

In Kissimmee, **Murphy's Vine Street Emporium Dance Palace** at 4763 West Route 192, ((407) 396-6500, has a dance floor as

endless as its name and the sounds of a live dance band until the early hours.

WHERE TO STAY

Walt Disney World and environs has a truly vast selection of hotels to chose from. The first decision you will have to make is whether to stay inside or outside the grounds of Disney World. The main advantages of being in the grounds are that you are close to all the things you want to see, and use of the quick and efficient internal transportation is free. Moreover, on-site guests receive a guest identification card which allows them to charge anything at Disney World (except in the Magic Kingdom) to their hotel room.

Your second decision will be whether to stay in one of the hotels owned by Disney World, most of which overlook Bay Lake next to the Magic Kingdom, or to stay in one of the independently owned hotels within the grounds at Lake Buena Vista in the Walt Disney World Village. These hotels are further away from the main attractions, but most run their own shuttle service to and from the theme parks. Some of the hotels in the village have self-catering facilities and there is a supermarket in the shopping complex nearby.

To reserve a room in any on-site hotels contact the **Walt Disney Central Reservation Office**, Box 10100, Lake Buena Vista FL 32830, ((407) 824-8000, as far in advance of your stay as possible. All-in packages, including admission tickets, car rentals, and hotel reservations inside or outside the Disney World grounds, can be made through the **Walt Disney Travel Company**, 1675 Buena Vista Drive, Lake Buena Vista FL 32830. ((407) 828-3232.

All on-site hotels, whether Disney-owned or not, range from the expensive to the very, very expensive.

On-Site Hotels Owned by Walt Disney World

All of the hotels mentioned below should be contacted through the Central Reservation Office mentioned above. They include:

The **Polynesian Village** has 644 rooms and tries to re-create the atmosphere of a South Pacific island, with a miniature "rain forest" in the lobby consisting of palm trees and sundry exotic plants. The accommodation is in 11 three-story "longhouses". Most of the rooms have balconies and some overlook the Magic Kingdom. The hotel has its own beach and marina where you can rent canoes and boats for sailing, fishing, and water-skiing on the lake. The 1,053-room **Contemporary Hotel** has the monorail running straight through its lobby. This 15-story, ultra-modern hotel is constructed mainly of glass. The facilities

units, accommodating up to six people, in a delightful cedar structure next to the Lake Buena Vista golf course.

Other Disney hotels are the **Grand Floridian Beach Resort**, the **Disney Inn** by Bay Lake, **Club-Suite Villas** in the World Village, the **All-Star Sports Resort** and the **All-Star Music Resort.** The increasingly popular **Treehouses**, tucked away in quiet woods between the World Village and Bay Lake, will appeal to those who want to escape the crowds while remaining within striking distance of the theme parks. It is

include two swimming pools, a health club and sauna, and a fifteenth-floor lounge with dancing and entertainment every night. The hotel is next to Bay Lake.

The **Resort Villas** are in the Walt Disney World Village alongside the independently-run hotels. The villas enjoy all the extensive sporting facilities, shopping, and nightlife which the village has to offer. There are several villas to choose from. **Vacation Villas** offers 139 one-bedroom efficiency units which can accommodate up to four people, and 87 two-bedroom units, each accommodating up to six people and having kitchen facilities. Vacation Villas also has two swimming pools. **Two-Bedroom Villas** has 64 two-bedroom efficiency

now possible to be married in any of the Walt Disney attractions, and there are even secluded honeymoon cottages.

Independent Hotels in Walt Disney World Village

The **Buena Vista Palace** at 1900 Lake Buena Vista Drive, Lake Buena Vista, ((407) 827-2727, toll-free (800) 327-2990, is a 27-story, 841-room hotel which cost $93 million to build. Many of its modern, spacious rooms overlook Epcot Center. The facilities include swimming pools, tennis courts, a games room, and several bars and restaurants,

OPPOSITE: The Floridiana Hotel at Disney World.
ABOVE: Surely you joust: the Middle Ages live in Kissimmee, at the Medieval Times Restaurant.

including Arthur's 27, a splendid top-floor eatery offering great views of Disney World. The **Hilton Hotel** at 1751 Hotel Plaza Boulevard, Lake Buena Vista, ((407) 827-4000, toll-free (800) 445-8667, has the latest in electronic technology, including lights that turn themselves on and off as you enter or leave the room, and all sort of devices that control the central heating, the air conditioning, and the television.

At the Colonial-style **Grosvenor Resort**, 1850 Hotel Plaza Boulevard, Lake Buena Vista, ((407) 828-4444, toll-free (800) 624-4109, all the rooms are handsomely decorated and each has its own VCR (you can rent movies from the hotel). There are two swimming pools, basketball and volleyball courts, and a children's playground. Other luxury hotels in the Disney World Village include the **Hotel Royal Plaza** at 1905 Hotel Plaza Boulevard, ((407) 828-2828, toll-free (800) 248-2424; and the **Pickett Suite Resort** at 2305 Hotel Plaza Boulevard, ((407) 934-1000, toll-free (800) 742-5388.

As a budget-conscious alternative to these hotels, you can stay at the **Fort Wilderness Campground Resort**, which is next to Bay Lake in the Disney World grounds. You can rent efficiency trailers that accommodate four to six people, or bring your own trailer, or simply pitch a tent. There are two "trading posts" in the campground, and the recreational facilities include canoeing, riding, and Disney film shows. For prices and other information contact the Reservation Office, ((407) 824-8000.

Hotels Outside Disney World

There are two areas close by Disney World where you can find a wide selection of mid-range and inexpensive hotels: the *Maingate* area, east off I–4 just above Disney World's northern entrance, and the area east of Disney World known as the *Route 192 Corridor* running to Kissimmee. Here is a selection of the hotels to be found here:

MID-RANGE

In the *Maingate* area: the **Orlando Marriott Inn**, 8001 International Drive, Orlando, ((407) 351-2420, toll-free (800) 228-9290; the **Hilton Inn Florida Center**, 7400 International Drive, Orlando, ((407) 351-4600, toll-free (800)

327-1363; the **Holiday Inn International**, 6515 International Drive, Orlando, ((407) 351-3500; the **Days Inn Orlando Lakeside**, 7335 Sandlake Road, Orlando, ((407) 351-1900, toll-free (800) 777-3297; and the **Sheraton World**, 10100 International Drive, Orlando, ((407) 352-1100, toll-free (800) 325-3535.

In the *Route 192 Corridor* area: the **Colonial Motor Lodge**, 1815 West Wine Street, Kissimmee, ((407) 847-6121; the **Radisson Inn Maingate** 7501 West Spacecoast Parkway, Kissimmee, ((407) 396-1400, toll-free (800) 333-3333; the **Spacecoast Motel** 4125 Spacecoast Parkway, Kissimmee, ((407) 933-5732, toll-free (800) 654-8342; the **Gemini Motel** 4624 Route 192, Kissimmee, ((407) 396-2151; and the **Hawaiian Village Inn**, 4559 Route 192, Kissimmee, ((407) 396-1212.

INEXPENSIVE

In the *Maingate* area: the **Knight's Inn Orland Maingate West**, 7475 West Irlo Bronson Highway, ((407) 396-4200; the **Quality Inn Plaza**, 9000 International Drive, Orlando, ((407) 345-8585, toll-free (800) 228-5151; and the **Comfort Inn**, 8421 South Orange Blossom Trail, Orlando, ((407) 855-6060, toll-free (800) 327-9742.

In the *Route 192 Corridor* area: the **Golden Link Motel**, 4914 Route 192, Kissimmee, ((407) 396-0555; the **Casa Rosa Inn**, 4600 Route 192, Kissimmee, ((407) 396-2020; and the **Lakeside Cedar Inn**, 4960 Route 192, Kissimmee, ((407) 396-1376.

WHERE TO EAT

Every pavilion in Epcot Center's World Showcase has a restaurant offering a menu of the host nation's cuisine. Many of the restaurants also have special children's menu at reduced prices.

Making a reservation at World Showcase restaurants

Guests at any on-site hotel can make reservations by phoning (407) 824-4000 a day or two in advance. Take your guest identification card with you when you go to the restaurant.

Visitors to Disney World who are not staying in one of the on-site hotels cannot make telephone reservations, and can only book a table on the day of the meal. **Worldkey**

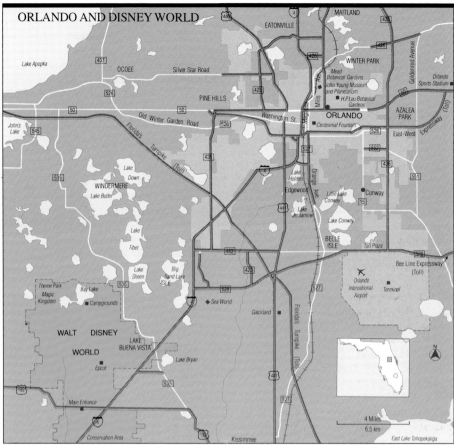

ORLANDO AND DISNEY WORLD

Information screens are the quickest way to make a reservation. They can be found at Earth Station in Future World's Spaceship Earth; there are more in a kiosk by the lagoon as you emerge from Future World. Of course you can also book in person at the restaurant of your choice, but you should do it early in the morning. All the World Showcase restaurants are moderately priced.

World Showcase Restaurants

Three eminent French chefs — Paul Bocuse, Roger Verge, and Gaston Lenôtre — have created a classic menu at **Les Chefs de France** in the French Pavilion. The **San Angel Inn** is a romantic, candlelit restaurant in the Mexican pavilion, where the atmosphere is enhanced by the sounds of a Mexican guitar. The menu is actually more Tex-Mex than Mexican; the specialties not to be missed are Baja lobster with peppers in white wine and red snapper with onions.

Alfredo's in the Italian pavilion is highly popular, thanks to its wide selection of traditional pastas and not to its selection of Italian singing waiters. Also recommended is the ploughman's lunch at the English pavilion's **Rose and Crown Pub,** or the couscous and pork bastilas of the **Marrakesh** restaurant in the Moroccan pavilion.

Restaurants in Walt Disney World Village

The **American Vineyards** in the Hilton at 1751 Hotel Plaza Boulevard, ((407) 827-4000, specializes in wine-based sauces that lend an exceptional flavor to their beef and veal. The menu also includes an extensive selection of seafood cooked with Cajun seasonings and papaya butter. Regarded as one of Florida's premier restaurants, **Arthur's 27** can be found at the top of the Buena Vista Palace Hotel, 1900 Lake Buena Vista Drive, ((407) 827-3450. In the same hotel is a more family-oriented restaurant, **The Outback,**

℃ (407) 827-3430, which, as you might expect, specializes in Australian-style barbecued lamb and beef, and lots of beer. **Planet Hollywood**, part owned by Arnold Schwarzenegger, Sylvester Stallone and other stars, serves "fun" food, 1506 East Buena Vista Drive, ℃ (407) 827-7827.

HOW TO GET THERE

No problem. Many international airlines and over 30 national airlines serve Orlando International Airport, including two which offer package tours to Disney World: Delta, toll-free (800) 827-7786, and Pan Am, toll-free (800) 221-1111. An airport limousine service, toll-free (800) 423-5566, goes to Disney World every half-hour, and costs $11 (the limos can carry up to 11 people). If you want to go from the airport to the door of your hotel, inside or outside the grounds of Disney World, you will have to pay about $30.

For those traveling in their own car, I–4 passes by the entrance to Disney World. From the northwest, you approach on Florida's Turnpike (a tollway) and join I–4 at Junction 75. You should also take the turnpike if you are coming from the Gold Coast. The I–4 approaches Disney World from the west and northeast (Tampa and Daytona). If you are traveling from the south, take Route 27 as far as Junction 54, where you join the I–4.

GREATER ORLANDO

The Greater Orlando area, with a population approaching one million, is one of the most rapidly expanding metropolises in America. The growth of the city, and its transformation into a business and tourist center, is largely due, of course, to the proximity of Walt Disney World. The city, however, does have its own character and attractions distinct from those of Disney World.

BACKGROUND

U.S. soldiers were the first inhabitants of the area when Fort Gatlin was established in 1838 as a military outpost to keep the local Seminole Indians in check. By 1875 the Seminoles had been subdued, increasing numbers of settlers were coming into the area, and the slowly growing community around the fort had been named Orlando. The city's early economy was based on citrus produce and cattle, although the exceptionally cold weather during 1884 and 1885 wiped out many of the citrus groves in the area. The local farmers, ever resourceful, turned to cereals and vegetables as replacement crops.

In the 1880s railroads reached central Florida, bringing tourists who were attracted by the waters and springs of the region. Orlando was a favorite base for these visitors, whose custom further boosted the city's economy. In those days Orlando could offer only a handful of hotels for visitors to choose from, but the city has steadily grown and prospered over the years and there are now some 60,000 hotel rooms in the Greater Orlando area.

GENERAL INFORMATION

The Greater Orlando Tourist Information Center is at 8445 International Drive, Orlando FL 32819, ℃ (407) 351-0412, where you can pick up a complimentary copy of the guidebook, *Discover Orlando*. The Orlando/Orange County Convention and Visitors Bureau is at 7208 Sand Lake Road, Suite 300, Orlando FL 32819, ℃ (407) 363-5800. For news of upcoming local events get the *Orlando Sentinel/Central Florida Guide*.

Other useful telephone numbers (all in area code 407):

Orlando International Airport	825-2001
Yellow Cabs	423-4455
Town and Country Cabs	828-3035
Orange County Medical Society	898-3338
Emergency Dental Care	425-1616

WHAT TO SEE AND DO

Sights
Route 192 west of Disney World is known locally as the "Tourist Trail", along which you will find, at 5770 West Route 192, Kissimmee, ℃ (407) 396-4888, **Old Town**, home to a variety of Old World-style shops and restaurants, as well as the **Museum of Woodcarving**, ℃ (407) 396-4422, which contains

over 400 beautifully carved works by Joseph T. Barta. A "Home of the Future" called **Xanadu** can be seen at 4800 West Route 192, Kissimmee, ((407) 396-1992. Like the spaceship in film *2001*, the house is controlled by an omnipotent and omnipresent computer, but a robot butler adds a "human" touch. Xanadu is open daily from 10 am to 10 pm, and admission is $4.75 for adults and $3.50 for children. At the **Alligatorland Safari Zoo**, 4580 West Route 192, Kissimmee, ((407) 396-1012, there are no prizes for guessing who runs the protection racket: 2,000 of the brutes live alongside over 100 other species of intimidated wildlife.

Splendid China, ((407) 397-8800, the area's latest attraction on U.S. 192, west of I–4, is home to over 60 replicas (full scale or miniature) of China's best known scenic, historic and cultural sites.

Further north, before you get to downtown Orlando, there are more attractions grouped around International Drive. The most popular of these is **Sea World** at 7007 Sea World Drive, ((407) 351-3600, which considers itself the world's premier marine life theme park. It features shows with killer whales, dolphins, and sea lions, plus a nerve-testing ride along a tunnel made of *very* (read: completely sharkproof) thick acrylic which passes through a shark-infested tank. Wild Arctic, the park's the latest attraction, is a thrill ride among exhibit featuring animals of the frozen north. There are also gardens and restaurants in the park, which is open from 9 am to 7 pm daily; admission is $34.95 for adults and $29.95 for children aged three to 11.

Other attractions in this area include the **Mystery Fun House** at 5767 Major Boulevard, ((407) 351-3355, which is full of haunting effects, mirrors, and moving floor; **Wet 'n' Wild** at 6200 International Drive, ((407) 351-1800, a 25-acre (10-hectare) waterpark with wave machines and huge water slides; **Fun 'n' Wheels** at 6739 Sand Lake Road at International Drive, ((407) 351-5651, where you can race go-carts or settle some scores in bumper cars, and **Church Street Station** at 129 West Church Street, ((407) 422-2434, a nighttime entertainment complex with Dixieland, folk music, bluegrass, discos and restaurants.

ABOVE: A killer whale rises to the occasion at Orlando's Sea World. OVERLEAF: The silent beauty of Lake Kissimmee State Park.

In downtown Orlando you will find, among other attractions, the beautiful grounds of **Lake Eola Park** off Orange Avenue, which retains the serene atmosphere of old Orlando. Watch out for the spectacular **Centennial Fountain**, especially at night, when water and light combine to dazzling effect. Another interesting collection can be seen at the **Cartoon Museum** 4300 South Semoran Boulevard, ((407) 273-0141, which features rare super-hero comic books from the earliest days of cartoon art. Just north of the downtown area is the **Orlando Science Center** at 810 East Rollins Street, ((407) 896-7151, which has a practical approach to teaching science: a computer will analyze your risk of a heart attack, and another machine will convert your bodily energy into electricity.

Universal Studios Florida, 1000 Universal Studios Plaza (off Kirkman Road), ((407) 363-8000 is the largest motion picture and television facility outside Hollywood. It offers more than 40 rides, shows and realistic backlot sets where famous scenes in cinematic history are recreated for visitors. Admission is $39.22 for adults, $31.80 for children aged three to nine. Parking is $5. Open at 9 am daily.

Orlando offers several ways of escaping the theme parks and the crowds, including **Scenic Boat Tours** which leave from 312 East Morse Boulevard in Winter Park, North Orlando, ((407) 644-4056, on a one-hour tour of the area's canals and lakes past some lovely countryside. Alternatively, you can go up and away with **Balloon Flights of Florida** at 129 West Church Street, Orlando, ((407) 422-2434.

Sports
Baseball fans might want to make the 40-mile (64-km) journey southwest, on I-4 and then Route 557, to Winter Haven to watch the Boston Red Sox in spring training at the Chain of Lakes Park, Cypress Gardens Boulevard, ((813) 293-2138. In Orlando, the Minnesota Twins train from mid-February to the end of March at Tinker Field on the corner of Tampa Avenue and Church Street, ((407) 849-6346. From April to September the minor-league Orlando Twins play at the same stadium.

Walt Disney World has three championship **golf** courses in its grounds, all of which are included on the PGA tour. Green fees are $55. Call (407) 828-3741 for details. The Cypress Creek Country Club at 5353 Vineyard Road in Orlando charges about $30 a round, including a cart. Golfpac, Box 484, Maitland (north of Orlando), ((407) 660-8559, prearranges rounds for visitors at numerous courses around Orlando.

Tennis players should head for Oak Street Park, Palm and Oak streets, Orlando, ((407) 847-2388, or the Orange Lake Country Club Resort at 8505 Route 192, Kissimmee, ((407) 239-0000.

Water sports enthusiasts can rent canoes, airboats, or motorboats from U-Drive Airboat Rentals at 4266 West Vine Street, Kissimmee, ((407) 847-3672, or receive lessons in jet-skiing, parasailing, windsurfing, or waterskiing on one of Orlando's lakes by contacting Splash-N-Ski at 10000 Turkey Lake Road, Orlando, ((407) 352-1494.

Shopping
The fashion-conscious tend to make tracks to the upmarket **Park Avenue** in Winter Park, North Orlando, which is lined with stylish boutiques and antique shops. The **Florida Mall** at 8001 South Orange Blossom Trail, near International Drive, Orlando, offers a wide selection of merchandise in over 160 shops. Nearby, at 8445 International Drive, you will find the brick streets and Mediterranean-style shopfronts of the **Mercado Shopping Village**, where over 50 shops specialize in arts, crafts, jewelry, and Oriental curios. Buskers, street entertainers, and some very decent restaurants add to the flavor of this charming shopping complex.

Nightlife
The **Mardi Gras** in the Mercado Shopping Village, ((407) 351-5151, offers one of the best dinner shows in town. The food has a Deep Southern accent, and a New Orleans jazz band plays during dinner. Caribbean and Latin American music, as well as Dixieland, follow dinner, allowing you to dance away the calories. With any luck, you will be able to catch such golden oldsters as Fats Domino and Bo Diddley at **Little Darlin's Rock 'n' Roll Palace** in the

old town, 5770 West Route 192, Kissimmee, ((407) 396-6499, which has live music from the Fifties and Sixties seven nights a week.

The most vibrant night spot in downtown Orlando is probably the **Church Street Station** complex at 129 West Church Street, ((407) 422-2434, which offers a great variety of entertainment, including Dixieland bands, cancan dancers, and vaudeville acts at **Rosie O'Grady's**, the live country-and-western bands of the **Cheyenne Saloon**, which also has a traditional American restaurant, and the live folk and bluegrass music at **Apple Annie's Courtyard**. The Church Street Station also houses one of the trendiest discos in town, **Phileas Phogg's Balloon Works**, where you can dance until 2 am.

WHERE TO STAY

The hotels along the "Route 192 Corridor" and those around International Drive are all within half an hour's drive of Orlando. For more information about the city's seemingly endless list of hotels contact the Greater Orlando Tourist Information Center or the Orlando/Orange County Convention and Visitors Bureau. Here is a small selection of the hotels in the area:

Luxury

The **Park Plaza Hotel** is in Orlando's exclusive Winter Park suburb at 307 Park Avenue, ((407) 647-1072. It is an especially welcoming hotel with a genuine southern feel and 29 handsome rooms which all open out on to flower-bedecked balconies overlooking modish Park Avenue. At the **Colonial Plaza Inn**, 2801 East Colonial Drive, Orlando, ((407) 896-9858, there are four suites with their own small swimming pools, but all the hotel's guests can enjoy the Jacuzzi facilities. Victorian antiques contribute tastefully to the interior of the **Norment-Parry Inn** at 211 North Lucerne Circle East, Orlando, ((407) 648-5188, which is in a choice position overlooking Lake Lucerne.

In downtown Orlando at 151 East Washington Street, ((407) 841-3220, toll-free (800) 321-2323, the **Harley Hotel** is in a beautiful spot next to Lake Eola Park. The Harley has a gorgeous swimming pool and an elegant restaurant with a lovely view over the park.

Mid-range

In Winter Park at 300 East New England Avenue, ((407) 644-3400, is the friendly, family-run **Langford Hotel**, one of the best values in town considering the extensive facilities, which include a courtyard swimming pool, a jacuzzi and sauna, and the Empire Room restaurant with its excellent food and live musical entertainment. The **Fugate House**, a small and *gemütlich* hotel, can be found in Orlando's Lake Cherokee district, tucked away at 545 Margaret Court *(sic!)*, Orlando, ((407) 423-8382, and is particularly recommended for its friendly service. **Howard Johnson's** at 2014 West Colonial Drive in midtown Orlando, ((407) 841-8600, offers the usual reliable service and quality of any Howard Johnson's but in this case is distinguished for the mouth-watering Southern-style food up at its restaurant, Aunt Polly's.

Inexpensive

Good budget bets in Orlando include the **Econo Lodge Orlando Central** at 3300 West Colonial Drive, ((407) 293-7221, the **Howard Vernon Motel** at 600 West Colonial Drive, ((407) 422-7162, **TraveLodge Downtown Orlando** at 409 Magnolia Avenue, ((407) 423-1671.

WHERE TO EAT

Expensive

For the most romantic ambience, and some of the best seafood in town, go to **Park Plaza Gardens** at 319 Park Avenue South, Orlando, ((407) 645-2475, where in absolutely delightful surroundings you can enjoy such specialties as flounder meunière and shrimp in curry sauce. There is another elegant garden setting at the **Ran-Getsu**, 8400 International Drive, Orlando, ((407) 354-0044, a Japanese restaurant that includes on its menu such innovations as Florida rolls — sushi rice, avocado, cucumber, and crab — as well as the more traditional fare. **Christini's** at the intersection of Sand Lake Road and Dr. Phillips Boulevard in the Marketplace Shopping Center, Orlando, ((407) 345-8770, is a highly-regarded Italian restaurant which has invented its own *zuppa di pesce alla Mediterrania* — lobster, shrimp, clams, and mussels in a light red sauce.

Another restaurant worth visiting is the **Royal Orleans** in the Mercado Shopping Village at 8445 International Drive, Orlando, ((407) 352-8200, which specializes in Cajun food, with Creole variations.

Moderate

For traditional French cuisine your best bet is the **Coq au Vin** at 4800 South Orange Avenue, Orlando, ((407) 851-6980, where Louis and Magdalena Perotte have created an excellent menu and a charming atmosphere. You would also do well to try the chateaubriand and the fish in wine sauce at **La Belle Verrière**, 142 Park Avenue South, Orlando, ((407) 645-3377. The tandoori cooking of northern India can be enjoyed at the elaborately decorated **Darbar**, 7600 Dr. Phillips Boulevard, Orlando, ((407) 345-8128. Despite its name, **La Cantina** at 4721 East Colonial Drive, Orlando, ((407) 894-4491, is a splendidly straightforward American restaurant, which means, among other things, that it serves wonderful steaks.

Inexpensive

It's friendly and informal, it serves six-ounce martinis and tasty fresh seafood, and it's called **Gary's Duck Inn**. It can be found at 3974 South Orange Blossom Trail, Orlando, ((407) 843-0270. **The Greek Place** in the Mercado Shopping Village, 8445 International Drive, Orlando, ((407) 352-6930, is a *good* Greek place. The quaint **British Tearoom** at 1917 Alona Avenue, Winter Park, ((407) 677-0121, offers such typical (yawn) English fare as ale pie, Cornish pasties, and cheese on toast, all washed down by tea. **Skeeter's**, by contrast, is a rough-and-ready place where you can tuck into hash browns, waffles, pancakes, hot dogs, and fried eggs, all washed down with beer. This very popular local diner is at 1212 Lee Road, Orlando, ((407) 298-7973.

OTHER ATTRACTIONS IN CENTRAL FLORIDA

SOUTH OF ORLANDO

Baseball fans will want to head for **Boardwalk and Baseball**, ((813) 424-1526, at the

intersection of I–4 and Route 27 (near Haines City), which has nine cages in which you can practice your batting, and a machine which tells you whether you've pitched a ball or a strike. The National Baseball Hall of Fame has some fascinating exhibits here, and the Baseball Theatre shows a film entitled The Eternal Game which traces the history of baseball. There's also an amusement park on the site, with roller-coaster rides and a Wild West show. It's open daily from 9 am to 9 pm; admission is $18.95 for adults and $14.95 for children.

Further down Route 27, on Route 540 near Winter Haven, ((813) 324-2111, are the **Florida Cypress Gardens**, a 223-acre park with beautifully-tended botanical gardens,

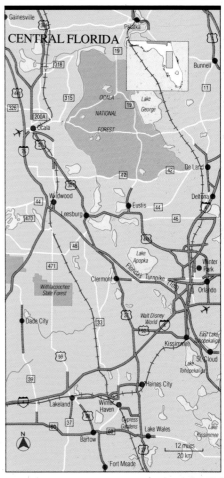

OPPOSITE: An orange juice cannery in central Florida.

a zoological park, and a miniature railway. You can also see the Great American Ski Show, which features water-skiing, power-boat racing, and water-ski jumping. The gardens are open daily from 9 am to 6 pm, and admission is $26.45 for adults and $17.40 for children aged three to 11.

For somewhat more natural surroundings, head further south down Route 27 until you reach **Bok Tower Gardens**, ((813) 676-1408, just before the town of Lake Wales. A Gothic tower 200 ft (61 m) high, with a 57-bell carillon, is surrounded by 123 acres of tranquil gardens and nature trails. Classical music recitals are performed in the gardens on selected summer evenings. The gardens are open daily from 8 am to 5 pm, and admission is free for children up to 11, and $3 for everyone else.

If you prefer something wilder you should head east out of Lake Wales to the **Lake Kissimmee State Park** at 14248 Camp Mack Road, Lake Wales, ((813) 696-1112, which has excellent fishing, hiking trails, and also features rodeos. There are campsites in the park for those wishing to camp.

Some useful addresses and telephone numbers for tourist information south of Orlando:
The Kissimmee/St. Cloud Convention and Visitors Bureau, P.O. Box 422007, Kissimmee FL 32742. ((407) 847-5000.
The Haines City Chamber of Commerce, P.O. Box 986, Haines City FL 33844. ((813) 422-3751.
The Lake Wales Area Chamber of Commerce, 340 West Central Avenue, Lake Wales FL 33859. ((813) 676-3445.

NORTH OF ORLANDO

About 20 miles (32 km) northeast of Orlando on I-4 is the town of Sanford, where you have the choice of two excursions up the St. Johns River. **Captain Hoy's Riverboat Fleet** specializes in daytime narrated tours which point out the abundant wildlife of the river; the boats leave from Sanford Boat Works, Route 415, Sanford, ((407) 330-1612. Catamarans leave on evening cruises, which include, cocktails, dinner, and dancing, from **River Romance** at 433 North Palmetto Avenue, Sanford, ((407) 321-5091; tickets

start at $25. Just north out of Sanford on I-4 in Lake Monroe, you will come to the **Central Florida Zoological Park**, ((407) 323-4450, which houses over 400 exotic animals and has picnic areas set in the woods.

Fifty miles (80 km) northwest of Orlando on Route 441 is the town of Ocala, well known for its Victorian architecture but better known as the state's racehorse center and home to some of the nation's best thoroughbreds. Some of the horse farms in the hills surrounding Ocala will welcome visitors, including **Grosse Point Stud Farm** at 8998 West Fort King Street, ((904) 237-3348, and **Bonnie Heath Farm** at 5400 Southwest College Road, ((904) 237-2121. If you go to Ocala you can see a varied and interesting collection at the **Appleton Museum of Art**, 4333 East Silver Springs Boulevard, ((904) 236-5056, which includes Persian, Oriental, Peruvian, and Mexican artifacts.

To the east of Ocala is the **Ocala National Forest,** over 300,000 acres of unspoiled woodland, springs, rivers, and lakes, through which there is a scenic drive known as the Backwoods Trail. The recreational activities include canoeing, hiking, hunting, fishing, and tubing (a new craze among collegians, involving floating downstream on an inner tube). Maps of the forest, and information on campgrounds and picnic sites, and everything else, can be obtained from the USDA Forest Service, 227 North Bro nough Street, Suite 4061, Tallahassee FL 32301. ((904) 625-2520. The forest is home to the state's oldest attraction, **Silver Springs**, which dates from 1890 as a leisure park. The limestone artesian springs are the largest in the world, beautifully clear and teeming with fish life, as the glass-bottom tour boats will demonstrate. The springs are off I-75 on Route 40, east of Ocala, ((904) 236-2121, and are open from 9 am to 5:30 pm daily (extended in the summer); admission is $24.50 for adults and $16.50 for children.

For further information, contact the Ocala/Marion County Chamber of Commerce, P.O. Box 1210, Ocala FL 32678. ((904) 629-8051.

OPPOSITE: The Bok Tower at Lake Wales.

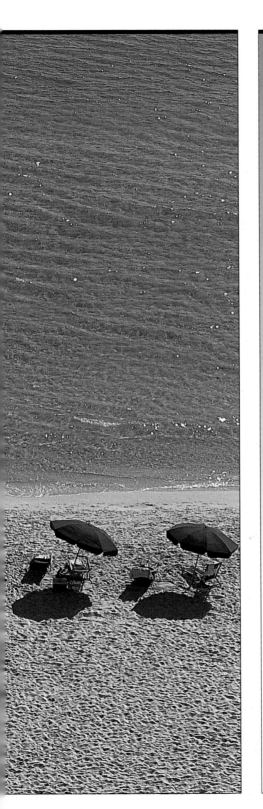

The
Panhandle

FIRST-TIME visitors to Florida's Panhandle are invariably surprised by the diversity of its attractions. There is the state's sophisticated capital city, Tallahassee, and there are all the small towns that have not yet Gone With The Wind; there are the rich resort spots such as Fort Walton Beach and Destin (on a stretch of coast east of Pensacola sometimes referred to as the "Redneck Riviera"), and the quaint old fishing villages on the marshy coastline between the mouths of the Suwannee and St. Marks rivers. There are crystalline streams flowing through pine and oak forests southwest of Tallahassee, and there are miles of deserted white sand beaches married to the azure Gulf waters west of Panama City. The Panhandle has all this to offer, plus inhabitants who are as welcoming and hospitable as any in Florida.

After the Civil War the east and west coasts of Florida were transformed by commercial enterprises and by tourism, but the Panhandle remained relatively underdeveloped, which could help to explain why the region has so successfully retained its distinctive characteristics. The only substantial commercial activity in the region after the Civil War was in the ports, which thrived on the business of sending out wood and forest products to the peninsula's developing east and west coast cities. But for the most part the Panhandle was and remained until the middle of this century, a region of sharecroppers and tenant farmers working a meager living from the land. As many of these people had come from Alabama and Georgia, they gave the Panhandle a Deep South character not found in other parts of Florida.

Many people only see the Panhandle from the inside of a car, as they hurry to the warmer climate and more loudly trumpeted attractions further south. But it would be well worth your while to get off the beaten Interstate tracks and take the time to explore this often overlooked but thoroughly charming region of the state.

TALLAHASSEE

Like the entire region, Tallahassee is an interesting blend: it is the capital city of Florida, it is the most important commercial city in the Panhandle, it is home to two universities, Florid State and Florida A & M, and it has an historic district dating from the early nineteenth century.

BACKGROUND

When Spain ceded Florida to the United States in 1821 the territory's two most-important cities were Pensacola and St. Augustine. In 1823, the legislature of the territory, recognizing the need for one capital, proposed that it be established midway between Pensacola and St. Augustine. Thereupon two delegates set out, one from each city; they met in the foothills of the Appalachians and named the site Tallahassee (an Indian word meaning "old town").

From the 1830s, Tallahassee was the distribution center for cotton grown in Florida and the Deep South, and its commercial prominence in the region was secured when the state's first railway was built from the town to the coast at St. Marks. During the Civil War the town was fiercely Confederate, and the defeat of Union troops at the nearby battle of Olustee ensured that Tallahassee remained the only town east of the Mississippi not to be taken by the Union. Since then the state's center of gravity has moved steadily southward towards Miami, but Tallahassee still remains the home of Florida's government.

GENERAL INFORMATION

The Tallahassee Area Convention and Visitors Bureau is at 200 West College Avenue, P.O. Box 1639, Tallahassee FL 32302. ((904) 681-9200.

Other useful telephone numbers (all in area code 904):

Tallahassee Regional Airport	574-7800
Capital Medical Society	877-9018

OPPOSITE: Between palm and flag: lining up the putt.

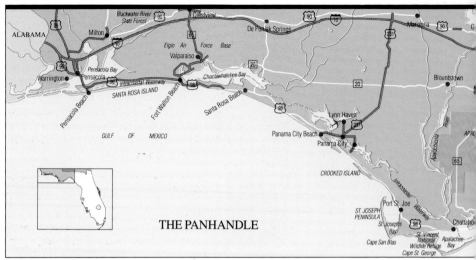

THE PANHANDLE

Sights

The modern **Florida Capitol** and the **Old Capitol** (which dates from 1845) stand next to each other at Apalachee and South Monroe Streets. You can tour the new Capitol on weekdays from 8:30 am to 4:30 pm; there is a wonderful view of the city from the Capitol's dome. The Old Capitol is now home to exhibits tracing Florida's political history and is open daily to visitors. ℂ (904) 488-6167. The oldest commercial building in the state is the **Old Union Bank** at South Carolina Street and Apalachee Parkway, ℂ (904) 487-3803, which houses a display of old state currency. For a look at the city's antebellum houses and buildings stroll around the historic district along Park and Calhoun streets.

Four blocks west of the Old Union Bank can be found the **Museum of Florida History** in the R.A. Gray building, 500 South Bronough Street, ℂ (904) 488-1484, home to a collection of historic artifacts and relics portraying the state's past; admission is free. The **Tallahassee Museum of History and Natural Science** is a 52-acre park which includes an 1880s farm with demonstrations of blacksmithing, sheep-shearing, and weaving. The opening hours are 9 am to 5 pm Tuesday to Saturday, and 12:30 pm to 4:30 pm on Sunday; admission is $5 for adults and $2.50 for children. The museum is at 3945 Museum Drive, ℂ (904) 575-8243.

The **University Gallery and Museum** on the Florida State University campus, in the Fine Arts Building at Copeland and Call streets, ℂ (904) 644-2098, features American, Japanese, and Dutch painting, and the **LeMoyne Art Foundation** at 125 North Gadsden, ℂ (904) 222-8800, has displays of local art, sculpture, and photography.

Just to the north of the city, off Route 27 at 1313 Crowder Road, ℂ (904) 562-0042, are the **Lake Jackson Indian Mound**s, where excavations have discovered evidence of an Indian ceremonial site dating from 1100 AD. There are also picnic areas and a nature trail on the site, which is open from 8 am to dusk every day.

If you would like an overview of the city and surrounding area, take a balloon ride from **Aeronauts & Balloons** at 1355 Market Street, Tallahassee, ℂ (904) 893-1282: If you take the ride you will see that the **Apalachicola National Forest** comes right up to the city's southwest limit. Tallahassee is a good base from which to explore the forest and enjoy its unparalleled fishing, hiking, canoeing, swimming, and picnic facilities — on which you can get more information from the city's Visitors Bureau, ℂ (904) 643-2282.

Other attractions in the Tallahassee area include the **Lafayette Vineyards and Winery** just east of the city at 6505 Mahan Drive, off I-10, ℂ (904) 878-9041, which offers a tour of the cellars and wine-tasting free of charge; there is also a shop selling wine, crystal

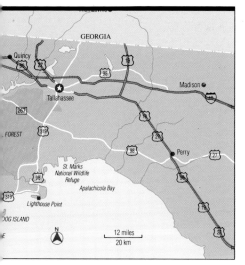

Nightlife

The Moon at 1105 Lafayette Street, ℂ (904) 222-6666, is a disco with live music some evenings, while **Studebaker's** at 1103 Apalachee Parkway, ℂ (904) 656-2191, is a disco serving up popular music from the Fifties and Sixties. If you want to join the student crowd, go along to the **Flamingo Café Lounge** at 525 West Tennessee Street, ℂ (904) 224-3534, where live bands play into the early hours on most nights.

WHERE TO STAY

Luxury

What sort of place is it that serves complimentary breakfast, with the morning newspaper, in rooms with four-poster beds and antique furniture, and has a free limousine service to any point within five miles of the hotel, and allows free local calls, and serves complimentary cocktails in the evening? It's the place where the Governor of Florida stays when he's in town, and it's called the **Governor's Inn** and can be found next to the Old Capitol at 209 South Adams Street, ℂ (904) 681-6855. The **Radisson Hotel** is in a good downtown position at 415 North Monroe Street, ℂ (904) 224-6000, and has very handsome rooms to go with its elegant lounge and restaurant. Also in the downtown area is the **Tallahassee Hilton** at 101 South Adams Street, ℂ (904) 224-5000, which has 246 attractive and spacious rooms, as well as 25 plush suites.

Mid-range

The **Leisure Inn** at 202 Apalachee Parkway, off Route 27, ℂ (904) 877-4437, is a reasonably priced hotel with a tasteful sunken parlor where you can enjoy your complimentary Continental breakfast. Every room has a view over the city and surrounding countryside at the **Holiday Inn University Center**, 316 West Tennessee Street, ℂ (904) 222-8000. The Camelot dining room has copious seafood and salad buffets each night, after which you can relax in the rooftop Viking Lounge. The Parkway Holiday Inn, a mile from the downtown area at 1302 Apalachee Parkway, off Route 27, ℂ (904) 877-3141, is surrounded by lawns and has a swimming pool.

glasses, and other gifts. Ten miles south of Tallahassee, at 1 Springs Drive, Wakulla Springs, off Route 267, is the **Edward Ball Wakulla Springs State Park**, ℂ (904) 222-7279, where you can swim in the clear springs, take a riverboat tour, or walk in the lovely grounds.

Sports

You can play golf at the Seminole Golf Course, 2550 Pottsdamer Road, ℂ (904) 644-2582. You can also play a nine-hole course at the Jake Gaither Community Center and Golf Course on Bragg Drive, ℂ (904) 222-7259. The center also has basketball and **tennis** courts. The city's recreation department, ℂ (904) 222-7259, can provide you further information on the city's tennis facilities. **Canoeists** should contact the Canoe Shop at 111-B Orange Avenue, ℂ (904) 576-5335, which rents canoes and will direct you to all of the local rivers.

Shopping

The **Market Square** at Thomasville and Timberlaine roads is the place for gift shops and stalls selling local produce. At 3251 Thomasville Road, ℂ (904) 368-4180, is the **Outdoors Shop**, which has everything for the hiker, camper, angler, and hunter, as well as a good selection of sportswear. The staff can also give you a lot of helpful information about the area. Overall, Thomasville Road probably has the best selection of shops in Tallahassee.

Inexpensive

With free in-room movies and a children's playground among its amenities, the **Days Inn South** at 3100 Apalachee Parkway, off Route 27, ((904) 877-6121, is very good value. The same can be said of the **Tallahassee Motor Hotel** at 1630 North Monroe Street, ((904) 224-6183, which has pleasant rooms and a swimming pool. Also on North Monroe Street at Nº 745 is the **Prince Murat Motel**, with 28 rooms which overlook an historic mansion and its grounds.

For those who would rather stay in the countryside around Tallahassee, the Convention and Visitors Bureau at 100 North Duval Street, P.O. Box 1639, ((904) 681-9200, will be happy to send you the *Tallahassee Area Fishing Camps and Lodges Guide*.

WHERE TO EAT

Expensive

Having tasted the food at **Andrew's Second Act,** 102 West Jefferson Street, ((904) 222-2759, one wonders what the first act was like, but do try the exceptional *tournedos St. Laurent*

— lean tenderloin coated with garlic, scallion, and parsley butter, and served with asparagus. The fanciest restaurant in town is **The Golden Pheasant** at 109 East College Avenue, ((904) 222-0241, which has a Continental atmosphere to go with its French haute cuisine. Hint: Have the pheasant baked in pastry.

Moderate

American cuisine is given a Greek accent at **Brothers Three**, 2696 North Monroe Street, ((904) 386-4193. Their Apalachicola oysters

are a house specialty. If you want to choose from a menu that has a good selection of both Chinese and Japanese dishes you should try **Ms. Lucy's Bamboo Gardens** at 2814 Apalachee Parkway, ((904) 878-3366, where you will be greeted by Lucy Ho, a charming and graceful Chinese lady. **Anthony's** at Betton Place, ((904) 224-1477, is an intimate restaurant serving traditional Italian food. If you would prefer a fondue you should head for the **Melting Pot** at 1832 North Monroe Street, ((904) 386-7440, which has delicious cheese, meat, seafood, and chocolate fondues.

Inexpensive

Restaurants with names like **Julie's Place** are normally friendly, and Julie's is no

Tallahassee: ABOVE: Governor's Inn and RIGHT State Capitol.

exception. Her place—which has very good nachos, pizzas, and quiches — is in the La-Quinta Motor Inn, 2905 North Monroe Street, ((904) 368-7181. Another popular and cheap eatery is the **Adams Street Café** at 228 South Adams Street, ((904) 222-3444. An especially down-home atmosphere can be found at 4175 Apalachee Parkway,((904) 877-4518, where the Violante couple run **Mom and Dad's**, a very nice little Italian restaurant.

HOW TO GET THERE

The Tallahassee Regional Airport is served by a number of national airlines. Tallahassee Taxis and Yellow Cabs both operate from the airport, where you can also find the offices of the major car rental firms.

Approaching Tallahassee by car from the east or west, drivers should take I–10. Routes 27 and 319 enter the city from the north, and you should take Route 319 if you are traveling from the south.

PANAMA CITY

The city lies on that stretch of coast often jokingly called the "Redneck Riviera", and is one of the Panhandle's most popular resorts, having a lively nightlife, an amusement park with arcades and rides overlooking one of the finest white-sand beaches anywhere, and good facilities for water sports. Quieter (even deserted) stretches of beach can be found to the east and west of Panama City, and two state parks — St. Andrews and Dead Lakes—are within striking distance of the city. In short, there are attractions to suit all tastes and age groups, which is why Panama City is a particular favorite with tourists traveling *en famille*.

GENERAL INFORMATION

The Panama City Beach Convention and Visitors Bureau is at P.O. Box 9473, Panama City Beach FL 32407. ((904) 234-6575. It can provide you with all the information you may need about the area.

Other useful telephone numbers (all in area code 904):

Bay Walk-In Clinic	234-8442
Beach Taxi	234-5202
Tallahassee Regional Airport	574-7800
The Panama City–Bay County International Airport	763-6751

WHAT TO SEE AND DO

Sights

The **Miracle Strip Amusement Park** at 12000 West Highway 98-A, Panama City Beach, ((904) 234-5810, the biggest on the city's Gulf-front road, has arcades, roller-coasters, carousels, and dozens of other rides. Admission is $16 for adults and $12 for children under 11. You can see performing porpoises and sea lions at **Gulf World**, 15421 West Highway 98-A, Panama City Beach, ((904) 234-5271, from 9 am to 7 pm daily in the summer; admission $8 for adults and $6 for children aged five to 12. If you would like to take a boat trip to the wonderfully scenic Shell Island off the coast of Panama City, you should go to **Captain Anderson's Marina** at 5550 North Lagoon Drive, Panama City Beach, ((904) 234-5940, whence excursions leave for the island at 9 am and 1 pm daily.

There are two interesting museums in the city: the **Museum of Man and the Sea** at 17314 Hutchinson Road,((904) 235-4101, has exhibits of early diving equipment, treasures from Spanish shipwrecks, and great moments in man's exploration of the ocean; the **Junior Museum of Bay County** has exhibits showing how Indians and early settlers lived and worked, and is located at 1731 Jenkins Avenue, ((904) 769-6128.

The **St. Andrews State Recreation Area** at 4415 Thomas Drive, ((904) 233-5140, southwest of the city at the end of Route 392, includes marshes, pinewoods, dunes, and beaches, as well as sites for camping. The **Dead Lakes State Recreation Area**, ((904) 639-2702, about 30 miles (48 km) east of Panama City on Route 22, near the village of Wewahitchka has some lovely nature trails and wonderful fishing.

Sports

Golf enthusiasts can take on the challenge of the par-70 Signal Hill Golf Course at 9615 Thomas Drive, Panama City Beach, ((904)

234-5051, or play the attractive course at the Creek Golf and Country Club, off Route 22 East, Panama City, ((904) 871-2623.

Golf and **tennis** players are catered for at the Holiday Golf and Tennis Club, 100 Fairway Boulevard, Panama City Beach, ((904) 234-1800. The city's recreation department, ((904) 763-6641, will give you information about the city's 19 public tennis courts.

Panama City Beach offers a variety of **water sports**: The Hydrospace Dive Shop at 3605 Thomas Drive, ((904) 234-9463, runs **diving** trips offshore in waters up to 98 ft (30 m) deep, and will also take you **snorkeling**. Trained divers from the Panama City Dive Center at 4823 Thomas Drive, ((904) 235-3390, can take you diving in some of the freshwater springs in the area. **Surfers** can rent a board from Lawrence Rentals at 15000 West Highway 98, ((904) 234-2432, and Jet Winds at 12705 West Highway 98-A, ((904) 235-0338, rents **jet skis** for $35 an hour, and sailboats for $25 an hour.

Shopping

For swimwear and everything else for the beach, try the variety of shops in **Field's Plaza** at 12700 West Highway 98-A, Panama City Beach, open from 9 am to 9 pm. The **Galleria** at 2303 Winona Drive, Panama City, is the place for gifts and specialty shops. For local crafts and souvenirs check out the **Olde Towne Mini Mall** at 441 Grace Avenue, Panama City.

Nightlife

There's a Caribbean flavor to the live music and the cocktails at **Pineapple Willie's**, 9900 Beach Boulevard, Panama City Beach, ((904) 235-0928, one of the liveliest night spots in town.

BELOW: Spring break at Panama City.

Spinnaker III is set among the dunes at 8813 Thomas Drive, Panama City Beach, ℂ (904) 234-7882; the music and dance goes on until 4 am, but it's open from 11 am to give you plenty of time to get warmed up.

At 5550 North Lagoon Drive, Panama City Beach, ℂ (904) 234-5940, you can board a boat and enjoy **Captain Anderson's Dinner Cruise**, on which the meal is followed by music and dancing. Alternatively, you could take the **Southern Elegance**, another cruise boat, which leaves from 5505 West Highway 98, Panama City Beach, ℂ (904) 785-3006; dinner, live music, and film shows are included in the price, and there is also a casino on board.

The place for live country music is the **Ocean Opry** at 8400 West Highway 98-A, ℂ (904) 234-5464, which is a large venue with more than a whiff of Nashville about it.

WHERE TO STAY

Luxury

The **Edgewater Beach Resort** is one of the best hotels in the Panhandle. The efficiency apartments have everything from marble sinks to washing machines, and overlook either the ocean or the beautifully landscaped grounds. The amenities include a swimming lagoon with waterfalls and a bar, nine tennis courts, a beachside clubhouse, and a nine-hole golf course. It is at 11212 West Highway 98-A, Panama City Beach, ℂ (904) 235-4977, toll-free (800) 874-8686. Matching the Edgewater for luxury is the **Bay Point Resort** at 100 Delwood Beach Road, Bay Point, Panama City Beach, ℂ (904) 234-3307, toll-free (800) 874-7105, which has a 200-room hotel and efficiency villas in its 1,000-acre grounds, which also include two golf courses, over 30 lakes and ponds, a forest, and restaurants and shops. The resort's own boat takes patrons across St. Andrews Bay to the superb beaches of Shell Island.

Mid-range

The **Sugar Sands Hotel** at 20709 West

The town of Seaside quietly, handsomely confronts the Gulf.

Highway 98-A, ℂ (904) 234-8802, is in a splendid situation right on the beach, and offers comfortable rooms and suites, with a cook-it-yourself barbecue next to the hotel's swimming pool. All the rooms face the ocean and have private balconies at the **Rendezvous Inn** at 17281 West Highway 98-A, Panama City Beach, ℂ (904) 234-8841. The **Flamingo Motel** at 15524 West Highway 98, Panama City Beach, ℂ (904) 234-2232, has a delightful courtyard where palmettos and tropical plants surround a swimming pool. The rooms are cozy, and some have kitchenettes. Small and intimate, **Cobb's Gulfview Inn** at 21722 West Highway 98-A, Sunnyside Beach, ℂ (904) 234-6051, has five charming rooms and serves a delicious full breakfast.

Inexpensive

There is a reasonable choice of cheaper places to stay in Panama City Beach, including the **Bikini Beach Motel** at 11001 West Highway 98, ((904) 234-3392, and at 8601 Surf Drive, ((904) 234-2201, there is the **Silver Sands Motel**. In Panama City you can expect good deals at **Howard's Motor Lodge,** 4911 West Highway 98, ((904) 763-4998, and **La Brisa Motor Inn** on East Highway 98 at Nº 5711, ((904) 871-2345.

WHERE TO EAT

Expensive

The beamed ceiling, stone walls, and fireplace make for a genuinely English ambience at the **Boar's Head**, 17290 West High-

way 98-A, Panama City Beach, ((904) 234-6628, where prime rib of beef with Yorkshire pudding adds an English accent to an excellent Continental menu which also has some very tasty Greek dishes. **Sylvia's** at 9850 South Thomas Drive, Panama City Beach, ((904) 234-0184, has a most attractive multilevel design and a resident pianist whose notes reach all levels. Try the lobster meat *en croute* in sherry and mushroom sauce.

Moderate

The food is Italian-American at **Caporelli's**, 8713 West Highway 98, Panama City Beach, ((904) 763-2245, as is the promenading violinist who adds a sweetly romantic touch. At the **Harbour House**, 3001-A West 10th

Street, Panama City, ((904) 785-9053, the luncheon buffet of salads, cold cuts, and vegetables is a big hit, as is every charcoal-broiled steak served in the evening.

Continental cuisine with a French bias is on the menu at the café-like **Greenhouse**, 443 Grace Avenue, Panama City, ((904) 763-2245, while **Claudio's** at 1013 Beck Avenue, Panama City, ((904) 769-8722, specializes in spicy Italian fare.

Inexpensive

There is a distinctly Louisianan flavor to the interior and to the menu of the **Cajun Inn** at 477 Beckrich Drive, Panama City Beach, ((904) 235-9987. Don't miss the Bayou Teche jambalaya with a side order of Cajun-spiced potatoes. Good Mexican food is available at Los Antojitos 4809 West Highway 98, Panama City Beach, ((904) 769-7081, which serves memorable Margaritas. Bargain crepes, quiches, and pastas are the stars at **The Cheese Barn**, 425 Grace Avenue, Panama City, ((904) 769-3892. For seafood go to the **Gulf Cafeteria**, 12628 West Highway 98, Panama City Beach, ((904) 234-6457.

HOW TO GET THERE

Several national airlines serve the Panama City–Bay County Regional Airport, notably Eastern and Piedmont. If you are arriving by car, Route 98 enters the city from the east and west, and Route 231 from the north.

PENSACOLA

Florida's westernmost city has a population of over a quarter of a million people, who live mainly on the hillsides which climb away from the downtown area next to the bay. The downtown area contains the historic district, whose heart is the Seville Quarter, where most of the museums, antebellum houses, and restaurants are to be found.

BACKGROUND

A Spanish explorer called Tristan de Luna established a colony at Pensacola in 1559. Two years later, however, particularly

ferocious tropical storms destroyed much of his fleet and the colonists were forced to abandon the settlement. The Spanish did not return to Pensacola until the 1690s, when they formed a military garrison at the bay. They co-existed peacefully with the French — their main rivals in the region — but were forced to abandon Pensacola again in 1821 due to American military strength rather than the weather. There is still a military connection in the city, however, as the Pensacola Naval Air Station became the U.S. Navy's first flight training center in 1914.

GENERAL INFORMATION

The **Pensacola Area Chamber of Commerce Visitor Information Center** is at 1401 East Gregory Street, Pensacola FL 32501. ((904) 434-1234.

Other useful telephone numbers (all in area code 904):

Pensacola Regional Airport	435-1746
Blue and White Cab	438-1497
Escambia County Health Department	438-8571

ABOVE: A balcony in the Seville Quarter of Pensacola.

WHAT TO SEE AND DO

Sights

In the downtown historic district, around Seville Square, you will learn all about the city's and the region's past — Indian, European, and American — at the **Pensacola Historical Museum** in the Old Christ Church at 405 South Adams Street, ((904) 433-1559, and at the **West Florida Museum of History**, 200 East Zaragoza Street, ((904) 444-8905. Where Zaragoza Street meets

Tarragona Street you will find the **Historic Pensacola Village**, full of old restored houses and stores.

The **Zoo and Botanical Gardens**, off Route 98, 10 miles (16 km) east of Pensacola at 5801 Gulf Breeze Parkway, Gulf Breeze, ((904) 9832-2229, is home to more than 500 animals, including Colossus, a lowland gorilla who at 600 lb (1,320 kg) is believed to be the largest in captivity in the world. Elephant rides and a children's petting zoo are other features. Admission is $6.50 for adults and $3.75 for children aged three to 11; the zoo is open daily from 9 am to 5 pm in the summer.

Aviation enthusiasts will not want to miss the **National Museum of Naval Aviation**, which has over 50 aircraft on display,

including the NC–4 (the first to cross the Atlantic in 1919), jet fighters, and the Skylab command module. Take Route 98 west out of town to Navy Boulevard and enter the Naval Air Station, ((904) 452-3604. The famed air-display team, the Blue Angels, frequently perform at the Air Station.

Southwest of Pensacola, you will find the **Big Lagoon State Recreation Area** at 12301 Gulf Beach Highway, ((904) 492-1595, where you can swim, boat, fish, camp, and hike. The **Gulf Island National Seashore** is over the water, off Route 399, ((904) 934-2604; the Spanish fort **San Carlos de Barrancas**, open to the public, is on the seashore. To the north-east of Pensacola is the **Blackwater River State Park**, Route 1 off Route 90 at Holt, ((904) 623-2363, which has excellent canoeing.

Sports

You can play **golf** at the Santa Rosa Shores Country Club on Pensacola Beach, ((904) 456-2761, the Carriage Hills Golf Course at 2355 West Michigan Avenue, Pensacola, ((904) 944-5497, or the Green Meadow Par–3 at 2500 West Michigan Avenue, Pensacola, ((904) 944-5483.

There are 18 **tennis** courts at the Scott Tennis Center, Cordova Park, ((904) 432-2939, and the Pensacola Racquet Club at 3450 Wimbledon Drive, ((904) 434-2434, has 10 courts.

Scuba diving and snorkeling off the coast of Pensacola can be arranged through the Southern Breeze Dive Shop at 10121 Sinton Drive, Pensacola, ((904) 492-3492, or Aquatic Orientations at 31 Hoffman Drive, Gulf Breeze, ((904) 9832-1944. **Surf and sail boards** can be hired from the Key Sailing Center at 289 Pensacola Beach Road, ((904) 932-5520, and **sailing** boats can be hired from Break Away in Harbor Village, ((904) 438-1711.

Shopping

In **Seville Square** and the streets off it there are numerous shops selling craft items and artwork, antiques, jewelry, and gifts; there are similar items on offer at the charming **Quayside Thieves Market**, 712 South Palafox Street, Pensacola. For designer

ABOVE: Vintage wheels enter a vintage part of town.
OVERLEAF: Bass fishing on the Suwannee River.

boutiques, try the **Harbourtown Shopping Village**, a modern mall at 913 Gulf Breeze Parkway, Gulf Breeze.

Nightlife

Live bands play every night at the popular **Flounder's Ale House**, 800 Quietwater Beach, Pensacola, ((904) 932-2003. Lively bars include the **Seville Inn** at 223 East Garden Street, ((904) 433-8331, the **Red Garter Saloon** on South Palafox Street in Pensacola, ((904) 433-9229, and, liveliest of all, **McQuire's Irish Pub** at 600 East Gregory Street,

French, Spanish, or English furnishings and decor. The hotel's restaurant also has a splendid Continental menu. On Pensacola Beach the best hotel is **The Dunes** at 333 Fort Pickens Road, ((904) 932-3526, where children can stay free. Most of the rooms here overlook the Gulf, and there are indoor and outdoor swimming pools.

Mid-range

The accommodation at the **Residence Inn**, 7230 Plantation Road, Pensacola, ((904) 479-1000, toll-free (800) 331-3131, surrounds

Pensacola, ((904) 433-6789, which has live Irish music and good food to go with the beer.

WHERE TO STAY

Luxury

Pensacola's old railway station concourse has been restored and converted into the lobby of the **Pensacola Hilton** at 200 East Gregory Street, Pensacola, ((904) 433-3336. The hotel has penthouse suites with jacuzzis and bars, and rooms on the upper floors have terrific views over the city. There is an international flavor to the **New World Inn** at 600 South Palafox Street, Pensacola, ((904) 432-4111, toll-free (800) 258-1103, where the 16 tasteful rooms have either American,

a courtyard which has basketball and tennis courts, a jacuzzi and a swimming pool. The hotel serves a complimentary Continental breakfast, and has a cocktail party for guests at weekends. If you book in advance, the **Lenox Inn** will send a car to pick you up if you arrive at the airport. The hotel is near the historic district downtown at 710 North Palafox Street, Pensacola, ((904) 238-4922, toll-free (800) 874-0710. A delightful Colonial-style hotel surrounded by pines, the **Homestead Inn** is at 7830 Pine Forest Road, Pensacola, ((904) 944-4816, where Neil and Jeanne Liechty provide a warm welcome and delicious breakfasts. There are cottages and rooms with kitchenettes to choose from at the **Sandpiper Inn**, which is next to the ocean on Pensacola Beach at 23 Via de Luna, ((904) 932-2516.

Inexpensive

There are 120 small but comfortable rooms at **Motel 6**, 5829 Pensacola Boulevard, Pensacola, ((904) 477-7522, and you will receive a similarly good deal at **Days Inn**, 6911 Pensacola Boulevard, ((904) 477-9000. The **Gulf Aire Motel** has rooms with kitchens, and is close to the beach at 21 Via de Luna, Pensacola Beach, ((904) 932-2319, and **Two Tom's Bed and Breakfast** has six pleasant rooms looking out on some lovely scenery close to Navarre Beach, east on Route 98 at Navarre, ((904) 939-2382.

WHERE TO EAT

Expensive

There is nowhere in town that you will find better French food than at **Jamie's**, 424 East Zaragoza Street, Pensacola, ((904) 434-2911 in a cozy Victorian-style cottage. The elegant **Jubilee** restaurant at 400 Quietwater Beach Road, ((904) 934-3108, has a large skylight to accentuate the decor and a menu which includes the most delicious sweetbreads and sautéed chicken breasts with crayfish. The **Driftwood** at 27 West Garden Street, ((904) 433-4559, successfully mixes an American atmosphere with a Continental cuisine.

Moderate

There is much to recommend at the **Angus Steak Ranch**, 1101 Scenic Highway, Pensacola, ((904) 432-0539, where chef Spero Athanasios has not limited himself to steaks; try his snapper casserole with oysters, shrimps, and scallops, accompanied by a Greek salad. The Scotto family will make you feel welcome at **Scotto's Ristorante Italiano**, 300 South Alcaniz Street, Pensacola, ((904) 434-1932. The home-made desserts are the highlights here. The Oysters Rockefeller steal the show at the **Dainty Del**, 286 North Palafox Street, ((904) 438-1241, a friendly seafood restaurant very popular with the local cognoscenti. For Creole cuisine, try **Beignet's** at 312 East Government Street, ((904) 434-7225, which also has live jazz on Sundays.

Inexpensive

Arkie "Ma" Hopkins established **Hopkins' Boarding House** in 1948, and her son Ed continues to serve your basic fried chicken, beef stew, and black-eyed peas at 900 North Spring Street, Pensacola, ((904) 438-3979. The freshest and, for the quality, the cheapest seafood in Pensacola can be found at **Captain Joe Patti's**, 610 South C Street, ((904) 434-3193. Simple but satisfying fare is available at **E.J.'s Food Company**, 232 East Main Street, ((904) 432-5886, while filling but tasty breakfasts and lunches are availa-

ble at the **Coffee Cup**, 520 East Cervantes, ((904) 432-7060.

HOW TO GET THERE

The Pensacola Regional Airport is served by several national airlines, and taxis and car rental firms operate from the airport.

If you are traveling by car, the principal east-west route into and out of Pensacola is I–10. From Panama City you would take Route 98, and from the north Route 29.

OPPOSITE AND ABOVE: the Panhandle coastline at Destin shows off its many shades of blue.

The
Gulf Coast

FLORIDA'S Gulf Coast, which extends almost 200 miles from Cedar Key in the north down to Marco Island in the south, is punctuated by offshore sandbars and numerous inlets, islands, lagoons, bayous, and estuaries. Ideal conditions, in other words, for the coast's first commercial enterprise: piracy. Pirates such as Black Caesar, José Gaspar and others operated along this coast during the eighteenth century, using their knowledge of the labyrinthine coastline to spring attacks and avoid capture. Their activities played a large part in discouraging European settlement of the Gulf Coast; in any case, the Spanish, French, and English were more concerned with consolidating themselves on Florida's east coast and protecting its important sea routes.

The pirates and the regions' indigenous Timucan, Calusas, and Seminole Indian tribes remained relatively undisturbed until 1824, when U.S. Army bases were established at Tampa and Fort Myers for the purpose of subduing the Seminoles. The bases attracted civilian settlers, two towns were born, and then more settlements began to appear all along the coast once the army had defeated the Seminoles and gained complete control of the region. Many fishing villages emerged, some of which survive to this day between Naples and Marco Island, where the inhabitants live much as their forebears did.

From the 1880s onward the Gulf Coast's story is similar to that of the east coast. Developers suddenly realized that what Flagler was doing from Jacksonville to Miami could certainly be done from Tampa down to Naples — *i.e.*, entice rich northerners with prospects of good transportation, luxury hotels, and year-round sunshine. The last condition being guaranteed, Henry Plant got to work on the first two, bringing a railway to Tampa by 1884 and completing the Tampa Bay Hotel by 1891 and the Bellview Hotel in Clearwater by the end of the century. In Sarasota, further south, John Ringling, founder of the Ringling Brothers, Barnum and Bailey Circus, built hotels and an art museum (sometimes using circus elephants on the job), as well as his own winter home, which was modeled on the Doges Palace in Venice.

The tourists took the bait and the Gulf Coast has flourished ever since, to the extent that between Venice and Tampa towns are now gradually merging as their suburbs sprawl and overlap. To the south, the beaches of the Charlotte Harbor area and the coastline and offshore islands below Naples are largely protected areas or wildlife reserves. In these areas the laws on development are very strict, but the rest of the Gulf Coast continues to be developed, with Fort Myers being one of the fastest growing cities in the country.

TAMPA

Tampa is Florida's third largest city with a population of 300,000, including the Hispanics of Ybor City, a western district, and a large number of Greeks who first arrived at the turn of the century to dive for sponges off the coast at Tarpon City, which became the largest sponge center in the world during the 1930s. Tampa is also the seventh largest port in the country, and the most important commercial and industrial city in western Florida. Unfortunately, because of the volume of traffic in and out of the port (ships carrying 51 million tons of cargo annually), and the industrial waste, Tampa Bay is seriously polluted and unfit for swimming. On the coast to the north of the city and around St. Petersburg there are beaches washed by clear seas.

BACKGROUND

In its early days in the first half of the nineteenth century, Tampa (an Indian word meaning "sticks of fire") was a small community of fishermen and farmers clustered around Fort Brooke. The city's growth accelerated dramatically in 1885 when Vincente Martínez Ybor, due to labor problems in Key West and the prospect of lower taxes in Tampa, moved his cigar factory to the city. This brought with it a wave of immigrant workers who settled in the area now known as Ybor City, whose clubs, restaurants, shops, and culture remain overwhelmingly Cuban-Hispanic.

East meets West in downtown Tampa.

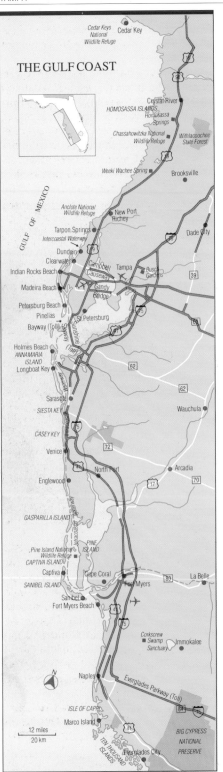

THE GULF COAST

The arrival in 1898 of one man and his army of 30,000 gave Tampa its next big boost —both to the city's economy and to its status as one of Florida's most important cities. Theodore Roosevelt set up his headquarters in the Tampa Bay Hotel, and his force of "Rough Riders" trained in its grounds before going on to Cuba to fight in the Spanish-American War. The hotel now houses the University of Tampa administration offices and a museum.

GENERAL INFORMATION

The Tampa/Hillsborough Convention and Visitors Association is at 111 Madison Street, Suite 1010, Tampa FL 33602. ((813) 223-1111, and the Greater Tampa Chamber of Commerce is at 801 East Kennedy Boulevard, Tampa Fl 33602. ((813) 228-7777. For information on the area's hotels call (813) 596-9944 to get through to the Tampa/St. Petersburg Reservations Center.

Two newspapers, the *Tampa Tribune* and the *Tampa Times*, and a magazine, *Tampa Bay*, are full of information on local attractions and upcoming events.

Other useful telephone numbers (all in area code 813):

Tampa International Airport	870-8700
Yellow Cabs	253-0121
Emergency clinic	877-8450

WHAT TO SEE AND DO

Sights

Busch Gardens — The Dark Continent, home to over 3,000 predominantly African animals, birds, and reptiles, is one of the most highly rated zoos in the world, and the second most popular tourist attraction in the state after Disney World. The park has different areas, each with a particular theme. For example, the *Serengeti Plain* has free-roaming zebras, giraffes, rhinos, lions, and cheetahs, among other "plains" animals, all of which you can view from a monorail; the *African Queen* is a jungle cruise on which you can see all kinds of wildlife in the water and on the riverbanks; and *Eagle Canyon*, a vast structure, allows you a rare opportunity to watch American bald eagles and the magnificent golden eagles. There is also an amusement area with rides, stalls, shops, and restaurants. The park is at 3000 Busch Boulevard, ((813) 987-5082, and is open from 9:30 am to 6 pm daily, admission $29.95, children under two free.

Near Busch Gardens at 4545 Bougain-villea Avenue, ((813) 987-5000, is **Adventure Island**, a water theme park for all the family. The fun includes wave-pools, beaches, water slides, inner-tube runs, swimming pools, stalls, and shops. In the peak holiday season between May 26 and August 19 the park is open from 9 am to 8 pm daily. For an insight into the old way of life of the state's most famous Indian tribe visit the **Seminole Culture Center** at 5221 North Orient Road, ((813) 623-3549, which has a reconstruction of a Seminole village, a museum with various artifacts, and shops selling Seminole crafts. There is also a poisonous snake show and the ever-popular alligator wrestling.

The city is home to a couple of interesting collections, one of contemporary American art and one of exhibits from ancient Rome, Greece, and Egypt, at the **Tampa Museum of Art**, 601 Doyle Carlton Drive, ((813) 223-8130. Exhibits which chart the history of the city and portray its culture are on display at the **Henry Plant Museum**, which is in the old Tampa Bay H tel at 401 West Kennedy Boulevard, ((813) 254-1891. For lots of fresh air and views of Davis Island in Tampa Bay, stroll along the longest continuous sidewalk in the world — six and a half miles (10.5 km) alongside Bayshore Boulevard. At one point you won't be able to miss the 300-ton pirate ship **José Gasparilla**, named after a legendary buccaneer of the Gulf Coast, which is docked on the bayshore and fully rigged out as it would have looked in the eighteenth century. The ship is open to the public.

The heart of Ybor City, Tampa's old Cuban and Hispanic quarter, is **Ybor Square** at Eighth Avenue and 13th Street, where there is a selection of arts and crafts shops, boutiques, and some very good restaurants. At **Tampa Rico Cigars** in the square you can watch cigars being rolled by hand, and then you can try them. The **Ybor City State Museum** will show you how this district originated and how it has changed

over the years; you will also find the Ybor City Visitors Center, ((813) 248-3712, in the museum, which is at 1818 East Ninth Avenue.

The best beaches near Tampa are **Clearwater Beach**, an island 15 miles (24 km) west of Clearwater across the Memorial Causeway; **Dunedin Beach**, north of Clearwater, near the charming neo-Scottish village of Dunedin (from which you can take ferries to the beautiful Caladesi or Honeymoon islands); and **Sand Key Beaches**, just south of Clearwater off Gulf Boulevard.

Sports

Baseball fans will be interested to know that three major-league teams converge on the Tampa area for spring training and to play exhibition games during February and March: the Philadelphia Phillies can be seen at the Jack Russell Stadium in Clearwater, the Toronto Blue Jays at Grant Field in Dunedin, and the Cincinnati Reds in Tampa itself at Al Lopez Field. Call (904) 488-0990 for information on all the teams' training schedules and games.

You can see NFL **football** from August to December at Tampa Stadium, 4201 North Dale Mabry Highway, ((813) 461-2700,

ABOVE: Boats stacked in Dunedin.

which is the home of the Tampa Bay Buccaneers. It is also where the Tampa Bay Rowdies **soccer** team plays from April to August.

Two municipal **golf** courses which offer lessons and a lounge/snack bar among their facilities are Rocky Point at 4151 Dana Shores Road, ((813) 884-5141, and Rogers Park at 7910 North 30th Street, ((813) 234-1911. There are also several private clubs around the city which welcome non-members. There are numerous **tennis** courts in Tampa, including 11 courts at Riverfront Park, 900 North Boulevard, ((813) 253-6038, and good facilities at the City of Tampa Courts, 15 Columbia Drive, ((813) 253-3782. For details on all golf courses and tennis courts, call the city's recreation department, ((813) 238-6451.

Shopping

The city has several large shopping malls, but you can find the best range of shops — including three major department stores — at the **Tampa Bay Center** at Himes and Buffalo avenues near the football stadium. Luxury shops and exclusive boutiques jostle for space at the **Harbour Island Market**, 601 South Harbour Island Boulevard. You can rummage through antiques in over 20 shops in the **Interbay Antique Row District** along MacDill and El Prado avenues, and you are bound to find something authentically Cuban to take home with you in the gift shops of **Ybor Square** at Eighth Avenue and 13th Street.

Nightlife

There is a good choice of live music in Tampa, including **MacDinton's Tavern** at 405 South Howard Avenue, ((813) 254-1661, which features rhythm and blues and rock bands; **Parker's Lighthouse**, which offers live rock and jazz in the Harbour Island Market mentioned above, ((813) 229-3474; and **Dallas Bull** at 8222 Route 301, ((813) 985-6877, which specializes in country and western music. Another popular live venue which serves up jazz, reggae, blues, and new wave music is the **Skipper's Smokehouse** at 910 Skipper Road, ((813) 971-0666.

A windsurfer's sail echoes the geometric shape of the Sunshine Skyway bridge, over Tampa Bay.

Stingers at 11921 North Dale Mabry Highway, ((813) 968-1515, is one of the city's liveliest night clubs, where women can get free drinks between 8 pm and 11 pm from Thursday to Sunday. Another popular night spot is **Killians Backbeat Lounge**, 4235 West Waters, ((813) 884-8965, which features live bands from Wednesday to Sunday, and a disco the rest of the week. It also has large-screen television during the football season.

WHERE TO STAY

Luxury
One of the few Tampa hotels to have its own beach is the **Bay Harbour Inn,** toll-free (800) 282-0613, at 7700 Courtney Campbell Causeway, ((813) 885-2541, toll-free (800) 282-0613, on the eastern shore of Tampa Bay, which most of the rooms' balconies overlook. Free sailing and windsurfing lessons are among the amenities. Another first-class place to stay around Tampa Bay is the **Harbour Island Hotel** at 725 South Harbour Island Boulevard, ((813) 229-5000, nicely designed and furnished, with an attentive and friendly staff. Fifteen miles (24 km) north of Tampa, off Route 54 (exit 58) at 100 Saddlebrook Way, Wesley Chapel, ((813) 973-1111, is the award-winning **Saddlebrook Golf and Tennis Resort**, which is regularly ranked among the top 50 resorts in the world. The extensive sports facilities in the scenic wooded grounds include a golf course designed by Arnold Palmer, 17 tennis courts, and an Olympic-size swimming pool.

Downtown Tampa offers the ultra-modern **Lincoln Hotel** at 4860 West Kennedy Boulevard, ((813) 873-4400, which has a highly-regarded restaurant, J. Fitzgerald's. Another sleek downtown hotel is the **Hyatt Regency** at 2 Tampa City Center, ((813) 225-1234, toll-free (800) 228-9000, where there are suites with jacuzzis and kitchenettes, and complimentary Continental breakfasts served in the stylish Regency Club.

Mid-range
The **Holiday Inn Busch Gardens** at 2701 East Fowler Avenue, ((813) 971-4710, is especially welcoming to families and has a

swimming pool, sauna, health club, in-room movies, and a free shuttle service to Busch Gardens. Also near the African theme park and zoo is the **Safari Resort Inn** at 4139 East Busch Boulevard, ((813) 988-9191, where the decor and furnishings are determinedly exotic, with lush color schemes and plenty of tropical plants and bamboo chairs.

You can take a free shuttle to local shopping malls and golf courses from the **Days Inn** at 7627 Courtney Campbell Causeway, on Rocky Point Island, ((813) 884-2000, which has tennis courts and a swimming pool, and a lounge featuring evening discos. In the heart of the downtown area, on the riverfront, is the **Ashley Plaza Hotel** at 111 West Fortune Street, ((813) 223-1351, whose modern and attractive rooms are very reasonably priced, considering the enviable position of the hotel.

Inexpensive
The **Expressway Inn** at 3696 Gandy Boulevard, ((813) 837-1971, has simple but well-furnished rooms and a swimming pool. The same facilities can be found at the **Tahitian Inn**, 601 South Dale Mabry Highway, ((813) 877-6721. Conveniently placed for Busch Gardens, at bargain prices, is the **Garden View Motel** at 2500 East Busch Boulevard, ((813) 933-3958.

WHERE TO EAT

Expensive
The Lincoln Hotel at 4860 West Kennedy Boulevard, ((813) 873-4400, is home to one of Tampa's finest restaurants, **J. Fitzgerald's**, which serves exquisitely-prepared Continental dishes. At the **Monte Carlo**, 3940 West Cypress Street, ((813) 879-6245, the chef, Romeo Berranini, specializes in seafood, and particularly in new ways to serve lobster. At **Bern's Steak House**, 1208 South Howard Avenue, ((813) 251-2421, there are 38 different cuts of beef to choose from and nearly 7,000 different wines. The **Lauro Ristorante** at 4010 West Waters Avenue, ((813) 884-4366, is regarded as one of the best Italian restaurants in west Florida, and the pick of the Hispanic restaurants in Ybor City is the **Columbia** at 21st Street and Broadway, ((813) 248-4961, which features

on its menu traditional Spanish dishes such as paella, pork salteado, and delicious bean soups — all served in a romantic setting with tableside serenades by Spanish troubadours.

Moderate
One of Florida's best-liked seafood restaurants, **The Colonnade**, can be found at 3401 South Bayshore Boulevard, ((813) 839-7558, overlooking Tampa Bay. At **Selena's**, 1623 Snow Avenue, ((813) 251-2116, you can choose from Creole or Sicilian food, and from

4115 South MacDill Avenue, ((813) 832-4115, while **Coyotes**, another friendly eatery, specializes in ribs at 4426 Gandy Boulevard, ((813) 831-9759. If you want a jolly bohemian atmosphere in which to enjoy a masterpiece like *capelli di l'Angelo* — smoked salmon and caviar, tossed with spinach and pasta in a vodka and cream sauce — at unbelievable poor-student prices, go to the **Bella Trattoria** at 1413 South Howard Avenue, ((813) 254-3355. In Ybor City there are many cheap Cuban restaurants; I like **La Tropicana** at 1822 East Seventh Avenue.

some subtle combinations of the two. The **Café Pepe** is a very popular Spanish/Cuban restaurant at 2006 West Kennedy Boulevard, ((813) 253-6501, serving spicy food in a cosmopolitan atmosphere. For expertly prepared sushi, sashimi, and teriyaki in a beautifully simple restaurant, try the **Kaoribana** at 13180 North Dale Mabry Highway, ((813) 968-3801; and for equally masterful Thai cuisine, such as curried crab meat and cheese in wonton pockets, go the nearby **Jasmine Thai** at 13248 North Dale Mabry Highway, ((813) 968-1501.

Inexpensive
Attractively priced steaks, seafood, and hamburgers are on offer at **Club Key West**,

HOW TO GET THERE

Tampa International Airport is served by a large number of national and international airlines, and there are half a dozen car rental companies with offices at the airport.

Motorists approaching Tampa from the Panhandle should take Route 19. From the northeast or the south you want I–75; from the east take either I–4 (from Orlando) or Route 60 (from Lake Wales).

Tall masts and skyscrapers jut into the evening sky at Tampa harbor.

ST. PETERSBURG

For many years the popular image of St. Petersburg was of a sleepy retirement town for the elderly who began to arrive in large numbers after the American Medical Association declared the area's environment and sea air to be good for the constitution. In recent years, however, St. Petersburg Beach and other beaches to the north have been developed, giving the area a younger, springtlier image. Tourists — not just retir-

ees — now come to the city in ever greater numbers, lured by the wonderful beaches and pristine waters of the "Suncoast" between St. Petersburg and Clearwater. The city itself has a developing downtown area and some delightful parks and gardens.

GENERAL INFORMATION

The St. Petersburg Chamber of Commerce is at 100 Second Avenue North, Suite 150, St. Petersburg FL 33701, ((813) 821-4069. St. Petersburg/Clearwater Convention and Visitors Bureau is at 1 Stadium Drive, Suite A, St. Petersburg FL 33705, ((813) 582-7892. For information about the beaches and resorts north of St. Petersburg, contact the Pinel-

las County Tourist Development Council at Newport Square, 4625 East Bay Drive, Suite 109, Clearwater FL 34624. ((813) 530-6132.

WHAT TO SEE AND DO

Sights

The city's cultural renaissance is happening down on the cosmopolitan bayfront, where in the **Salvador Dali Museum** at 1000 Third Street South, ((813) 823-3767, you can see the largest collection in the world of the Spanish surrealist's works, including oils, watercolors, drawings, and graphics. Admission is $5 for adults and $3 for students; the museum is open from 10 am to 5 pm Tuesday to Saturday, from noon to 5 pm on Sunday. Many excellent paintings by the French Impressionists are on exhibit at the **Museum of Fine Arts** at 225 Beach Drive, ((813) 896-2667, alongside Oriental and American art, and photographic exhibits. The opening hours are the same as those at the Dali museum, and admission is free.

One of the strangest sights on the bayfront is **The Pier**, which has a five-storey inverted pyramid structure at the end of it, containing Continental stores, restaurants, and a viewing platform at the top affording great views over the bay, which The Pier juts into from 800 Second Avenue, ((813) 821-6164. Among the most beautiful on the Gulf Coast, the **Sunken Gardens** is a well-ordered tropical jungle with over 50,000 varieties of plants, flowers, and trees, and an exotic bird aviary. The gardens are downtown at 1825 Fourth Street North, ((813) 896-3187, and are open from 9 am to 5:30 pm daily. Admission is $11 for adults and $5 for children. If you would like to go on a day cruise of the bay, with entertainment and food included, go to the Port of St. Petersburg at First Street and Eighth Avenue and board the **SeaEscape**, ((813) 432-0900.

Fort DeSoto Park at 34th Street on Mullet Key is in the mouth of the bay. You can explore the fort, which was built during the Spanish-American War, or simply relax on the island's beaches. If you head north from Mullet Key on Route 679 and then join Gulf Boulevard you will reach St. Petersburg Beach. Gulf Boulevard continues north along an island chain which includes Madeira

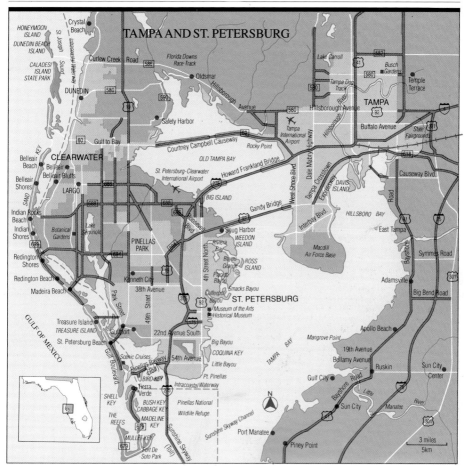

TAMPA AND ST. PETERSBURG

Beach, Indian Rocks Beach, Belleair Beach, and Clearwater Beach, which with St. Petersburg Beach comprise the "Suncoast".

Sports

There are 31 **golf** courses in the St. Petersburg area (Pinellas County), including Mangrove Bay three miles (five kilometers) north of the city at 875 62nd Avenue, ((813) 893-7797, which is one of the best known in the state. Tarpon Springs Golf Club at 1310 Pinellas Avenue South, ((813) 937-6906, and Pasadena Golf Club at 6100 Gulfport Boulevard, St. Petersburg, ((813) 345-9329, are two of 15 public courses.

Tennis players should head for the St. Petersburg Tennis Club at 650 18th Avenue South, ((813) 894-4378, which has 15 courts, or call the city's recreation department, ((813) 893-7441, for information on other courts.

Windsurfers and **surfers** can receive instruction and rent a board from Windsurfing Florida Suncoast Inc. at 6200 Gulf Boulevard, St. Petersburg Beach, ((813) 360-3783. **Sailboats** are for rent at Gulfcoast Sailboat Charters, 9600 West Gulf Boulevard, Treasure Island, ((813) 367-4444. **Divers** should contact the Madeira Dive Shop at 13613 Gulf Boulevard, ((813) 392-8978, for information about diving trips, instruction, and renting of equipment.

Shopping

The Pier (already mentioned) at 800 Second Avenue contains exclusive boutiques and expensive gift shops. On Madeira Beach at 12925 East Gulf Boulevard is the

OPPOSITE: Greek girl in Tarpon Springs.

Johns Pass Village and Boardwalk, which is home to gift shops and sportswear outlets. For the best arts and crafts shops in town head for the **St. Petersburg Arts and Crafts Emporium**, at 333 First Street Northeast. Further north you can find shops selling Greek products in the old fishing village of Tarpon Springs, and Scottish tartan in Dunedin.

Nightlife

The two joints that do the most jumpin' in the downtown area — which is rather musically re-live the Fifties, and for a good laugh the **Coconuts Comedy Club at Barnacle Bill's** in Howard Johnson's, 6110 Gulf Boulevard, St. Petersburg Beach, ((813) 360-4575.

WHERE TO STAY

Luxury

The Aga Khan has been a guest at the downtown **Presidential Inn**, 100 Second Avenue South, ((813) 823-7552, which was modeled on the famed Governors Inn in

supine in the evening — are the **Bayfront Center** at 400 First Street South, ((813) 893-3367, which features live rock and country bands, and the **Alessi Café at the Pier**, 800 Second Avenue, ((813) 804-4659, where you can hear live jazz on weeknights and live rock at weekends.

Most of the action, however, is on the islands, especially at **The Beach Place**, 2405 Gulf Boulevard, Indian Rocks Beach, ((813) 596-5633, and **Cadillac Jack's** at 145 107th Avenue, Treasure Island, ((813) 360-2099. Also recommended are **Don's Beach Bar** at the Bilmar Hotel, 10650 Gulf Boulevard, St. Petersburg Beach, ((813) 360-5531, **Studebaker's** at 2516 Gulf Boulevard, Clearwater, ((813) 799-4147, where you can

Tallahassee. The rooms are indeed fit for a president, and all of them overlook Tampa Bay. A lounge/bar serves complimentary breakfast and, in the evening, complimentary cocktails. Another lovely downtown hotel, **The Heritage**, can be found at 234 Third Avenue North, ((813) 822-4814, where mahogany bars, oak floors, and antique furnishings lend a turn-of-the-century ambience; the indoor swimming pool and the jacuzzis add late-in-the-century appeal.

There are several luxury hotels in St. Petersburg Beach, including the exotic **Tradewinds** at 5500 Gulf Boulevard, ((813) 367-6461, toll-free (800) 282-5553, where gondolas or paddleboats, operating on an internal canal system, deliver guests to their rooms. The recreational facilities are outstanding and feature a water sports center on the hotel's own beach, which has equipment for windsurfing, jet-skiing, water biking, and parasailing. Similar amenities are available at the pink Mediterranean-style **Don CeSar Beach Resort**, 3400 Gulf Boulevard, ((813) 360-1881, toll-free (800) 237-8789, home of the celebrated King Charles restaurant, and a hotel long frequented by celebrities ranging from Scott Fitzgerald to Babe Ruth.

beach. There are 43 rooms and apartments overlooking the sea at the **Cadillac Motel** 3828 Gulf Boulevard, ((813) 360-1748, and the **Dolphin Beach Resort** boasts 174 spacious rooms and, like the Cadillac Motel, its very own swath of white sandy beach at 4900 Gulf Boulevard, ((813) 360-7011.

Inexpensive
For more economical rates in St. Petersburg you should check out the **Avalon Hotel** at 443 North Fourth Avenue, ((813) 822-4783, or the **Beach Park Motor Inn** at 300 North-

Mid-range
In St. Petersburg, the **Edgepark Hotel** is a quiet and comfortable hostelry at 256 First Street North, ((813) 894-9435. A veranda with wicker chairs is provided for post-prandial relaxation, and all the rooms are very neatly turned out. The **Bayboro House** is one of the city's oldest buildings, with conch shells lining the porch, and marble tables and grandfather clocks dotting the interior. The hotel is at 1719 Beach Drive Southeast, ((813) 823-4955.

In St. Petersburg Beach, the **Colonial Gateway Resort Inn** at 6300 Gulf Boulevard, ((813) 367-2711, toll-free (800) 282-5245, has a children's play area with a pool, a pool with a bar for adults, and 800 ft (244 m) of

east Beach Drive, ((813) 898-6325. In St. Petersburg Beach, try the **Carlida Apartments and Motel** at 610 69th Avenue, ((813) 360-7233, which stands out for its good value on this otherwise pricey stretch of the coast.

WHERE TO EAT

Expensive
The **King Charles**, already mentioned, on the fifth floor of the Don CeSar Beach Resort at 3400 Gulf Boulevard in St. Petersburg

The Don CeSar Beach Resort OPPOSITE in St. Petersburg and the Belleview Biltmore Hotel ABOVE in Clearwater are two examples of the luxurious accommodations found along the Gulf Coast.

Beach, ((813) 360-1881, offers superb Continental cuisine which you can enjoy while looking at the Gulf through the restaurant's French windows. Another treasure is **Peter's Place** at 208 Beach Drive Northeast, St. Petersburg, ((813) 822-8436, which has a delicious Moroccan couscous and a nicely prepared filet wrapped around garlic-buttered shrimp. Rather more imaginative, however, is the Veal Kentucky in bourbon sauce at the **Palm Court** restaurant in the Tradewinds Hotel, 5500 Gulf Boulevard, St. Petersburg Beach, ((813) 360-0061. If you have a yearning for charcoal-grilled seafood, you can satisfy it at **Girard's** up the coast at 3580 Ulmerton Road, Clearwater, ((813) 576-7076.

Moderate

You can watch the fishing boats docking from the comfort of the **Crab Market** at 955 Blind Pass Road in St. Petersburg Beach, ((813) 360-4656, which specializes in varieties of tenderly cooked crabmeat. Those who prefer non-shell fish should go to **Ted Peters** at 1350 Pasadena Avenue South, St. Petersburg, ((813) 381-7931, where mullet and mackerel are smoked over red oak. In St. Petersburg there is good Italian food at the inaptly-named **Bahama Bill's**, 320 Fourth Street North, ((813) 821-4931.

Inexpensive

There are numerous inexpensive restaurants in St. Petersburg, among the best of which are **China City** at 1221 Fourth Street North, ((813) 822-3713, which serves simple and well-prepared Chinese food, and the very popular **Big Tim's Bar-B-Que** at 530 34th Street, ((813) 327-7388, a local legend for its rib and pork barbecue sandwiches with spicy sauce. You should also try **Carol's Seafood and Steak House** at 7220 Fourth Street North, ((813) 522-9907. And in St. Petersburg Beach the **Pelican Diner**, 7501 Gulf Boulevard, ((813) 363-9873, serves up some great home cooking in an old dining car.

The pier at Naples sillouetted by the coppery sunset. Located along the Shell Coast, Naples has 41 miles (66 km) of beaches.

How to Get There

The St. Petersburg–Clearwater International Airport, 10 miles (16 km) southeast of Clearwater, is served by a reasonable number of national and international airlines. Probably, though, you will prefer to fly in to Tampa International Airport, on the eastern side of Old Tampa Bay.

Motorists should use the same roads for St. Petersburg as for Tampa. If you are coming from the south you can leave I–75 north of Ellenton and take the Sunshine Skyway over the mouth of Tampa Bay to reach St. Petersburg.

SARASOTA

Known as the "Culture Capital" of Florida, Sarasota offers theater, classical music, opera, and a number of much-respected art galleries. Over the years increasing numbers of artists, musicians, and writers have settled in Sarasota, attracted by the city's reputation for being hospitable to the arts. So if you are looking for Culture to go with your sand, sea, and sun, this is the place for you.

BACKGROUND

Sarasota only began to make itself noticed in 1927 when John Ringling of circus fame established a winter residence for his family — and his circus — in the city. An avid art collector, with a special passion for Italian Renaissance and Baroque works, he built a museum to house his acquisitions. He also invested heavily in civic improvements for his adopted city, building hotels and island causeways and generally subsidizing the arts. The theaters and art galleries which proliferate in the city today testify to Ringling's enthusiastic patronage.

GENERAL INFORMATION

The Sarasota Convention and Visitors Center is at 655 North Tamiami Trail, Sarasota FL 34236. ((813) 957-1877. The Sarasota Chamber of Commerce is at 1551 Second Street, Sarasota FL 33577. ((813) 955-8187.

Other useful telephone numbers (all in area code 813):

Sarasota–Bradenton Airport	355-5200
Airport Taxi	365-1360
Yellow Cabs	955-3341
Sarasota County Health clinic	365-2020

WHAT TO SEE AND DO

Sights

Three miles (five kilometers) north of downtown Sarasota, at 5401 Bayshore Road off Route 41, are the 68 landscaped acres of

the **Ringling estate**, now open to the public. You can tour the 32-room mansion — modeled on the Doges Palace in Venice and built at a cost of $1.5 million at a time when $1.5 million was serious money — which served as Ringling's winter residence, **Ca'd'Zan** (venetian patois meaning "House of John"). Also on the estate, the **Ringling Museum of Art**, ((813) 359-5700, is home to one of the nation's premier collections of Italian Renaissance and Baroque art, as well as a valuable series of paintings and cartoons by Rubens and works by Rembrandt and El Greco.

Next to the art museum is the rococo-style **Asolo Theater**, ((813) 351-9010, which Ringling brought in pieces from an

Italian castle in Asolo to his estate, where he had it reassembled. You can also see all kinds of circus memorabilia from the great days of the Big Top at the **Circus Galleries**. The Ringling estate is open from 10 am to 5:30 pm. Admission (which covers the house and the museums) is $8.50 for adults and $3.75 for children aged six to 12.

There are some rare and beautiful plants in the attractive **Mary Selby Botanical Gardens** at 800 South Palm Avenue off Route 41, ((813) 366-5730, which has an international reputation for its collection of orchids. There are another 15 acres of tropical growth at the **Sarasota Jungle Gardens** 3701 Bayshore Road, ((813) 355-5305, which features jungle animals, and daily bird and reptile shows.

At the **Mote Marine Science Center**, 1600 City Island Park, ((813) 388-4441, swimmers will be keen to learn that 27 species of shark inhabit the Gulf of Mexico. There is little you can't learn here about the Gulf and its creatures, and the center's aquarium contains specimens such as "Nibbles" the nursing shark. If you prefer classic cars to deadly nurses go to **Bellm's Cars and Music of Yesterday** at 5500 North Tamiami Trail, ((813) 355-6228, where there is a collection of 200 lovely old cars, along with antique bicycles and old musical contraptions such as the hurdy-gurdy and the nickelodeon.

For beaches, I would recommend **South Lido** on the southern tip of Lido Key, which has 100 acres of beach and leisure facilities, or **Siesta Beach** on Siesta Key, which has 40 acres of beach and superb sports facilities.

Two rural attractions are near Sarasota: the **Oscar Sherer Recreation Area**, about 10 miles (16 km) south on Route 41, which has campsites, nature trails, and fishing; and the **Myakka River State Park**, 15 miles (24 km) east at 13207 Route 72, where you can go on airboat tours of the 29,000-acre wildlife sanctuary, or rent canoes and stay in log cabins.

Sports

Baseball fans should know that the Chicago White Sox and the Pittsburgh Pirates hold their spring training and play their exhibition games here — the White Sox at Payne

Park off Route 301, and the Pirates at McKecknie Field, 17th Avenue West and Ninth Street in nearby Bradenton.

There is a good choice of **golf** courses in Sarasota, including the Sarasota Golf Club at 7280 Leeswynn Drive, off Route 301, ((813) 371-2431, and the Bobby Jones Golf Club at 1000 Circus Boulevard, ((813) 955-5188.

There are free public **tennis** courts at Siesta Beach on Siesta Key, and the Forest Lakes Tennis Club at 2401 Beneva Road, ((813) 922-0660, also has public courts. For more information on golf courses and tennis courts, call the Sarasota recreation department at ((813) 365-2200.

For **water sports** go to Don and Mike's Boat and Ski Rental at Marina Plaza on the waterfront downtown, ((813) 366-6659, where you can get surfboards, water skis, jet skis, wave jammers, miniboats, as well as windsurfing and waterskiing instruction. Sailing enthusiasts should go to O'Leary's Sarasota Sailing School near Marina Jack's restaurant off Route 41 on the bayfront, ((813) 953-7505, where you can rent sailboats and receive instruction on how to sail them.

Shopping

One of the best known — and exclusive — shopping complexes on the Gulf Coast, **St. Armand's Circle** has over 100 specialty stores, including expensive gift shops and designer fashion outlets. Take Route 41 south to Route 789, turn right and cross Ringling Causeway to reach the circle of shops. For an equally wide choice at considerably lower prices head for the **Sarasota Square Mall** at 8201 South Tamiami Trail, or **Siesta Village** at 5000 Ocean Boulevard on Siesta Key.

Nightlife

The **Asolo Performing Arts Center** in the Ringling estate at 5401 Bayshore Road, ((813) 359-5700, is home to a professional troupe who perform a well-balanced repertoire during a season that runs from December to August. On Monday evenings the Ringling Fine Arts Film Series shows classic and foreign films in the center. A small professional company presents contemporary

drama, comedies, and musicals at the **Florida Studio Theater**, 1241 North Palm Avenue, ((813) 366-9796, and the **Players of Sarasota** enact comedies, thrillers, and musicals in a community theater at Route 41 and Ninth Street, ((813) 365-2494.

The **Florida Symphonic Band** is comprised of 50 musicians who perform a classical concert each month at the Van Wezel Hall, 709 North Tamiami Trail, ((813) 955-6660, and in February–March you can hear internationally known artists, supported by young in-house apprentice singers, at the

Sarasota Opera in a charming old theater at the corner of First and Pineapple streets, ((813) 953-7030.

For rawer entertainment, try the **Beach Club** at 5151 Ocean Boulevard on Siesta Key, ((813) 349-6311, which has live music, or **Club Paradise**, another bustling night club featuring rock music, at 1927 Ringling Boulevard in Sarasota, ((813) 366-3830. You can down a few pints with the locals at the no-nonsense **The Pub** 760 Broadway, Longboat Key, ((813) 383-2391, and there's more hard drinking to be done in the delightfully

OPPOSITE AND ABOVE: Exterior and interior views of John Ringling's winter residence, *Ca'd'Zan* in Sarasota.

seedy **Hemmingway's** at 325 Ringling Boulevard in Sarasota, ☎ (813) 388-3948.

WHERE TO STAY

Luxury

The **Hyatt Sarasota** is downtown next to a marina at 1000 Boulevard of the Arts, ☎ (813) 366-9000, toll-free (800) 228-9000. The hotel's restaurant, Peppercorn's, is much acclaimed, and its other amenities include a sauna, health club, and sailboats. Offering an excellent selection of water sports, the **Harley Sandcastle Hotel** is on the oceanfront at 1540 Ben Franklin Drive, ☎ (813) 388-2181. There is also a playground and games room for children, and two swimming pools, one with a bar. There are 232 beach houses, villas, and apartments set in scenic grounds next to the ocean at the **Colony Beach Resort**, 1620 Gulf of Mexico Drive on Longboat Key north of Sarasota, ☎ (813) 383-6464, toll-free (800) 282-1138. All the accommodations are modern efficiencies with full conveniences, and the resort's sporting and beach facilities are outstanding.

Mid-range

Set in three acres of landscaped grounds, the **Golden Host** at 4675 North Tamiami Trail has stylish rooms with balconies, a palm-ringed swimming pool, and a cocktail lounge with a tropical decor. On South Tamiami Trail at № 6660, ☎ (813) 924-4900, is the modern and very comfortable **Days Inn Sarasota**, which is only a mile from the beach. Facing the ocean at 459 Beach Road, ☎ (813) 346-1786, on Siesta Key is a small, comfortable hotel with friendly service, the **Crescent House**, which serves a complimentary Continental breakfast each morning.

Inexpensive

With its own swimming pool and very spacious rooms, the Old Florida-style **Our Hacienda** is great value at 2803 Browning Street, ☎ (813) 951-1920. There are several inexpensive hotels on North Tamiami Trail, among them the **Econo Lodge** at № 5340, ☎ (813) 355-8867, and the **Hampton Inn** at № 5000, ☎ (813) 351-7734.

WHERE TO EAT

Expensive

Fresh seafood with crisp salads are served up at **Marina Jack's**, 2 Marina Plaza, downtown, ☎ (813) 365-4232, which affords a marvelous view over Sarasota Bay. The **Marina Jack II** is a paddle-wheel boat which leaves from Marina Plaza on lunch and dinner cruises. There is a northern Italian bias to the food at **Osteria**, 29-1/2 North Boulevard of Presidents, ☎ (813) 388-3671, a charming restaurant bedecked with flowers, where the house specialty is their wonderful veal layered with prosciutto. One of the best Continental restaurants in the entire area is the **Café L'Europe** at 431 Harding Circle on Lido Key, ☎ (813) 388-4415, where I would urge you to try the *mignonettes aux poivres* and the red snapper *belle meunière*. For good solid American cuisine try **Michael's on East** at 1212 East Avenue, Sarasota, ☎ (813) 366-0007, where the desserts are sensational.

Moderate

In the nautical surrounds of **Charley's Crab** at 420 Harding Circle on Lido Key, ☎ (813) 388-3964, you can choose from a splendid selection of inventively concocted seafood dishes. The **Indian Cuisine** at 1522 Main Street in Sarasota, ☎ (813) 953-5102, has apart from its eponymous dishes, some interesting Trinidadian dishes. Nearby at 1551 Main Street, **Ristorante Bellini**, ☎ (813) 365-7380, features northern Italian cooking, which happily includes a *sogliota aurora* — sole in a wine, shrimp, and lemon sauce. For real down-home American cooking try **Poki Joe's Greatest Hits** at 6614 Superior Avenue, ☎ (813) 922-5915, where spinach pie and sausage soup are among the greatest hits.

Inexpensive

Everything on the menu is homemade at the simple, café-like **Der Dutchman**, 3713 Bahia Vista, ☎ (813) 955-8007. At **Wildflower**, 5218 Ocean Boulevard, Siesta Key, ☎ (813) 349-1758, food for the health-conscious unfairly has to compete with Mexican food. **Walt's Fish Market, Raw Oyster Bar, and Restaurant** is probably all you need to know about

Walt's food at 560 North Washington Boulevard in Sarasota, ((813) 365-1735. For hot dogs and barbecued ribs and mountains of fries, head out to Siesta Key and the **Old Salty Dog Pub** at 5023 Ocean Boulevard, ((813) 349-0158.

HOW TO GET THERE

The Sarasota–Bradenton Airport is served by most of the major national airlines; in any case, the larger Tampa and St. Petersburg airports are both convenient for Sarasota.

have some of the best "shelling beaches" in the world.

Further south, the city of Naples has 41 miles (66 km) of beaches and some of the best shopping on the entire Gulf Coast. Continuing down the coast, you come to Marco Island, with its modern Gulf-front condominiums and its carefully preserved fishing villages such as Goodland. At the southern end of the Shell Coast are the Ten Thousand Islands, which are still largely undeveloped and provide a home for a dazzling array of wildlife.

By car, I–75 is the main route in from the north and south (the more scenic Route 41 also comes in from the south). Routes 64 and 70 enter Sarasota from the east.

THE SHELL COAST

The Shell Coast runs from Captiva Island, near Fort Myers, to the Ten Thousand Islands in the south, near Everglades City. Fort Myers is one of the fastest growing cities in the U.S. and an important center of commerce, while Fort Myers Beach is a resort community on the offshore island of Estero. There are also luxury resort facilities on the islands of Captiva and Sanibel, which

GENERAL INFORMATION

The Fort Myers Chamber of Commerce is at 1365 Hendry Street, P.O. Box CC, Fort Myers FL 33902, ((813) 334-1133, and the Fort Myers Beach Chamber of Commerce is at 1661 Estero Boulevard, P.O. Box 6109, Fort Myers Beach FL 33931, ((813) 463-6451. The Sanibel-Captiva Chamber of Commerce is at Causeway Road, Sanibel FL 33957, ((813) 472-1080, and the Naples Chamber of Commerce is at 1700 North Tamiami Trail, Naples FL 33940, ((813) 262-6141.

The Ringling Museum of Art, home of one of the nation's best collections of Italian Renaissance and Baroque works.

WHAT TO SEE AND DO

Sights

Thomas Edison wintered in Fort Myers, which means you can visit **Edison's Winter Home** at 2350 McGregor Boulevard, ((813) 334-7419. There is a museum which displays some of the 1,096 (!) inventions which Edison patented, and there are 'beautiful botanical gardens in the 14-acre grounds which the great man nurtured. The home and gardens are open daily, and admission is $10 for adults and $3 for children.

The world's largest collection of shells can be seen at the **Shell Factory** 2787 North Tamiami Trail, off Route 41 north of Fort Myers, ((813) 995-2141, which also has a souvenir shop and a children's theme park.

On Sanibel Island you can explore the **J.N. "Ding" Darling National Wildlife Refuge**, which is home to 300 species of birds and 50 species of reptiles. You can walk along nature trails or rent a canoe or boat from the Visitors Center at 1 Wildlife Drive, ((813) 472-1100. At the southern tip of the island is the historic Sanibel Lighthouse on **Lighthouse Beach**, a popular spot for swimming, lazing in the sun, and shell-searching.

The best shells on Sanibel Island can be found on **Bowman's Beach**, to the north, which is less crowded than the island's southern beaches.

A good way to visit the islands near Fort Myers is to join the **Adventure Sailing Escape Flotilla** whose 16 full-berth yachts sail for a week and spend each afternoon docked at a resort on a different island, including Useppa, Captiva, Sanibel, and Cabbage Key. Contact the Royal Palm Tours Inc., 6296 Corporate Court, Fort Myers, ((813) 489-0344, for more information.

The main attractions in the Naples area are the **Corkscrew Swamp Sanctuary** at Sanctuary Road off Route 41 north of Naples, ((813) 657-3771, where you can see some of the oldest cypress trees in America as well as some rare species of birds, and **Jungle Larry's Zoological Park** at 1590 Goodlette Road, off Route 41 south of Naples, ((813) 262-5409, which has hundreds of exotic animals and a children's petting zoo.

The Marco Island Area Chamber of Commerce situated at 1102 North Collier Boulevard, Marco Island, ((813) 394-7549, will provide you with information about Marco Island and the Ten Thousand Islands region to the south. One of the best ways to see the islands is on a boat tour which leaves from the Gulf Coast Ranger Station in Everglades City;

contact the **Everglades National Park Boat Tours** in Everglades City, ((800) 445-7724, for more details.

Sports

There is no shortage of **golf** courses along the Shell Coast, including the Bay Beach Golf Club at 7401 Estero Boulevard in Fort Myers Beach, ((813) 463-2064, the Beachview Golf Club at 110 Parkview Drive South on Sanibel Island, ((813) 472-2626, and Naples Beach Hotel and Golf Club at 851 Gulf Shore Boulevard, ((813) 261-2222.

There are **tennis** courts at the Bay Beach Racquet Club at 120 Lenell Street, Fort Myers Beach, ((813) 463-4473, The

Dunes at 949 Sand Castle Road on Sanibel Island, ((813) 472-3522, and at the Forest Hills Racquet Club, 100 Forest Hills Boulevard, Naples, ((813) 774-2442.

Opportunities for **water sports** abound on the Shell Coast. In Fort Myers Beach you can rent sailboats, aquacycles, and jet skis from Happy Sailboat Rental at 1010 Estero Boulevard, ((813) 463-3351; Windsurfing of Sanibel at 1554 Periwinkle Way on Sanibel Island, ((813) 472-0123, will fix you up with a sail-board; you

The best-quality shops on the Shell Coast, however, are in Naples at the **Old Marine Market Place**, 1200 Fifth Avenue South.

Nightlife

The Fort Myers area is the best place for living it up after dark on the Shell Coast. In Fort Myers itself there is live music in the open air at **The Beach Club**, 1915 Colonial Boulevard, ((813) 939-2582. Live rock bands play Top 40 hits at **Edison's Electric Lounge** in the

can receive instruction in scuba diving from Underwater Explorers at 12600 McGregor Boulevard, ((813) 481-4733; and you can arrange an offshore diving trip and equipment rental from Sealandia Scuba Center at 625 Eighth Street in Naples, ((813) 261-3357.

Shopping

For the best selection of shops in Fort Myers go to the **Royal Palm Square Shopping Center** located at 1400 Colonial Boulevard.

On Sanibel Island, **Periwinkle Way** is lined with gift shops, shell shops, and a good selections of outlets for sports and swimwear.

Holiday Inn at 13051 Bell Tower Drive, ((813) 482-2900. A lively singles crowd dances to disco music at **Norma Jean's** 4797 Route 41, ((813) 275-9997. In Fort Myers Beach, simply go along Estero Boulevard and sooner or later you will find what you're looking for.

OPPOSITE: An elegant snowy egret stalks through the still waters of the J. N. "Ding" Darling National Wildlife Refuge on Sanibel Island.
ABOVE: Fishermen and pelicans wind up a tranquil evening of fishing on a pier at Sarasota.

WHERE TO STAY

Luxury

In Fort Myers, the **Sheraton Harbor Place** is downtown by the waterfront at 2500 Edwards Drive, ((813) 337-0300, with 417 luxurious rooms. In Fort Myers Beach you can find a similar standard at **Seawatch-on-the-Beach**, 6550 Estero Boulevard, ((813) 481-3636, which has two-bedroom efficiency suites overlooking the gulf. An excellent hotel on Sanibel Island with superb recre-

((813) 597-3123, is particularly recommended for families.

Inexpensive

There are not too many budget deals on the Shell Coast, but three places that I know to be good value for money are the **Ta Ki Ki Motel** at 2631 First Street, Fort Myers, ((813) 334-2135; the **Beacon Court Motel** at 1240 Estero Boulevard, Fort Myers Beach, ((813) 463-5264; and the **Fairways Motel**, 103 Palm River Boulevard, Naples, ((813) 597-8181.

ational facilities, the **Sanibel Beach and Tennis Resort**, is at 1415 Middle Gulf Drive, ((813) 472-4151. In Naples there is the deluxe **Ritz-Carlton** at 280 Vanderbilt Beach Road, ((813) 598-3300.

Mid-range

The comfortable **Fountain Motel** at 14621 McGregor Boulevard, Fort Myers, ((813) 481-0429, has both rooms and apartments; and the **Outrigger Beach Resort** at 6200 Estero Boulevard, ((813) 463-3131, is on the oceanfront in Fort Myers Beach. On Sanibel Island, the **Kon Mai Motel** is a charming Hawaiian-style resort at 1539 Periwinkle Way, ((813) 472-1001. **La Playa**, near Vanderbilt Beach at 9891 Gulf Shore Drive, Naples,

WHERE TO EAT

Expensive

There is some quite exceptional seafood on the menu at **La Tiers** restaurant in the Sheraton Harbor Place Hotel, 2500 Ewards Drive, ((813) 337-0300, in Fort Myers. In Fort Myers Beach, the **Snug Harbor Restaurant and Lounge** at 645 San Carlos Boulevard, ((813) 463-4343, is another restaurant featuring wonderful seafood from local waters. Roast duckling in fruit sauce is the house specialty at **Jean-Paul's French Corner**, 708 Tarpon Bay Road, Sanibel Island, ((813) 472-1493. At the **Chef's Garden**, 1300 Third Street South,

Naples, ((813) 262-5500, there is an interesting choice of Italian, Californian, and Cajun cooking, backed up by an equally eclectic wine list.

Moderate

The seafood is impeccably prepared and presented at **The Prawnbroker**, 6535 McGregor Boulevard, ((813) 489-2226, in Fort Myers. Another popular seafood restaurant is the **Mucky Duck** at 2500 Estero Boulevard, ((813) 463-5519, in Fort Myers Beach, where you can enjoy fish-and-chips

((813) 463-6139. For a cheap sandwich or pizza go to **Island Pizza** at 1619 Periwinkle Way, ((813) 472-1518, on Sanibel Island. Omelettes, fondues, and crepes are the order of the day at the **Venetian Café**, 4050 Gulf Shore Boulevard, Naples, ((813) 261-4050.

HOW TO GET THERE

The Southwest Florida Regional Airport is 10 miles (16 km) southeast of Fort Myers and is served by many national airlines.

and bacon-wrapped barbecued shrimps in a quasi-English-country-style-pub ambience. For Creole and Cajun food go to the **Thistle Lodge** at 2255 West Gulf Drive on Sanibel Island, ((813) 472-9200. For good, honest just-about-everything in Fort Myers you should head for the **Riverwalk Fish and Ale House** at 1200 Fifth Avenue South, ((813) 263-2734.

Inexpensive

In Fort Myers, **Woody's Bar-B-Q** at 6701 North Tamiami Trail, ((813) 997-1424, is exactly what you would expect — and excellent. In Fort Myers Beach, the **Pelican Restaurant and Inn** offers good bargains in seafood dishes at 3040 Estero Boulevard,

The principal north-south roads through the region are I–75 and Route 41. Route 17 approaches the Shell Coast from the northeast, and Everglades Parkway ("Alligator Alley") is the main road from the east into Naples. Route 80 enters Fort Myers from the east.

OPPOSITE AND ABOVE: Two ways of approaching the Gulf.

The
Everglades

EVERGLADES NATIONAL PARK

Many, if not most, people imagine a swamp filled with alligators when they think of the Everglades. But the reality is something that more closely resembles a vast midwestern wheat field: an expanse of sawgrass, interrupted by copses of hardwood and cypress trees, which, at the end of winter before the spring rains, appears totally dry. When the rains do come, and the water levels rise, this grassy plain is transformed into a unique

"river", over 60 miles (about 100 km) wide and six inches deep, which flows slowly southward to the Gulf Coast and Florida Bay. The "river" drops only 13 ft (four meters) over its 100-mile (160-km) length, which gives you some idea of the flatness of the Everglades.

The Indian name for the region is Pa-hay-okee, meaning "the grassy waters". An early white surveyor came up with the name "River Glades", but later maps changed "River" to "Ever", and the new name stuck. The water sources of the Everglades start with the rivers of central Florida's Kissimmee Valley, which runs into the huge Lake Okeechobee, which in

ABOVE: In the Everglades, a pelican thinks things over. OPPOSITE: An anhinga dries its wings.

turn feeds "the grassy waters". On its course southwards, the river passes through a zone where temperate and subtropical climates blend, which is one of the reasons for the great diversity of animal and plant life in the region, which includes such rarities as the manatee and the Florida panther, not to mention half of the 650 species of birds found in North America, as well as 45 kinds of flora that cannot be found anywhere else in the world.

The Everglades are also a source of water for farmlands to the east around the city of Homestead and Florida City, and for the homes of millions of people who live along Florida's southeast coast. The drainage this has involved has had its effect on the ecological balance of the Everglades, with water levels dropping in recent years as demands increase from the thirsty and booming populations of the coast cities.

Everglades National Park consists of 1.4 million acres (over 500,000 ha) of protected land and coastline stretching from Everglades City in the northwest down to the coast near Key Largo in the southeast, all policed by park rangers and carefully tended by conservationists.

BACKGROUND

Calusas, Tequestas, and Mayaimis Indians lived in Pa-hay-okee for two thousand years before white settlers arrived in the latter half of the nineteenth century and set about requisitioning the marshland for agricultural purposes. By 1909, a canal running from Lake Okeechobee to Miami was completed, and numerous dikes and irrigational canals had been installed across the plains, impeding the natural rise and fall of water levels. In the 1920s a series of hurricanes whipped up the waters of Lake Okeechobee, causing floods in the surrounding area which killed 2,000 people. In response, the U.S. Army Corps of Engineers ringed the lake with the Hoover Dike and constructed a further 1,400 miles (2,254 km) of canals and levees and to control and channel the waters of the lake and Everglades.

All of this drastically upset the ecosystem, which demands that the marshes should be "dry" in winter and crossed by the river in summer. Sometimes, due to water

mismanagement, the cycle was reversed, with devastating results for flora and fauna alike: since 1930 the Everglades have lost about 90 percent of their marsh and wading birds, and without great conservation efforts even the alligator would have disappeared.

A conservationist named Marjorie Stoneman Douglas published a book in 1947 entitled *The Everglades: River of Grass*, which began: "There are no other Everglades in the world." She went on to warn that the region was in danger of being destroyed if action

wasn't taken urgently. The book had an effect. That same year President Truman created Everglades National Park, which was created to the north, and in 1989 a further 107,000 acres of the ecologically crucial Shark River Slough in the northeast were added to Everglades National Park. There is a water purity project well under way at this writing, and the Army Corps of Engineers have been called back in to undo their well-intentioned but ultimately damaging work.

Meanwhile, and perhaps most importantly, the politicians have realized that the protection of the Everglades is a popular vote-getter. The "grassy waters" may survive after all.

GENERAL INFORMATION

The Greater Homestead–Florida City Chamber of Commerce is at 43 North Krome Avenue, Homestead FL 33030. ((305) 247-2332. For full details of accommodation, tours, and activities available in the park,

plus literature and maps, contact the Everglades National Park, P.O. Box 279, Homestead FL 33030. The Everglades City Chamber of Commerce is at Routes 41 and 29, Everglades City FL 33929. ((813) 695-3941.

There are three main entrances to the park — at Shark Valley in the northeast, off Route 41; at Everglades City in the northwest on Route 29, off Route 41; and the entrance southwest of Homestead at the main Visitor Center on Route 9336, which is the one I would recommend if you can spend only one day in the park. At this Visitor Center you can see a short film about the wildlife and ecology of the Everglades, and there are free guides and maps explaining the attractions and trails you can find in the park. There are naturalists to give talks, and to lead hikes or canoe trips, but you are free to make your own way from the Visitor Center by taking a 38-mile (61-km) park road, the Ingraham Highway, which passes through sawgrass plains, hardwood and cypress copses, and mangrove swamps on its way to the fishing village of Flamingo, 35 miles (56 km) to the southwest.

Along the road there are trails and boardwalks branching off, some of which lead to "hammocks" — raised, tree-clad mounds in the swamps — which serve as observation points and campsites. The first turning on the left will take you to the Royal Palm Visitor Center, which has slide shows and rangers who will direct you along the various nature trails which branch out from the center. The Anhinga and Gumbo Limbo trails are particularly popular boardwalks, from which you can see alligators, egrets, herons, raccoons, opossums, and lizards, among other wildlife. There are several more turnings before you reach Flamingo; the maps and official guides will tell you where they are and what you can expect to see there.

When you arrive in Flamingo, go to the Visitor Center for any information about trails, boat routes, picnic areas, campsites, and special attractions in the area. There is a restaurant, a shop, a motel, and a marina in the village, plus a bayfront observation deck with telescopes with which to view the islands and wildlife offshore.

The best time of year to visit the Everglades is winter — the "dry" season — for two reasons: that is when you will see the greatest concentration of birdlife, and there are far fewer mosquitoes and biting insects, which can be a real problem at other times of the year. (If you do visit in the summer, be sure to take plenty of insect repellent, because there are plenty of repellent insects.) At any times of the year you should be aware of the presence of poisonous plants and snakes (particularly coral snakes, water moccasins, diamondback and pigmy rattlesnakes), all of which the printed guides will clearly identify for you. If you keep to the official trails and follow all written and oral instructions you will have no problems.

If you do decide to head out on your own, be sure to file your planned walking or boating route with the nearest ranger station. The park is vast and there are very few navigational points of reference; reckless amateur explorers have been known to disappear without trace in the Everglades. What you have to remember is that this is not a theme park or a zoo: this is the real thing, this is one of the great wild areas in the world.

Finally, *don't* (yes, it has been known to happen) go near or try to touch the alligators, however somnolent they may appear. They have an incredible turn of speed, which could well be your last great surprise if you get too close to one.

WHAT TO SEE AND DO

Sights

The Tamiami Trail (Route 41) runs from Miami to Everglades City on the Gulf Coast, and is a good way to view the park's northern attractions. Twenty five miles (40 km) west of Miami you will find the **Miccosukee Indian Village** on the Tamiami Trail, ((305) 223-8380, where 600 contemporary Miccosukees live and work. You can watch the Indians at work and buy their handmade ornaments and crafts. Or you can watch alligator wrestling, or you can take the boardwalks or the airboat rides into the surrounding wilderness. The village is open daily from 9 am to 5 pm. A mile down the road from the village is the **Shark Valley** entrance to the park. You

can take a tram ride around a 15-mile (24-km) loop road; the tram stops at an observation tower which affords panoramic views of the surrounding countryside and such local denizens as alligators, otters, wood storks, and kites. Reservations are advisable for the December–March period — call (305) 221-8455. The trams run from 9 am to 4 pm daily.

In Everglades City you can take a 12-mile (19-km) boat tour through the offshore Ten Thousand Islands region. The **Everglades National Park Boat Tours** leave from a dock

just under one mile south of the Gulf Coast Ranger Station on Route 29, off Route 41, ((813) 695-2591. If you are in Chokoloskee Bay at sunset you will be treated to the sight of as many as 20,000 birds returning to the mainland to roost. For more information on the area contact the Everglades National Park Visitor Center on Route 29 south of Everglades City, ((813) 695-3311.

Further south down the coast, the *Bald Eagle* leaves from **Florida Bay Cruises** at Flamingo Marina, ((305) 253-2241, on a 90-minute tour of the islands in Florida Bay, providing close-up views of the islands'

OPPOSITE: An osprey keeps a look-out from its lofty vantage point. ABOVE: A boat operator in Everglades National Park.

fascinating birdlife. The **Back Country Tour**, ((305) 253-2241 again, is a two-hour cruise also out of Flamingo Marina, which explores the tropical estuaries and mangrove swamps of the coast, giving you a chance to see manatees, dolp ins, sharks, and a variety of birds, among them the bald eagle. Reservations can be made — and are strongly recommended in the winter season — for all the boat tours.

There is also an inland water route, called the **Wilderness Waterway**, from Flamingo to Everglades City; the route's

course is marked with posts along its 99-mile (159-km) length. You can receive more information about it from the Visitor Center in the village. Outboard motorboats take about six hours to make the trip, and can be rented from Flamingo Marina.

If you want to rent a canoe, go the **Everglades Canoe Outfitters** at 39801 Ingraham Highway (the road between Homestead and Flamingo), Homestead, ((305) 246-1530. Guided trips are available or you can simply get good advice on the planning of your own route. **Coopertown Airboat Ride** operates from Southwest Eighth Street, off Krome Avenue, west of Miami, ((305) 226-6048, and offers 30-minute excursions, taking in hardwood hammocks and alliga-

tor holes. It's open from 8:30 am to dusk, and charges $6 for a ride.

For a comprehensive guided tour of the park, including an airboat ride, a visit to the Indian Village, Shark Valley, nature trails, and lunch, contact **Safari Sightseeing Tours** at 6547 Southwest 116th Place, Miami, ((305) 226-6923. Tours run on Wednesday, Saturday, and Sunday from 8:30 am to 5 pm, at $29.50 for adults and $14.75 for children under 12.

Sports

You can rent a canoe and go on a guided **canoeing** trip from North American Canoe Tours at Glades Haven, 800 Southeast Copeland Avenue, Everglades City, ((813) 695-2746. The daily trips run from November to March; they cost $18 for the first day and $15 for each day thereafter. There are six canoe trails in the Flamingo area, including the southern end of the Wilderness Waterway. Canoes can be rented at the Flamingo Marina, along with skiffs and houseboats.

If you want to go **diving**, contact Pirate's Cove Dive Center at 116 North Homestead Boulevard in Homestead, ((305) 248-1808. It offers equipment for sale or rent as well as diving trips from Homestead Bayfront.

Shopping

The shop at the Flamingo Marina sells the usual gifts and souvenirs, guides to the Everglades, some local crafts, camera film, sun lotion, and the all-important insect repellent. Homestead is the only place in the vicinity of the Everglades with any sort of selection of shops. But then you haven't come to the Everglades to shop.

WHERE TO STAY

Some people choose to stay at hotels in the Greater Miami area, but having to struggle through traffic to get to one of the park's entrances seriously reduces one's "quality time". Besides, in Homestead there are several comfortable and moderately-priced hotels, including the **Holiday Inn** at 990 North Homestead Boulevard, ((305) 247-7020, which has 139 rooms and a swimming pool, and the recently renovated **Greenstone Motel** at 304 North Krome Avenue, ((305) 247-8334. In Florida City there are two similarly attractive hotels: the **Park Royal Inn** at 100 Route 1, ℂ (305) 247-3200, and the **Knights Inn** at 401 Route 1, ℂ (305) 245-2800, which also has efficiency suites.

In Everglades City, there are tasteful rooms and efficiency villas at the **Captain's Table Resort**, 102 Broadway Street, ℂ (813) 695-4211. Probably the best-known hotel in the Everglades, the **Flamingo Lodge Marina and Outdoor Resort** in Flamingo, ℂ (305) 253-2241, has 121 rooms and 17 cottages with kitchenettes, a very friendly staff, rooms overlooking Florida Bay, and of course a

purposes and to control the numbers of campers) is $7 per day in winter and free in summer.

WHERE TO EAT

The Tamiami Trail (Route 41) between Miami and Shark Valley and the area from Homestead to Florida City offer the best possibilities of eating well in or near the Everglades.

The **Miccosukee Restaurant,** ℂ (305) 223-8388, has such native specialties as pumpkin bread, Indian taco, breaded catfish, and

marina. Advance reservations are strongly advised for the winter season. Like the Captain's Table, the Flamingo Lodge is moderately priced.

Campsites in the Everglades are basic (read: no electricity). You must provide your own food and water (and — again — insect repellent). Note: the park rangers come down hard on litter bugs. Information on the campsites, and permits to stay in them, are available from the ranger stations in Flamingo and Everglades City, or at any of the Visitor Centers at the entrances to the park and inside the grounds. There are almost 300 sites in the Flamingo area alone, and during the winter a stay is limited to 14 days. The charge (a permit is required for registration

frogs' legs. The restaurant is by the Shark Valley entrance to the park on Route 41 and is very reasonably priced. By contrast, the expensive **Le Kir** restaurant at 1532 Northeast Eighth Street, Homestead, ℂ (305) 247-6414, has a distinctly Gallic menu, on which I would recommend the medallions of veal. **El Toro Taco** in Homestead at 1 South Krome Avenue, ℂ (305) 245-5576, has superb Mexican food at superbly low prices. For southern-style bargains try **Potlikker's** at 591 Washington Avenue in Homestead, ℂ (305) 248-0835, where the chicken pie and pot roast are both worth having. In Florida City,

OPPOSITE: Visitors focus on the local fauna.
ABOVE: A squadron of black skimmers.

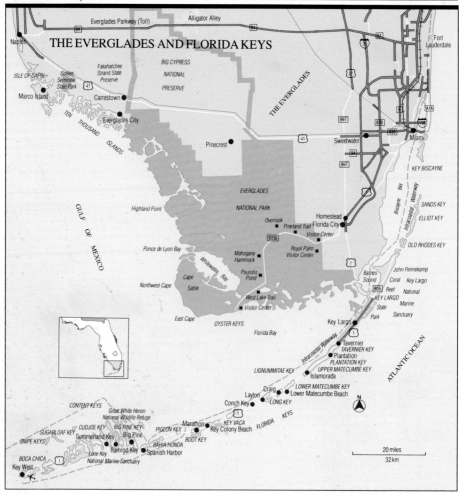

Captain Bob's at 326 Southeast First Avenue, ((305) 247-8988, specializes in reasonably-priced, Greek-influenced seafood.

In Everglades City you must try the **Rod and Gun Club** at 200 Riverside Drive, ((813) 695-2101, which serves delicious steaks, poultry, and seafood on its porch where you can watch boats drift by as you eat. On the second floor of the Visitor Center in Flamingo, the **Flamingo Re**staurant, ((813) 695-3101, has wonderful views over Florida Bay and an eclectic menu featuring Cuban pork loin roasted with garlic and lime, teriyaki chicken, and fried marlin.

HOW TO GET THERE

Most visitors to the Everglades fly in to Miami International Airport. The Airporter,

((305) 876-7077, operates a regular shuttle service from the airport to Homestead; one can also, of course, rent a car at the airport. An alternative is to fly into Naples Municipal Airport north of Everglades City.

Traveling by car from the north down the east coast, you will take either Route 1 or Route 997 (Krome Avenue) to reach the Homestead–Florida City area. From there you continue on until you reach Route 9336, where you turn right: this will take you to the main Visitor Center and, eventually, to Flamingo. Route 41 — AKA the Tamiami Trail — runs from Miami to the Shark Valley entrance, and then on to Everglades City. Route 41 is also the principal highway down the Gulf Coast to the Everglades.

OPPOSITE: An anhinga nest in the Everglades.

The Florida Keys

THE sequence of coral and limestone islands known as the Florida Keys, running in a southwesterly curve from Biscayne Bay almost 124 miles (200 km) out to Key West, appears on a map like a long sea wall, battered and breached, but still preventing the waters of the Atlantic from washing over southern Florida's marshlands.

In fact, the Keys have their own sunken defensive wall in the form of a live coral reef (the only one in America) which lies off their eastern coasts. This protective reef means that there is little surf and surprisingly few beaches on the Keys' eastern shores.

The name "key" is derived from the Spanish word *cayo*, meaning "little island", and the islands have been known as the Keys since early last century. The name first given to them, by the sixteenth-century explorer Ponce de León, was *Los Martires*, and throughout the seventeenth and eighteenth centuries the coves and inlets of Los Martires were ideal bases for such infamous pirates as Blackbeard and Lafitte, who regularly attacked treasure-laden Spanish ships traveling from South America.

By the early nineteenth century piracy had died out and the islands were renamed the Florida Keys. The first American community on the islands was at Key West, which became a major salvaging town with a deep-water port and continued to boom throughout the nineteenth century, while the rest of the Keys remained virtually undeveloped and largely uninhabited — except for a few Indian tribes and a handful of small salvaging villages in the Middle and Upper Keys.

It was in 1905 that the Keys attracted the attention of Henry Flagler, who decided to extend his Florida East Coast Railroad to Key West. He envisioned the railway carrying wealthy sportsmen to lavish resorts, as well as export cargo to Key West. The rail line was completed in 1916 and included one bridge that was over seven miles (11 km) long. In 1935 much of the railroad was destroyed by a terrible hurricane. A few years later a road followed literally in the tracks of the railroad, and the Ocean Highway — Route 1 — remains to this day the world's longest ocean-going road. The Ocean Highway is lined with green mile-markers (MMs), and as it is the only major road through the Keys most hotels, restaurants, and shops have the number f the nearest mile-marker as their address (*e.g.*, The Caribbean Club, Route 1, MM 104).

Nowadays the Keys are extremely popular holiday destinations, offering all kinds of fishing, diving, and water sports facilities. You can also enjoy the uniquely romantic experience of watching the sun rise over the Atlantic and later, after you have wandered over to the other side of the Key, watching the sun set into the Gulf of Mexico. Added to this, at the tip of the Ocean Highway, is America's southernmost city, with one of the most evocative names on the entire continent: Key West, once the home of Ernest Hemingway, Tennessee Williams, Wallace Stevens, and a host of other great American writers.

KEY LARGO TO LONG KEY

The string of islands from Key Largo to Long Key are known as the Upper Keys. Touristically, they are the busiest of the Keys as they are within a few hours' drive of Miami and Palm Beach. Key Largo is the starting point of the 113-mile (182-km) journey along the Ocean Highway to Key West, and is perhaps best known as the setting for the Bogart-Bacall film of that name. As it is the nearest island to the John Pennekamp Coral Reef State Park — the world's first underwater park — it is also the area's premier diving site.

Further south are the Upper and Lower Matecumbe Keys, whose name derives from the Spanish *matar* ("to kill") and *hombre* ("man"), which is a self-explanatory reference to the welcome originally given to shipwrecked sailors by the islands' Indians. These Keys are particularly renowned for their fishing. Islamorada is known as the "purple island" because of the color of the snails that once thrived on its shores; Indian Key is an island of lush tropical growth; Long Key is noted for the quality of its beaches and camping facilities.

A favorite local pastime; cruising the Keys.

GENERAL INFORMATION

The Upper Keys Chamber of Commerce is at 105950 Overseas Highway, Key Largo, ((305) 451-1414. The Islamorada Chamber of Commerce can be found at MM 82.5, Islamorada, ((305) 664-4503.

Note: The mile-markers (MMs) start on Route 1 a mile south of Florida City with MM 126 and end with MM 0 in Key West. If an address falls between two mile-markers, the designation .5 is used — as

There are also beaches and nature trails on the park's coast. An aquarium, gift shop, and Visitor Center can be found in the park, which is open from 8 am to sunset every day. Admission is $1, and you pay extra for the diving and boat tours, for which you are urged to make reservations.

Fans of Bogart will be interested to know that the original *African Queen* boat, the one used in the film, is on display outside the Holiday Inn Dock, Route 1, MM 100.

with the two chambers of commerce mentioned above.

WHAT TO SEE AND DO

Sights

The main attraction in the Key Largo area is the **John Pennekamp Coral Reef State Park,** Route 1, MM 102.5, ((305) 451-1202. It is 21 miles (34 km) long and eight miles (13 km) wide, covering over 2,000 acres of land and 178 sq miles (287 sq km) of water, and containing 40 types of coral and 650 species of fish. Scuba and snorkeling tours, as well as glass-bottom boat tours, are available for you to view the coral, fish, and shipwrecks in the park's waters.

In Islamorada you can take glass-bottom tours to the coral reefs from **Holiday Princess Cruises,** Holiday Isle Marina, Route 1, MM 84.5, ((305) 664-2321, and visit the **Theater of the Sea**, Route 1, MM 84.5, ((305) 664-2431, which is one of the nation's top marine parks; here you will find dolphin and sea lion shows, as well as collections of sharks and stingrays. The park is open from 9:30 am to 4 pm daily, and admission is $12.25 for adults and $7.50 for children aged four to 12; for a small extra charge you can swim with the dolphins.

The **Indian Key State Historic Site** can be reached by taking a boat from MM 78, Indian Key Fill, between Upper and Lower

Matecumbe Keys, to the 10-acre **Indian Key**. Guides lead you on a tour of a reconstructed salvaging village and of the surrounding tropical vegetation. Boats also leave MM 78 for **Lignumvitae Key**, an uninhabited virgin hammock with tropical growth of the kind that once covered most of the Keys. On Long Key, the **Long Key State Park**, Route 1, MM 67.5, ((305) 664-4815, is popular for its beaches and camping facilities.

Sports

Water sports, not surprisingly, are *the* sports

boards and offers lessons. All along Route 1 in the Key Largo area you will find shops catering to fishermen and water sportsmen. There is also a **golf** course with nearby **tennis** courts open to the public at the Cheeca Lodge Hotel in Islamorada, ((305) 644-4651.

Shopping

Key Largo's streets are lined with department stores, groceries, hardware stores, gift shops, fishing shops, and shops selling everything you might need for the beach — in other words, here you will find

on the Keys. **Fishing** trips are arranged in Key Largo at Miss Kitty Reef Fishing, Route 1, MM 100, ((305) 451-2220, and in Islamorada at the Holiday Isle Resort Marina, Route 1, MM 84.5, ((305) 664-2321; the marina also offers **diving** courses, wreck trips, equipment for rent, as well as boats and yachts. The John Pennekamp Coral Reef State Park, Route 1, MM 102.5, has a water sports center, ((305) 451-1621, which has **snorkeling** tours three times a day for $18, **scuba diving** trips twice a day for $27.50, and a **sailing** plus snorkeling trip for $50 a day. The center's dive shop also rents all sorts of equipment, sailboats, canoes, and **windsurfing** boards.

Windsurfing of the Florida Keys, Route 1, MM 104, Key Largo, ((305) 451-3869, rents

the best selection of shops in the Upper Keys. In Islamorada, Irene and George's on Route 1 at MM 82 is a personalized emporium with nine departments, and the Bimini Town Shops alongside the Holiday Isle Resort, Route 1, MM 84, have beach and swimwear.

Nightlife

At the **Caribbean Club**, Route 1, MM 104, ((305) 451-9970, you can sit on the veranda with a drink and watch the sun fall into the Gulf of Mexico. This, by the way, is the club

OPPOSITE: Crab floats. ABOVE: Sportfishing boats at Key West.

where part of the film *Key Largo* was shot. Bogart would have liked the place now, as it is open 24 hours a day. The liveliest night spot in Key Largo is **Coconuts**, MM 100 at Marina del Mar, ((305) 451-4107, which features disco music and live reggae bands. In Islamorada, the nightlife centers around the Holiday Isle Resort, Route 1, MM 84, ((305) 664-2321, where you can find the **Tiki Bar**, the **Bilge Bar**, the **Kokomo Beach Bar**, and the **Horizon Restaurant** at the top of the hotel, which has mellow but live music for dancing.

WHERE TO STAY

Luxury

Offering some of the best facilities in Key Largo, the **Marina del Mar,** Route 1, MM 100, ((305) 451-4107, toll-free (800) 253-3483, has a marina with water sports equipment, several tennis courts, a fitness center, a swimming pool, a night club, and spacious, well-equipped rooms, some of which are efficiencies. The hotel is also in an excellent position near the offshore diving areas. The other top hotel in Key Largo is the Sheraton Key Largo, Route 1, MM 97, ((305) 852-5553, which faces the Gulf.

In Islamorada there is a hotel that has just about everything: seven lounge bars, five restaurants, beachside shops, two swimming pools, a famous marine park next door, and accommodation ranging from luxurious rooms to fully-equipped suites and apartments. The hotel is the **Holiday Isle Resort** and it's off Route 1 at MM 84, ((305) 664-2321. Two markers down Route 1 at MM 82, the **Cheeca Lodge,** ((305) 327-2888, is an old fishing lodge which has recently been renovated. It has a health spa, tennis courts, and a nine-hole golf course in its 25-acre grounds. A pier poking out into the Atlantic affords fishing, diving, and snorkeling facilities.

Mid-range

There are six delightful two- or three-bedroom cottages set in tropical gardens at **Largo's Lodge**, Route 1, MM 101.5, ((305) 451-0424, next to the beach; and at the stucco-style **Stone Ledge Lodge**, Route 1, MM 95–96, ((305) 852-8114, you can have a simple room or a studio apartment overlooking a small beach. Very similar accommodation can be found at the **Drop Anchor**, Route 1, MM 85, Islamorada, ((305) 664-4863, which also has a swimming pool. One of the best-bargain hotels — considering the quality of its rooms and amenities — is **The Islander** in Islamorada at Route 1, MM 82, ((305) 664-2031, which is built on 25 acres of beach, and has saltwater and freshwater swimming pools, as well as a fishing pier. Most of the hotel's 114 rooms have a kitchen.

Inexpensive

There are not many cheap hotels in the Keys, especially the nearer one gets to Key West, but in Key Largo there is the charming **Rock Reef Resort,** which offers efficiency cottages and one- or two-bedroom suites, on Route 1 at MM 98, ((305) 852-2401.

Expensive

There is a natural ambience at **The Quay**, Route 1, MM 102, Key Largo, ((305) 451-0943, which overlooks the Gulf and features alligator meat sauteed in garlic-lemon butter. Such is the reputation of **Marker 88** that you should book well in advance if you are to have any hope of getting a table. The reputation is well-deserved, and the address is predictable: MM 88, Route 1, Plantation Key, ((305) 852-9315. Atop the Holiday Isle Resort in Islamorada at MM 84 is the **Horizon Restaurant**, with wonderful views over the ocean, and in the Cheeca Lodge Hotel at MM 82 there is the **Atlantic Edge** restaurant, ((305) 664-4651, where George Bush once had a meal and said it was real swell.

Moderate

The very popular **Ziggy's Conch Restaurant**, Route 1, MM 33, Islamorada, ((305) 664-4590, offers some of the best seafood in the Keys. Some of the rest of the best is available at the **Italian Fisherman**, Route 1, MM 104, Key Largo, ((305) 451-4471, where you should definitely try the *linguini mareciaro* — clams, scallops, and shrimps in a garlic butter sauce and served with linguini. Steaks and excellent prime rib are on offer along with the seafood at the **Green Turtle Inn Restaurant**, Route 1, MM 81.5, Islamorada, ((305) 394-6248. The two-level **Coral Grill**, Route 1, MM 83.5, Islamorada, ((305) 664-4803, has a gourmet buffet upstairs and a seafood-soup-and-salad bar downstairs.

Inexpensive

It doesn't specialize in seafood and it's not elegant, but it's still worth a visit: **Mrs Mac's Kitchen** at MM 99.5 in Key Largo has good steaks, sandwiches, homemade soups, and a wide selection of beers. In Islamorada there are two places you might want to check out: **Lor-e-lei on the Gulf** at MM 82, ((305) 664-4657, which overlooks a small harbor and specializes in lamb and ribs, and **Papa Joe's** at MM 80, ((305) 664-8109, where the seafood is Italianate.

HOW TO GET THERE

Some national airlines have regular flights out of Miami International Airport into Marathon Regional Airport, which is about 20 miles (32 km) southwest of Long Key. Most people, however, drive from Miami down Route 1.

GRASSY KEY TO STOCK ISLAND

The islands between Grassy Key and Stock Island constitute the chain known as the Middle and Lower Keys (Key West is considered as being distinct from the other Keys). The population centers here are Marathon in the Middle Keys and Big Pine in the Lower Keys. Marathon, on Vaca Key, is a resort and fishing center, and the start of the Seven Mile Bridge, the country's longest, which reaches all the way to Sunshine Key,

next to Bahia Honda Key. Bahia Honda has some of the best beaches between Key Largo and Key West.

The vegetation is more lush in the Lower Keys, due to the slightly warmer, slightly more tropical climate, but the activities are the same as anywhere else in the Keys: water sports, fishing, beachcombing, swimming. On Big Pine Key, and the surrounding islands, you can see a unique and wonderful sight: the tiny, endangered Key deer, which you are frequently reminded by road signs to watch out for. From Big Pine Key the highway passes over various wild-looking

OPPOSITE: The southernmost house in the United States. ABOVE: A typical old Key West residence.

Keys with wide expanses of beach. Roadside motels, resorts, and restaurants begin to increase in number as you approach Key West.

GENERAL INFORMATION

The Greater Marathon Chamber of Commerce is at 3300 Overseas Highway, Marathon, ((305) 743-5417, and the Lower Keys Chamber of Commerce is in Big Pine, ((305) 872-2411.

WHAT TO SEE AND DO

Sights

Grassy Key is the home of the **Dolphin Research Center**, Route 1, MM 59, ((305) 289-1121, which — I am not joking — rehabilitates show dolphins suffering from stress-related conditions brought on by overwork, pressure to perform, and cramped pools. You can swim with one of these sweet, long-suffering creatures if you like. In the town of Marathon is the 63-acre **Crane Point Hammock** on Route 1, MM 50, ((305) 743-3900, an important nature reserve with exotic plants, trees, mangroves, and hardwoods. There are also archaeological sites and renovated conch-style houses in its grounds.

The **Seven Mile Bridge** between Vaca Key and Sunshine Key is a wonder to behold, as indeed is the vastness of the seas to either side of it.

On Bahia Honda Key at the **Bahia Honda State Park**, MM 37, you can find white sand beaches, tropical plants and birds, a nature trail, picnic areas, and a marina. Big Pine Key — which is covered in pines and cacti — contains the **National Key Deer Refuge**. In 1954 there were only 50 deer left, but protection and careful management of the park have enabled their numbers to reach something approaching 400, despite well-meaning tourists feeding them often-lethal snacks. (If you see a deer, *please* don't feed it *anything*: if you do the deer might die and you might be caught and heavily fined.)

Guided canoe tours of the Big Pine Key region run from **Canoeing Nature Tour** at MM 29, ((305) 872-2620. The final sight before Key West is the **Perky Bat Tower** at

MM 17, built in 1929 by one Richard C. Perky as a residence for the bats he brought in to decimate the swarms of mosquitoes plaguing his resort. The bats, alas, didn't take to their new accommodation, leaving the tower to stand as an amusing folly.

Sports

You can go on **fishing** trips out of Marathon from The World Class Angler at the Faro Blanco Resort, MM 48.5, ((305) 743-6139, and in the Lower Keys out of Big Pine from Fantasy Charters at MM 28, ((305) 872-3200. For offshore trips, instruction, and rental of **diving** equipment, go to Seaview Ocean Divers, MM 50.5, ((305) 743-8514, in Marathon, and Cudjoe Gardens Marina and Dive Shop, MM 21, ((305) 745-2357, in the

Lower Keys. You can rent boats in Marathon at Clyde's Seven Mile Marina, MM 47.5, ((305) 743-7712, and in the Lower Keys at Dolphin Marina on Little Torch Key at MM 28.5, ((305) 872-2685.

Sailing enthusiasts can rent a yacht from Sailmaster Charters at 1000 15th Street, Boot Key Marina, ((305) 743-4200, in Marathon, and from Amantha at the Faro Blanco Resort, MM 48.5, ((305) 743-9020, in the Lower Keys. The Key Colony Beach in Marathon, ((305) 289-0821, has a **golf** course and **tennis** courts open to the public.

Shopping

The only choice of shops in the Middle and Lower Keys is in Marathon, which has several shopping malls, and a selection of shops selling gifts, souvenirs, sportswear, and swimwear.

Nightlife

In the Middle Keys you might want to sample the atmosphere at **The Ship's Pub**, MM 61 on Duck Key, ((305) 743-7000, which has live bands and a dance floor. At 19 Sombrero Boulevard, ((305) 743-4108, in Marathon is **Good Times**, which features live music and even livelier cocktails. Rock bands perform at the **Looe Key Reef Resort** at MM 27.5, ((305) 872-2215 on Ramrod Key. At the **No Name Pub** on Big Pine Key at the north end of Watson Boulevard, ((305) 872-9115, you can play darts and pool, hear

Enjoying the fruits of the sea.

live bands, eat hearty pub grub, and choose from over 70 beers.

WHERE TO STAY

Luxury
Occupying its own 60-acre island, the **Hawk's Cay Resort** at MM 61 in Marathon, ((305) 743-7000, toll-free (800) 327-7775, is in a tropical setting which is cleverly echoed in the decor and furnishings of the rooms and suites. The resort has its own Atlantic lagoon, with beach, where you can swim or wind-

surf or take your boat out to sea. Tennis courts and a golf course are also in the grounds. At The Buccaneer, MM 48.5, Marathon, ((305) 743-9071, toll-free (800) 237-3329, there are rooms, cottages, and villas — not to mention the marina with windsurf boards, powerboats, yachts, and charter boats.

On Key Colony Beach at 351 Ocean Drive East, ((305) 289-0525, is the **Ocean Beach Club**, with its own beach, a swimming pool, and efficiency apartments. One of the most pleasant residences in the Lower Keys is the **Little Palm Island** at MM 28.5 on Little Torch Key, ((305) 872-2524, which has 14 two-suite villas in beautiful grounds, plus a full range of water sports facilities.

Mid-range
In Marathon there is the moderately-priced **Hopp-Inn Guest House** at 5 Man o' War Drive, ((305) 743-4118, which is family-run and very comfortable. The **Conch Key Cottages** off Route 1 at MM 62.5, ((305) 289-1377, occupy their own lovely island, which is reached by a causeway. The delightful wooden cottages are fully-fitted and are near a small private beach.

Inexpensive
There are 12 rooms, some of them efficiencies, at the **Valhalla Beach Motel**, which is by the ocean in Marathon at MM 56.5, ((305) 289-0616. On Ramrod Key in the Lower Keys, the **Looe Key Reef Resort** at MM 27.5, ((305) 872-2215, runs diving and charter trips to the distant Tortugas Islands out of its own dock. Further southwest on Sugarloaf Key, the **Sugarloaf Lodge** at MM 17, ((305) 745-3211, has a marina and swimming pool.

WHERE TO EAT

Expensive
Overlooking a marina, **Kelsey's** is the restaurant of the Faro Blanco Resort at MM 48.5, ((305) 743-9018, and offers some wonderful seafood dishes. **Chef's** at the Sombrero Resort, 19 Sombrero Boulevard, Marathon, ((305) 743-4108, is as unpretentious as its name, and as good. A boat will take you from MM 28.5 on Little Torch Key to the **Little Palm Island** restaurant, ((305) 872-2524, where the gorgeous seafood is only an accompaniment to the gorgeous before- and after-dinner drinks on the beach.

Moderate
The **Little Bavaria** in the Gulfside Village Shopping Center, MM 50, ((305) 743-4833, serves up your basic wienerschnitzel and some interesting Hungarian variations. **Bacchus by the Sea** at 725 11th Street in Marathon, ((305) 743-6106, is more seaside than Bacchanalian, but still good; while **Monte's Restaurant and Fish Market** at MM 25 on Summerland Key, ((305) 745-3731, has lovely conch chowders and fritters. And then there's **Cousin Joe's Supper Bar**, which

is good for Caribbean food on Drost Drive off Route 1 at MM 21, ((305) 745-1646.

Inexpensive
The intimate **Grassy Key Dairy Bar** at MM 58.5, ((305) 743-3816, has a different menu — Italian, Mexican, etc. — every night. Seafood and salads are predictably popular at **Shuckers Raw Bar & Grill,** 1415 15th Street, Marathon, ((305) 743-8686. On Big Pine Key there are two good budget restaurants: **Island Jim's at MM 31.5,** ((305) 872-2017, which specializes in steaks and prime

Only genuine Conchs are permitted to call themselves Conchs, although if you live there for seven years you can become an honorary "freshwater Conch".

The original Conchs came to the island from the Bahamas late in the eighteenth century. It became a part of the future state of Florida in 1822 when one of the settlers, John Simonton, bought it in a Cuban bar for $2,000. Also around this time a U.S. Navy commodore named David Porter cleared the Keys of all the pirates, enabling the settlers to establish their own form of *ex*

ribs, and **Dr. Feelgood's BBQ** at MM 31, ((305) 872-4752.

KEY WEST

Key West, the southernmost city in the United States, has a permanent population of 24,000 on a sub-tropical island four miles (6½ km) long and two miles (3.2 km) wide. The inhabitants are a mixed bunch: retired military personnel and their families, a black community whose ancestors originally came from the West Indies, writers, artists, Cuban exiles — and the Conchs (pronounced "konks") who are the descendants of the island's original settlers.

post facto piracy: shipwreck-plundering, or "wrecking". So profitable was wrecking that by 1830 the Conchs of Key West could claim the highest per-capita income in the country. By 1850 the Conch community (pop. 600) was earning a million dollars a year from wrecking. Then came a cigar-making factory set up by Cuban immigrants, and then a U.S. naval station. By 1880 Key West had a populatio of 10,000 and was the biggest city in the state.

But the cigar business packed up and moved to Tampa, which together with the Depression meant that by 1934 80 percent

OPPOSITE: One form of transport in Key West.
ABOVE: Another form — the Conch Tour Train.

of Key West's inhabitants were on welfare. Economic aid from the state eventually bailed the city out and enabled it to survive even the hurricane that destroyed Flagler's railway. And when the Ocean Highway reached the Keys, so did the tourists.

GENERAL INFORMATION

The Greater Key West Chamber of Commerce is at 402 Wall Street, Key West FL 33040. ((305) 294-2587. The Florida Keys Visitors Bureau, which covers all the

Keys, is at 416 Fleming Street, Key West FL 33040. Toll-free ((800) FLA-KEYS. *Key West* magazine will give you comprehensive information on local events and attractions.

WHAT TO SEE AND DO

Sights

A good way to see Key West and a lot of the sights is to take a ride on the **Conch Tour Train**, which has boarding points at Mallory Square, Roosevelt Avenue, and Duval and Angela Streets. It runs at regular intervals from 9 am to 4 pm daily. On the tour you will pass through the restored Old Town centered around **Duval Street**, which is lined with Spanish, Southern, and old Conch buildings (including the city's oldest house), and several old bars, among them **Sloppy Joe's**, where Hemingway used to drink and, occasionally, write.

Hemingway's House at 907 Whitehead Street, ((305) 294-1575, is where the great man lived and worked during the 1930s.

Here he wrote, among other works, *The Green Hills of Africa* and *To Have and Have Not*. You can see some of Hemingway's possessions in the study where he wrote, which is open from 9 am to 5 pm daily, for $6 adults and $2 children. **Tennessee Williams' House** is not open to the public, but you can see the outside of it at 1431 Duncan Street. Another of Key West's famous citizens was the painter and naturalist John James Audubon, who painted the local birdlife and also made engravings and prints; many of his works are on display in the **Audubon House** at 205 Whitehead Street, ((305) 294-2116. The house is open from 9:30 am to 5 pm daily, and admission is $5 for adults and $2 for children.

The world's largest display of treasure recovered from shipwrecks is at the **Mel Fisher Museum** (named after the man who found the wreck of the *Atocha*, a seventeenth-century Spanish ship which carried treasure with a modern value of $400 million). The ship's gold and silver bullion, coins, diamonds, and precious stones are on display in the museum at 200 Greene Street, ((305) 294-2633. It's open from 9:30 am to 5 pm, and admission is $5 for adults and $1 for children.

At **The Wrecker's Museum**, 322 Duval Street, ((305) 294-9502, you can learn all about the city's earliest industry. There are model ships and sundry maritime artifacts on display at the **Key West Lighthouse Museum**, 938 Whitehead Street, ((305) 294-0012, as well as such military peculiarities as a two-man Japanese submarine captured at Pearl Harbor. The view from the top of the lighthouse alone is worth the $2.50 entrance charge (50 cents for children). It is open from 9:30 am to 5 pm.

For more military history, go to the **Fort Zachary Taylor State Historic Site** at the western end of Southard Street, ((305) 292-6713. This museum has much historic weaponry, including the nation's largest collection of Civil War cannon. Here you can also learn the story of the fort, which was occupied by Union troops during the Civil War and re-armed in 1898 for the Spanish-American War. The park around the fort has picnic sites and one of the finest beaches on the island.

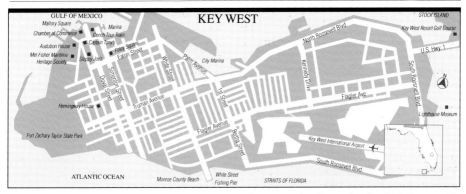

If you are feeling adventurous, you should go to Key West Seaplane Service at 5603 West Junior College Road, ((305) 294-6978, and arrange to fly the 68 miles (109 km) west to the **Fort Jefferson National Monument** in the Dry Tortugas, a group of small coral islands. The plane passes over the Marquesas Keys atoll and a number of coral reefs, sandbars, and shipwrecks before landing at the Dry Tortugas, where you can explore both the fort and the island.

Sports

For **fishing** trips out of Key West to both Gulf and Atlantic waters, or to the Dry Tortugas, try the Garrison Bight Marina at 711 Eisenhower Drive, ((305) 294-3093, or Sea Breeze Charters at 25 Arbutus Drive, ((305) 294-6027. **Scuba diving** and **snorkeling** trips and lessons can be arranged and equipment rented at the Key West Pro Dive Shop, 1605 North Roosevelt Boulevard, ((305) 296-3823, and at the Reef Riders Dive Shop, 109 Duval Street, ((305) 294-3635. **Boating** enthusiasts should point themselves at Key West Boat Rentals, 617 Front Street, ((305) 294-2628.

There is a **golf** course on Stock Island at the Key West Resort, ((305) 294-5232, and there are public **tennis** courts at Island City Tennis on Truman Avenue, ((305) 294-1346.

Shopping

Most of the shopping in Key West is done in the Old Town area around Duval Street, where you will find numerous souvenir and gift shops, boutiques, designer outlets, and artsy-craftsy shops. For the best selection of merchandise under one roof, go to Fast Buck Freddies at 500 Duval Street. There are also several galleries in the Old Town with quite decent works by resident and visiting artists.

Nightlife

Key West offers the most colorful and varied nightlife in the Keys. You mustn't miss, for example, **Sloppy Joe's** at 201 Duval Street, ((305) 294-8585, Hemingway's favorite watering hole. On the wall there is a sailfish that Hemingway is reputed to have caught. Short drinks and tall stories still abound here, as well as live rhythm and blues bands. Another Key West landmark is **Captain Tony's Saloon** at 428 Greene Street, ((305) 294-1838, where many of the town's bohemian characters hang out. Those who prefer to dance the night away to disco music have a good choice of venues, such as **The Copa** at 623 Duval Street, ((305) 296-8521, the **Havana Docks Bar** at Pier House, 1 Duval Street, ((305) 294-9541, and **Delmonico's** at 218 Duval Street, ((305) 294-4383, all in the Old Town district.

For a dinner-and-cabaret evening go to **Jan McArts Cabaret Theatre** at 410 Wall Street, ((305) 296-2120. The **Tennessee Williams Fine Arts Center** at 5901 Junior College Road, ((305) 294-6232, presents concerts, plays, and dance all year round. For one of the most enchanting and romantic experiences of your life go to Mallory Square at the northwest end of Duval Street and join the people who are watching the sun set into the Gulf while local musicians play gentle folk music.

OPPOSITE: A seaside bar at Key West provides plenty of maritime atmosphere.

WHERE TO STAY

Luxury

Among the destinations for travelers on Flagler's railway was the **Casa Marina Resort** at 1500 Reynolds Street, ((305) 296-3535, toll-free (800) 626-0777, which is still one of the city's most elegant hotels. It has its own beach with extensive water sports facilities, lighted tennis courts, a swimming pool, and a fishing pier.

There are some exceptional old Victorian

guest houses in Key West, including **Eaton Lodge** at 511 Eaton Street, ((305) 294-3800, where every room has a balcony overlooking a central tropical garden. Another fine guest house, with rooms facing the ocean, is **La Mer Hotel** at 506 South Street, ((305) 296-6577. At the edge of the Old Town at 901 Front Street, ((305) 296-9900, toll-free (800) 228-9000, you can find the **Hyatt Key West**, which has a beach, a marina, a swimming pool, jacuzzis, and an exercise room among its amenities, as well as rooms offering magnificent views of Key West's famous sunsets.

Mid-range

The **South Beach Motel**, with a small pier

for swimming and fishing, in addition to its bright and neatly furnished rooms, is at 500 South Street, ((305) 296-5611. At the 130-year-old **Duval House**, the 22 antique-furnished rooms surround a garden and swimming pool in the heart of the Old Town at 815 Duval Street, ((305) 294-1666. Another small and friendly guest house, **Eden House** at 1015 Fleming Street, ((305) 296-6868, has Twenties decor and furnishing, efficiency rooms, and a swimming pool. The amenities at the **Best Western Key Ambassador**, 1000 South Roosevelt Boulevard, include a pool with a bar, a fitness center, and shuffleboard courts.

Inexpensive

On Simonton Street there is the **Santa Maria** at N° 1401, ((305) 296-5678, and the **Hibiscus** at N° 1313, ((305) 296-6711, both of which are very comfortable. Also good value is the **Atlantic Shores** at 510 South Street, ((305) 296-2491, which has its own pier and swimming pool. There are some budget-priced rooms at the **Inn at the Wharf**, 2400 North Roosevelt Boulevard, ((305) 296-5700, which has a swimming pool with a bar.

For complete information on accommodation in Key West, get in touch with the Key West Chamber of Commerce, which will be happy to supply you with a guide to hotels and guest houses, or the Key West Reservation Service at 628 Fleming Street, ((305) 294-7713.

WHERE TO EAT

Expensive

Louie's Backyard at 700 Wadell Street, ((305) 294-1061, is a Revival Conch House listed in the National Register of Historic Places. Chef Norman Van Aken's fascinating menu features barbecued duck with Oriental noodles and Sichuan dressing, and Dijon-crusted rack of lamb with rosemary and roast garlic. It's probably the best restaurant in town. A close competitor is **Henry's** in the Casa Marina Resort at 1500 Reynolds Street, ((305) 296-3535, where you can get the best Cajun cooking in the Keys. There's a lovely veranda with hanging vines and banyan trees where you can enjoy the most wonderful American cooking at the **Pigeon House Patio**, 301 Whitehead Street, ((305) 296-9600. The **Café des Artistes** at 1007 Simonton Street, ((305) 294-7100, specializes in Provençal cooking and spicy Haitian food.

Moderate

Lovers of sushi, sashimi, teriyaki, sukiyaki, and other Japanese delights should try **Kyushu** at 921 Truman Street, ((305) 294-2995. You can eat outside under a straw roof or in a traditional tatami dining room. **La-**

294-7677, specializes in very reasonably priced French food. If you prefer Mexican, **El Loro Verde** serves the usual burritos, tacos, tostadas, and salsas, as well as the odd Bahamian dish, at 404 Southard Street, ((305) 296-7298. All the Cuban food served at **El Siboney**, 900 Catherine Street, ((305) 294-2721, comes with black beans, rice, and plantain or yucca. At the pleasantly bohemian **Full Moon Saloon** 1202 Simonton Street, ((305) 294-9090, the last orders (usually for conch or smoked fish) are taken around 3 am.

Te-Da is the restaurant in the La Terrazza de Marti Hotel at 1125 Duval Street, ((305) 294-8435, and offers mostly Continental cuisine. **Antonia's** at 615 Duval Street, ((305) 294-6565, has masterfully prepared northern Italian food, and cleverly offers half-servings of various pasta dishes. **The Bagatelle** is in a restored Conch house at 115 Duval Street, ((305) 294-7195, and serves a mixture of local seafood and more exotic Bahamian cooking. For good old southern-fried cooking go to **Pepe's Café** down near the old waterfront at 806 Caroline Street, ((305) 294-7192.

Inexpensive

La Crêperie at 124 Duval Street, ((305)

HOW TO GET THERE

Piedmont, Eastern, and Delta Airlines have regular flights to Key West. Motorists will take Route 1, which ends at the Key West Lighthouse. If you get this far, you have gone as far south as it is possible to go in the continental United States.

OPPOSITE: Self-captioning landmark in Key West. ABOVE: A watering hole near the water. OVERLEAF: The harbor at Key West.

Travelers'
Tips

THE best tip of all: Find a good travel agent. How? Ask the same questions of several different agents — questions that can't be answered out of a brochure. You can answer those questions yourself. The point of the exercise is not to find a travel agent who has all the answers — nobody does — but to find one who is willing to take the time and trouble to get the answers for you.

GETTING THERE

By Air

All major cities in Florida are served daily (often many times daily) by airlines from all corners of the U.S. Likewise, many international airlines have regularly-scheduled flights to Florida. These include, from Europe, British Airways, Pan Am, Continental, Virgin Atlantic, Lufthansa, Delta, KLM, Air France, and Icelandair. In addition, charter flights are available from Britain through Virgin Atlantic, Novair, Airtours, Intasun, and Thomson; from Germany through Condor and LTU; from Holland through Martinair; from Scandinavia through Sterling Air and Tower Air; from Switzerland through Balair.

There are, too, an infinite variety of special discount fares and package deals. Every airline has at least one, as does American Express and other travel companies. In London, The American Dream (℄ 081/470-1181) will create a package specifically to suite your requirements.

By Rail

Not to be outdone by the airlines, Amtrak now offers a variety of special fares (and much improved food and service) to try to bring more Florida-bound travelers back to earth. In particular, ask your travel agent about the "All Aboard America" fares. If you are coming from overseas, ask about the USA Railpass, which allows unlimited train travel for varying periods of time. Information about timetables and special fares, including tour packages, is available directly from Amtrak, P.O. Box 311, Addison, Illinois 60101. Toll-free ℄ (800) USA-RAIL.

By Bus

The two main American coach companies, Greyhound and Trailways, both now offer special cut-rate fares to Florida from all over the U.S. Greyhound's "Moneysaver" tickets, bookable 30 days in advance, are an especially good bargain.

By Car

Living as they do in a car-oriented, highway-blessed society, Americans do not need to be told of the pleasures or advantages of motoring. But visitors from abroad may be surprised to learn that these pleasures are not only available but extremely affordable

as well. This is due to the recent and rapidly growing phenomenon of "Driveaway" companies acting on behalf of clients who are in a hurry to get to Florida and who would like their cars to join them there later.

This means that there are companies in New York and elsewhere in the U.S. who are eager not to rent you a car but to *give* you a car (and free insurance and a free tank of gasoline!) so long as you deliver it to the car's owner in Florida within an agreed period of time. I have spoken to several people who took driveaway cars to Florida and they were unanimous in their opinion that this is the most delightful as well as economical way to get there from other parts of America. Of the driveaway companies in New York I would recommend All America

Transport (℄ 212/766-0700), Dependable Transport (℄ 212/840-6262), Transporters Inc. (℄ 212/594-2690), and Boutell Driveaway (℄ 212/227-1230).

TOURIST INFORMATION

All you need do to find yourself caught in a blizzard of facts and figures, maps and pictures, brochures and pamphlets, is to contact one of the following:
Florida Division of Tourism
126 West Van Buren Street
Tallahassee FL 32399-2000
℄ (904) 487-1462

The seaside at Seaside, Florida.

Florida Chamber of Commerce
P.O. Box 11309
Tallahassee FL 32302
((904) 222-2831

Florida Department of Natural Resources
Division of Recreation and Parks
3900 Commonwealth Boulevard
Tallahassee FL 32303
((904) 488-7326

Florida Attractions Association
P.O. Box 833
Silver Springs FL 32688
((904) 694-5444

Florida Tourist Information Center
2801 East Oakland Park
Fort Lauderdale FL 33306
((305) 566-0700

In Europe
U.S. Travel and Tourism Administration
22 Sackville Street
London W1X 2EA
((071) 439-7433

Florida Division of Tourism
18–24 Westbourne Grove
London W2 5RH
((0171) 727-1661   0891~600555

And this is not to mention the 200 or so Chambers of Commerce scattered around the state, each one of which will be more than happy to answer any queries or supply any information about the area in which it is located. There are also many tourist bureaus and information agencies designed to deal with specific enquiries; these you will find listed on the following pages under the appropriate categories.

CONSULATES

IN FLORIDA

BRITISH
Suite 2110
Brickell Bay Office Tower
1001 South Bayshore Drive
Miami FL 33131
((305) 374-1522

IN NEW YORK

AUSTRALIAN
636 Fifth Avenue
New York, NY
((212) 245-4000
CANADIAN
1251 Avenue of the Americas
New York NY
((212) 586-2400
IRISH
515 Madison Avenue
New York, NY
((212) 319-2555

TRAVEL DOCUMENTS

Canadians need only proof that they are Canadian: British need only a valid passport. Everybody else had better check with a travel agent, as the requirements are constantly changing (and usually for the better).

CUSTOMS

You may bring in, duty-free, 200 cigarettes or 50 cigars or three pounds of tobacco. I should add, however, that you would be stark raving mad to bring tobacco (especially cigars) into a state where you can buy all kinds of excellent tobacco products for a fraction of their price in the duty-free shops of the world's airports. The same goes for alcohol: you can bring in one U.S. quart, but it would be wiser and more economical to buy it when you get there. You may also bring in gifts up to $100 in value.

WHEN TO GO

Most people, like most birds, tend to flock to Florida in the winter. In the coldest month, January, the average daytime temperatures in the southern part of the state are 74°F (23°C) on land and 72°F (22°C) in the water. It is cooler, of course, in the evenings, but pleasantly so.

The summers are hot — but not *that* hot; it seldom gets over 90°F (32°C). It's the humidity that's bothersome, although the late afternoon showers tend to wring the moisture out the air. And the ubiquitous air conditioning blow-dries as it cools the air indoors.

As with most places in these latitudes, spring and autumn are the most agreeable times to visit.

WHAT TO TAKE

As always, the oldest advice is the best: take

GETTING AROUND

The only way to get around Florida is by car. For one thing, Florida is the cheapest place in the world to rent a car. All the major car rental firms (Hertz, Avis, Budget, *et al*) offer special deals, and the others don't need to. For another thing, fuel is astonishingly cheap by European standards. And lastly, of course, American roads and highways are a motorist's dream.

If you prefer to travel by train, Amtrak

half the clothes and twice the money you think you will need. This applies especially in Florida's case because everything you could possibly need or want is available there, at prices — here's the good news — that are much cheaper than you might expect.

Having said that, let me list a few of the things I personally would never travel without: a Swiss Army knife, nail clippers, tissues, plastic knife, fork and spoon, a plastic beaker, toothpicks, "wet wipes", sewing kit, eyedrops, aspirin, glue, antiseptic ointment, insect repellent, batteries for whatever battery-powered objects you take with you, and a flask for non-battery-powered situations. If you have sensitive skin, you might want to add a sunscreen.

serves 22 cities in the state. Your travel agent will have the details, or you can phone Amtrak General Information and Reservations toll-free (800) 872-7245. Greyhound and Trailways have buses going to every nook and cranny of the state, and Greyhound also has several package tours. For details write to Greyhound, 901 Main Street, Dallas, TX 75202.

For air travel within Florida, ask your travel agent about the specially-priced Visit USA tickets available and the many domestic shuttle flights between cities.

Pelicans waiting for a catch at Cedar Key on the Gulf Coast.

BASICS

The language spoken in Florida is English, right? Wrong, if you're in those parts of south Florida where Spanish (or, occasionally, Yiddish) is the *lingua franca*. And even the English that is spoken is very different from the British version; however, the differences are either so well-known or so easily decipherable (*e.g.*, "elevator" for "lift") that it would be a waste of time to catalogue them.

The electric current is 110-115 volts AC. Unless you buy your electrical appliances in America you will need an adaptor.

Except for the extreme western part of the Panhandle, Florida is on Eastern Standard Time, which is five hours behind Greenwich Mean Time (*i.e.*, when it is noon in London it is 7 am in Miami). If for some reason you feel the need to know the precise time, to the second, you can call (305) 324-8811.

HEALTH

The health care is excellent, as you would expect, but unbelievably expensive, so don't even *think* about going to Florida without some kind of short-term medical insurance. The best overseas insurer, in my opinion, is Europ Assistance Ltd., 252 High Street, Croydon, Surrey CR0 1NF, England, ((081) 680-1234, but your travel agent or private health insurance company will be able to advise you on the insurance you will need while visiting Florida.

The only other general advice I can offer is: don't underestimate the capacity of the local insects to ruin your holiday. Mosquitoes, ants (especially fire ants), flies (especially sand flies), and other tiny pests are abundant and obnoxiously happy to welcome you unless you have some kind of insect repellent with you.

MONEY

The old joke about the American tourist who asks, "How much is that in real money" is not so funny when a bank teller in America looks at your foreign currency as if it were a bank robber's note demanding cash. The dollar may have fallen on relatively hard times in recent years, but it is still the only currency that Americans understand and trust. Therefore you should only travel with dollars or travelers' checks in dollars. Also, in the land that invented plastic money, it's a very good idea to have a Visa Card or MasterCard or some other internationally recognized card with you. A *very* good idea, in fact, because many American firms prefer cards to cash — and some even insist on cards rather than cash.

ACCOMMODATION

The good news is that Florida has accommodation to suit every taste, every need, and every budget. The bad news is that it may already be taken unless you have booked well in advance.

The best news of all is that Florida has the most efficient system of matching visitors to their desired accommodation of any tourist destination in the world. If your travel agent can't find exactly what you want, try the

Florida Hotel/Motel Association, P.O. Box 1529, Tallahassee FL 32302. ((904) 224-2288. They will send you a free guide and any other specific information you may require. Or you can write to the local Chamber of Commerce in the area you intend to visit and they will happily circulate your request to all the hotels and motels and rental agencies in the area (but be prepared for an avalanche of letters and brochures in return).

If you are elderly and would prefer a package holiday that provides all of the fun

Youth Hostel Association, National Campus, Delaplane VA 22025.

EATING OUT

There are many fine restaurants in Florida featuring Continental cuisine, and indeed I have already recommended quite a few of them, but as a general rule, to enjoy the best meals in Florida you should stick to what is uniquely — or at least distinctively — Floridian.

without all of the hassle, you should write to Senior Vacation Hotels of Florida, 7401 Central Avenue, St. Petersburg FL 33710. ((813) 345-8123.

If you are traveling on a restricted budget I would suggest one of the chain motels — Days Inn, Motel 6, Best Western, TraveLodge, Econo Lodge, Scottish Inns, and Red Carpet Inns are the ones I have found to be the best value for money. If you are on very restricted budget, you can get a list of campsites from the Florida Department of Natural Resources, Bureau of Education and Information, 3900 Commonwealth Boulevard, Tallahassee Fl 32303. A list of youth hostels — you don't have to be a youth to stay in one — is available from the American

This means, among cuisines, you should sample the best of Old Southern, Cuban, and the Florida version of American cooking. Among the dishes from the Old South that you should try are southern fried chicken (of course), hush puppies (fried balls of cornmeal and onion), ham steak, stuffed turkey, catfish, grits (granulated white corn), rice with giblet gravy, okra, collard greens, black-eyed peas, cornbread, and pecan pie. The mainstays of Cuban cuisine are black beans and rice, fried plantains, paella, *arroz con pollo* (chicken with rice),

OPPOSITE: The Columbia restaurant in Tampa's Ybor City. ABOVE: The broadwalk at Madeira Beach.

picadillo (ground beef with olives and onions in a piquant sauce), and a scrumptious variety of pork dishes. For the best of American cooking, Florida-style, I would recommend the steaks (Florida ranks second in the nation behind Texas as a producer of beef), anything barbecued (particularly spare ribs), anything that calls itself a salad, any delicatessen sandwich, and — yes, I know it's heresy — the fare at fast-food restaurants. *Haute cuisine* it isn't, but for something quick, tasty, convenient, and inexpensive, you cannot beat the American fast food —

which is why it has colonized taste buds all over the world.

Florida's two great gastronomic glories are, of course, fish and fruit. Of its seafood specialties, easily the most famous are the stone crab claws. They come from the waters off the western side of the state, where the crab fishermen haul in the stone crabs, break off a large claw, and then — as required by law — throw the crab back into the sea, where it will grow another claw to replace the one you're eating. Stone crab claws are heavenly. Note, however, that during the closed season, mid-October to mid-May, there are only frozen ones available. Other seafood specialties include jumbo shrimp, oysters, crayfish (also known as "spiny lob-

ster" or "Florida lobster"), pompano, mullet, and grouper.

There is probably not much point in raving about Florida's fruit; after all, you have probably been eating it all your life, given that 70 percent of the world's grapefruit and 25 percent of the world's oranges come from Florida, not to mention the tangerines, lemons, limes, and other citrus fruits which Florida bestows on the world's dining tables. But it's better here because it's fresher here. And citrus is only half the story; the sub-tropical half includes the most delicious mangoes, papayas, carambolas, lychees, guavas, zapotes, and coconuts.

One further culinary delight deserves special mention: Key lime pie. This wonderful dessert is so sacred to Floridians that it is often the subject of almost theological debates: what sort of lime juice is best, to what temperature should the pie be chilled, should it be served with a meringue or should the eggs be beaten into the pie itself, etc. etc. Anyway, two things are certain — the pie should be made with Key limes (which are small and yellow, not green), and it should have a graham cracker crust.

Lastly, a couple of words about Florida restaurants. Except for the seriously upmarket eateries, restaurants in Florida tend to be very informal, and tend to open and close earlier (for all meals) than do restaurants in the rest of the world.

SHOPPING

My advice here is the same as my advice on eating out: look for what the natives do best, for what you can't get elsewhere. This means, if you are like me, you will come back with a whole suitcase stuffed with cigars and an innocent smile on your face as you pass through Customs. Florida, especially Tampa, is God's gift to budget-conscious cigar-lovers.

It is also God's gift to kitsch-lovers: if you like deliciously vulgar, outrageously colorful, unbelievably silly, totally useless things, you have come to the right place. Remember, only a relative handful of the pink flamingos in Florida exist outside the souvenir shops.

Of the items that you might want to bring back as gifts, the lightest and most beautiful are the seashells you can buy almost anywhere, but especially along the southwest coast. The heaviest and tastiest are the sacks and/or crates of Florida citrus, which any store will be happy to ship back home for you. Florida is also the place to buy any leisure wear that you might need for the beach, as well as any accessories such as suntan oil or beach towels, because the

fice, is available here, usually at a fraction of the prices these things sell for overseas. But do remember that American electrical items run on 110 volts, so if your home voltage is 220 volts, you will need an adaptor to make them work.

Finally, and unfashionably, I would like to put in a good word for the American shopping mall. If you want quality and value for money and convenience, plus a good return on your investment of time and effort, I would direct you to any of the thousands of shopping malls scattered around

competition to provide these things in a beach-fringed state is so intense that the prices are correspondingly low.

When it comes to things that are typically Floridian, aesthetically appealing, and attractively priced, your best bet is the range of handicrafts still produced by the Seminole Indians. These include colorful hand-sewn garments and wall hangings, leather goods, and turquoise jewelry.

The best bargains, however, if you are coming from outside the U.S., are indisputably to be found in the mouth-watering array of electronic gadgetry (well, it makes *my* mouth water). Everything you could possibly need — as well as everything you *couldn't* possibly need — for the home or of-

Florida. They are all — or almost all — open until 9 pm seven days a week, and all are worth a visit, regardless of what you are looking for.

TANNING

As the difference between a suntan and a sunburn can be the difference between a happy holiday and an unhappy one, it is well to remember that the Florida sun is very strong and should be not be

OPPOSITE: Cowboy boots for sale.
ABOVE: Fruit for sale beside the road in central Florida.

taken lightly if you want to go dark pleasantly. To begin with, in Noel Coward's memorable phrase, only mad dogs and Englishmen go out in the midday sun: from 11 am to 2 pm you are best advised to stay inside.

Secondly — and this is the hard part — you must wear a sunscreen, at least for the first few days, and you must be patient, increasing your exposure to the sun only gradually. Depending, of course, on the type of skin you have, you should only be out in the sun for half an hour (or less) the first few

TIPPING

Because a tip is an acknowledgement of a service rendered, the size of the tip depends ultimately on your opinion of the quality of the service. However, assuming that the service performed was at least adequate, and that no service charge has already been included in your bill (which it only rarely is in Florida), you should tip about 15 percent in restaurants and for room service. Porters and doormen who help with your bags

days, slowly increasing your exposure time to a couple of hours by the end of the first week. After that you should be ready for some serious sunbathing.

Another point to bear in mind is that some parts of the body are more sensitive to the sun's rays than others. Your nose, knees, and the tops of your feet should be particularly well protected by sun lotion, and your eyes should be protected by proper sunglasses. By "proper" sunglasses I mean ones that are UV-coated to keep out the harmful ultraviolet rays, and preferably also have Polarized filters if you plan to spend much time on the water, where your eyes are vulnerable to the reflected light.

should get 50 cents to a dollar per bag, depending on the size and weight; taxi drivers will expect a tip of 10 to 15 percent; and chambermaids should be tipped about $10 a week, or more for specially attentive service.

DRIVING

The most frustrating thing — in fact, about the *only* frustrating thing — about driving in Florida, or in the United States generally, is that the nation with the best roads in the world has the lowest speed limits in the world: 55 mph (88 kph) on highways and 20-40 mph (32-64 kph) in cities and residential areas. Obey the signs, for the speed limits are strictly enforced.

It is legal to turn right at red rights in Florida, provided that you come to a full stop first and there is no sign prohibiting a right turn. Two other laws with which visitors may not be familiar require all drivers to carry proof of personal injury insurance coverage, and all drivers must secure children five years old and younger in safety belts or child restraint seats.

For more detailed information contact the Florida Highway Safety and Motor Vehicles Department, Neil Kirkman Building, Tallahassee FL 32399, ((904) 488-3144. For help or travel information while on the road call the American Automobile Association, ((305) 573-6911.

Of the sights you can expect to see while motoring, perhaps the most remarkable are to be seen on the roads themselves, for Florida probably has more "customized" cars than any other state except California. The funniest one I saw when I was there was a yellow Volkswagen beetle with mouse ears, nose and tail. You also see a lot of amusing personalized license plates. My favorite: L8 4 WORK.

CAMPING

There are more than three dozen state parks in Florida, as well as campsites for recreational vehicles and wilderness areas, all of which provide camping facilities. Two essential guides, the *Florida State Parks Guide* and the *Florida State Parks Camping Reservation Procedures*, are available from the Florida Department of Natural Resources, Bureau of Education and Information, 3900 Commonwealth Boulevard, Tallahassee FL 32399. ((904) 488-7326. In addition, there is the valuable *Florida Camping Directory* published by the Florida Campground Association, 1638 North Plaza Drive, Tallahassee FL 32308. ((904) 656-8878.

You can expect to pay about $6 a night (slightly more in the Keys) for a campsite in a state park, and the maximum permitted stay is two weeks. You can reserve a site up to two months in advance by calling the park where you would like to camp. You will pay an extra $2 for electricity and $2 more for a second car on your site.

TENNIS

If Florida had an official state sport, it would undoubtedly be tennis. It is no accident that the queen of American tennis, Chris Evert, and the new crown princess, Jennifer Capriati, are both products of Florida tennis courts.

These courts — both public and private — are everywhere, including at all the larger hotels. The local recreation department can give you details of all the courts in the area you are visiting, or you can contact the Florida Tennis Association, 9620 Northeast Second Avenue, Room 200, Miami Shores FL 33138. ((305) 757-8568.

GOLF

Golf is a close second to tennis as the most popular pastime in Florida. Accordingly, the acreage given over to golf courses would be sufficient to accommodate your average banana republic. Not only are there splendid public courses in every corner of the state, especially near the more popular resort areas, but most of the private courses admit visitors for a nominal fee. Again, the local recreation department can provide you with a list of the courses in your area. Alternatively, you can get in touch with the Florida State Golf Association, P.O. Box 21177, Sarasota FL 33585. ((813) 921-5695.

If your interest in golf is purely spectatorial, you should plan on visiting Florida in February, March, or October, for those are the months in which the major PGA tournaments are held. In February the Doral Eastern Open is held in Miami, in March the Tournament Players Championship is held in Jacksonville, and in October you have both the Pensacola PGA Open and the Walt Disney World National Team Championship Golf Classic.

Florida's golf courses are among the most beautiful in the world.

FISHING

With 8,000 miles of tidal coastline, 30,000 lakes, and countless rivers and streams, it is hardly surprising that Florida is a fisherman's paradise. You will need a non-resident's license for freshwater fishing — which cost $10 for 10 days and $25 for a year — but no license is required for saltwater fishing. Licenses can be bought from any marina or tackle shop.

There are more than 600 different spe-

Branyon: *Florida Freshwater Fishing Guide* and *Florida Saltwater Fishing Guide*. They are available from P.O. Box 6512, Surfside FL 33154. Both cost $9.95, including postage and handling, in the United States; overseas readers should enquire before ordering.

CRUISES

There are so many ocean cruises from Florida ports that the peninsula could almost be considered one giant dock. There

cies of saltwater fish off the Florida coast, and there are almost as many species of boats for charter in every port to take you out to fish for them. For landlubbers, there are many public fishing piers from which one can fish in the ocean without going *deep* sea fishing. And for those fishermen who are not particularly good at sitting and waiting, there are ample opportunities for shellfishing among Florida's offshore population of crabs, scallops, and lobsters.

For a complete guide to fishing in Florida, write to the Florida Game and Freshwater Fish Commission, Farris Bryant Building, Tallahassee FL 32399. ((904) 488-1960. The *Orlando Sentinel* also publishes two excellent books by its fishing correspondent, Max

are morning cruises and afternoon cruises, sunlight and starlight cruises, half-day and one-day cruises, two-day and two-night cruises, week-long and longer cruises, cruises to the Bahamas and the Virgin Islands, to the West Indies and Mexico, even through the Panama Canal to Los Angeles and San Francisco.

Likewise, there are so many cruise lines operating out of so many port cities and catering for so many different tastes that it would be pointless to try to list them all. The one offering the most cruises, out of the most ports, is SeaEscape Ltd., 1080 Port Boulevard, Miami FL 33132. ((305) 379-0000. If they can't provide what you want, your travel agent can.

PUBLIC HOLIDAYS & FESTIVALS

Holidays

New Year's Day: January 1
Martin Luther King, Jr. Day: January 15
President's Day: February 20
Good Friday
Easter
Passover
Memorial Day: Last Monday in May
Independence Day: July 4
Labor Day: First Monday in September

FEBRUARY
Big Orange Music Festival in Miami
Coconut Grove Arts Festival
Miami International Boat Show in Miami Beach
Miami Grand Prix
Daytona 500 stock car race
Mardi Gras festivals in Orlando and Pensacola
Florida Derby festival in Hallandale
Old Island Days in Key West

MARCH
Carnival Miami

Rosh Hashanah
Yom Kippur
Columbus Day: Second Monday in October
Veterans' Day: November 11
Thanksgiving Day: Fourth Thursday in November
Christmas Day: December 25

Festivals

JANUARY
Polo season opens
Heritage Classic and Antique Automobile Show in Daytona Beach
Art Deco Weekend Festival in Miami Beach

Greek Festival in Tarpon Springs

Kissimmee Bluegrass Festival
Orange Blossom Festival in Davie
Sanibel Shell Fair on Sanibel Island
Arcadia All-Florida Championship Rodeo
Festival of Flowers in Boca Raton

APRIL
Lipton International Players Championship (tennis) on Key Biscayne
Spring Arts Festival in Gainesville
Easter Week Festival in St. Augustine
Daytona Beach Music Festival

OPPOSITE: Fishing boats at Tarpon Springs.
ABOVE: Waterever kind of fishing you want, Florida has it.

MAY
Sunfest Jazz Festival in West Palm Beach
Key West Fishing Tournament

JUNE
Silver Spurs Rodeo in Kissimmee
Sea Turtle Watch on Jensen Beach
Firecracker Festival on Daytona Beach

JULY
Hemingway Days Festival in Key West
Summer Beach Festival on Delray Beach
All-American Water Ski Championship in

Cypress Gardens
Summer Weekend Festival in Surfside

AUGUST
Boca Festival Days in Boca Raton

SEPTEMBER
Festival Miami
Pensacola Seafood Festival

OCTOBER
Florida National Jazz Festival in Jacksonville
Fantasy Fest in Key West
Florida State Air Fair in Kissimmee

ABOVE: Christmas in Miami.
OPPOSITE: Parading in Little Havana.

NOVEMBER
Sunstreet Festival in Miami's Liberty City
Banyan Art Festival in Coconut Grove
Greek Festival Bazaar in Pensacola

DECEMBER
Winterfest and Boat Show in Fort Lauderdale
Florida Tournament of Bands in St. Petersburg
Walt Disney World's Very Merry Christmas Parade in Orlando
Christmas Regatta of Lights in St. Augustine
Candlelight Processional at Lake Buena Vista
Christmas Boat Parade in Fort Lauderdale
Christmas Boat Parade in Pompano Beach
Orange Bowl Festival in Miami
    For details of these and other special events write to Festivals and Sporting Events, Department of Commerce, Division of Tourism, 126 West Van Buren Street, Tallahassee FL 32399.

MAIL

Post offices in Florida are generally open from 8 am to 5 pm weekdays, and from 8 am to noon on Saturday. If you do not know what your address will be, you can have your mail sent to you c/o General Delivery at the main post office in the town where you will be staying. You must collect such mail personally and have with you some form of identification. You can also have mail sent to you, marked "Client's Mail", c/o American Express.
    If the post offices are closed or inconveniently located, there are vending machines selling stamps all over the place. However, as there is an iniquitous mark-up on stamps sold through these machines, you will be better off paying your hotel or motel to send your mail for you.
    Telegrams and telex messages are handled by Western Union and International Telephone and Telegraph, private companies that you will find listed in the yellow pages of the telephone directory. Having dictated your message over the telephones, you can have the charge billed to your hotel room.

TELEPHONES

Most foreign visitors find the American telephone system a revelation. It is cheaper and more efficient by far than any other telephone system in the world; British visitors, in particular, are overcome by the experience of using telephones that actually work — and relatively cheaply. Public telephones are located on all major urban streets, as well as in hotel lobbies, restaurants, service stations, drugstores, shopping malls, and public buildings. At this writing, local calls are 25 cents everywhere in Florida. For information on local telephone numbers dial 411; for information on long-distance numbers call 1-555-1212. Rates for long-distance calls drop after 5 pm, and drop again after 11 pm.

Florida is divided into four telephone regions, with the area codes 305, 813, 407 and 904. To place a long-distance call within the same area code, you dial 1 + the number you are calling. To place a call outside your area code you dial 1+ area code + telephone number. If for any reason you need operator assistance, you dial 0 instead of 1 before dialing the rest of the number; an operator will come on the line before your call is connected. For direct dialing of international calls you dial 011 + country code + area code + telephone number.

RADIO AND TELEVISION

Like the rest of the U.S. Florida is media-intensive. And that's putting it mildly. The airwaves are a Babel of voices and a blizzard of images that will delight the media junkie and dismay those not similarly addicted. The radio dial features end-to-end music — classical, pop, rock, reggae, and a *lot* of country and western — interspersed with dozens of mind-numbing phone-in talk shows ("Hi Debbie, my name is Marcia and I live in Coral Gables and I would just like to ask if you think foreplay is …"). Still, Larry King, whose networked program from Washington comes on at 11 pm on stations all around the state, is well worth listening to.

As for television, I'll start with some numbers. There are 34 television channels in Miami alone—11 regular broadcast stations and 23 cable. In one week I counted 60 hours of soap operas. In one day I counted 22 talk shows. On CNN there is news 24 hours a day. Get the picture?

To help you wade through this avalanche of faces and voices, all I can do is report my personal choices. In my considered opinion, the best newscast is the MacNeil-Lehrer Newshour at 6 pm on PBS (the non-commercial Public Broadcasting Service),

although the main evening newscasts on the three major commercial networks (ABC, CBS, and NBC) are very good, despite being carved up into bite-size chunks to accommodate the advertisements. They air at either 6:30 pm or 7 pm, depending on which network station you are watching.

The best early-morning show is *Today* on NBC. The best early-morning weekend program is *CBS Sunday Morning*, hosted by the estimable Charles Kuralt — a delightful, gentle program to wake up to. In fact, CBS owns Sunday as far as I'm concerned, because after the NFL football games are over, the best magazine program on television, *60 Minutes* on CBS, comes on at 7 pm. The funniest talk show — the funniest show, period —

is *Late Night with David Letterman* on NBC at 12:30 am. All the other programs worth watching will already be familiar to overseas viewers.

Although I am not a great fan of American television, I have to admit that a TV station in Miami has come up with an idea of such wit that I would commend it to television producers anywhere in the world. The idea comes from the 10 pm news on Channel 7. During the sports segment of the program, there are all the usual interviews with players and coaches about yesterday's game or next week's game or the prospects for the seasons, etc. etc. What is not usual about these interviews is that the moment they begin a "Cliché Meter" appears in the bottom left-hand corner of the screen. Thus you still hear the usual rubbish — "the boys really want this one" and "will give it their best shot" and they "will take the game to them" because they will "come to play" and hope to "control the line of scrimmage" and "shut down their big guns" and "take them out of their offense" because after all "it's a game of inches" and "the best defense is a good offense" and vice versa and *(fill in the blank)* — and all the while the cliché meter in the corner is clicking away. Brilliant.

NEWSPAPERS AND MAGAZINES

With a very few exceptions — the *Wall Street Journal*, the *Christian Science Monitor*, the *International Herald Tribune* — American newspapers are all local newspapers. Even the great papers like the *New York Times*, the *Washington Post*, and the *Los Angeles Times* carry more local news than global news. And the one avowedly national newspaper, *USA Today*, is referred to derisively in the States as the McNewspaper, because its relationship to serious journalism is approximately the same as McDonald's is to serious food.

The local papers, as well as *USA Today* and, occasionally, the *New York Times*, are available from sidewalk vending machines in every major city, as well as from newsagents and drugstores. Foreign newspapers are hard to come by unless you find a newsagent that specializes in them.

Drugstore and supermarket racks groan under the overwhelming weight of magazines published in America on every conceivable subject, and for every conceivable taste (and some inconceivable). Worth bearing in mind, however, is that virtually every Florida city has its own city magazine, with comprehensive listings of upcoming events, entertainments, and exhibitions.

BUYING PROPERTY

Perhaps the greatest compliment that one can pay to Florida is to note the fact that a huge proportion of the people who go there for a holiday want to go back for good.

It is not only easy to buy property in Florida, but surprisingly inexpensive by current international standards. It is still possible, for example, to find luxurious accommodation, often right on the beach, for under $100,000. Considering that the down payments are low (20 percent), and the mortgage rates are extremely attractive to overseas buyers (an average eight to nine percent on a 30-year fixed mortgage at the time of writing), you could do a lot worse than put your money into a holiday or retirement home in Florida.

Whatever appeals to you, the local Chamber of Commerce will be eager to help you with information and introductions. For up-to-the-minute information on the latest housing developments, get a copy of the *Florida News Homes Guide*, One Park Place, 621 Northwest 53rd Street, Suite 140, Boca Raton FL 33487. It's free.

Recommended Reading

BARTRAM, WILLIAM. *Travels.* Penguin Books, New York 1988.

BENNETT, CHARLES E. *Settlement of Florida.* University of Florida Press, Gainesville 1968.

BIRNBAUM, STEVE. *Walt Disney World: The Official Guide.* Houghton Mifflin, Boston 1989.

BURNETT, GENE M. *Florida's Past.* Pineapple Press, Sarasota 1986.

DASMAN, RAYMOND F. *No Further Retreat: The Fight to Save Florida.* Macmillan, New York 1971.

DIDION, JOAN. *Miami.* Pocket Books, New York 1987.

DOUGLAS MARJORY STONEMAN. *Florida: The Long Frontier.* Harper and Row, New York 1967.

FICHTER, GEORGE S. *Birds of Florida.* E.A. Seamann, Miami 1971.

Florida Outdoor Guide. The Miami Herald, Miami 1989.

HATTON, HAP. *Tropical Splendor: An Architectural History of Florida.* Alfred A. Knopf, New York 1987.

HEMINGWAY, ERNEST. *Islands in the Stream.* Scribner's, New York 1970. *To Have and Have Not.* Scribner's, New York 1937.

JAHODA, GLORIA. *Florida: A bicentennial History.* W.W. Norton, New York 1976.

Kennedy Space Center Story. NASA, Cape Canaveral 1986.

LUMMUS, JOHN N. *The Miracle of Miami Beach.* Teacher Publishing, Miami 1940.

MACDONALD, JOHN D. *Condominium.* Lippincott, New York 1977.

MCGUANE, THOMAS. *Ninety-two in the Shade.* Farrar, Straus, New York 1973.

MCLENDON, JAMES. *Papa Hemingway in Key West.* E. A. Seamann, Miami 1972.

MARTH, DEL and MARTHA. *Florida Almanac.* A.S. Barnes, St. Petersburg 1988.

MORRIS, ALLEN. *The Florida Handbook.* Peninsula Publishing, Tallahassee 1989.

NEY, JOHN. *Palm Beach.* Little, Brown, Boston 1966.

RABKIN, RICHARD and JACOB. *Nature Guide to Florida.* Banyan Books, Miami 1978.

SMILEY, NIXON. *Florida: Land of Images.* E.A. Seamann, Miami 1977. *Yesterday's Florida.* E.A. Seamann, Miami 1974.

STACHOWITZ, JIM. *Diver's Guide to Florida and the Florida Keys.* Windward Publishing, Miami 1976.

WILLIAMS, TENNESSEE. *Memoirs.* Doubleday, New York 1975.

Quick Reference A–Z Guide to Places and Topics of Interest with Listed Accommodation, Restaurants and Useful Telephone Numbers

Illustrated Blueprints to Travel Enjoyment

INSIDER'S
GUIDES

The Guides That Lead